Dog Whistles, Walk-Backs, and Washington Handshakes

★ ★ ★ ★ ★ ★ ★

Dog Whistles, Walk-Backs, and Washington Handshakes
★ Decoding the Jargon, Slang, and Bluster of American Political Speech ★

Chuck McCutcheon and **David Mark**

FOREWORD BY JEFF GREENFIELD

ForeEdge

ForeEdge

An imprint of University Press of New England

www.upne.com

© 2014 Chuck McCutcheon and David Mark

All rights reserved

Manufactured in the United States of America

Designed by Richard Hendel

Typeset in Miller, Pacific Northwest, Patriotica,

and Klavika by Tseng Information Systems, Inc.

For permission to reproduce any of the material in this book,
contact Permissions, University Press of New England, One Court Street,
Suite 250, Lebanon NH 03766; or visit www.upne.com

Hardcover ISBN: 978-1-61168-700-2

Paperback ISBN: 978-1-61168-603-6

Ebook ISBN: 978-1-61168-657-9

Library of Congress Control Number: 2014933702

5 4 3 2 1

In memory of
Madeline Mark,
Dave Holden, and
Fran McCutcheon

Contents

Foreword

t is the stuff of urban legend, but the estimable journalist-author Joe Klein was an eyewitness. In his first, quickly aborted run for the presidency in 1980, Senator Bob Dole—already a twenty-year veteran of Congress—was asked by a young girl in New Hampshire what he would do about acid rain.

Without a second's pause, Dole replied: "That bill's in markup."

It's really not that puzzling why a United States senator would assume that a New England schoolgirl would understand the reference to the intricacies of the legislative process; two decades in the Capitol bubble will do that. For most of the population—let's call them "regular, normal people"—time spent listening to legislators, operatives, and journalists thrash over public policy on cable or a website can often result in something close to a fugue state, induced by the repeated use of words and phrases that have little if any connection to life as it is lived on planet Earth.

That's why this volume may prove a lifesaver—at least, to those who find politics a fascinating arena, who watch c-span2 the way others watch *Duck Dynasty* or *Storage Wars*, but who are often baffled by the conversation. Are you baffled by the way "frankly" is used to mean either its exact opposite ("Frankly, I'm the best candidate") or nothing at all ("Frankly, 2014 is an election year")? Incredulous at how "the American people" is trotted out every third sentence? In the words of a former vice president, "Help is on the way."

In one sense, it is utterly unsurprising that political discourse is encrusted with linguistic quirks; that is true of all enterprises. Listen to an nfl broadcast, where "he put the ball on the ground!" has replaced "fumble," and where "audibilizing" has added two syllables to a perfectly adequate word. Go to a corporate gathering, where attendees are urged to "think outside the box," and where no one is fired—only "downsized." Every profession has its own language, in part because it envelopes the enterprise in mystery, thus increasing the market value of those who have mastered the mystery (doctors can charge more for treating "contusions and abrasions" than "cuts and bruises.")

What's different about politics, though, is how practitioners consistently miss one of history's clearest lessons: the most memorable words spoken by political leaders shun the rarified language for simple, clear words that lodge in our memory.

"Government of the people, by the people, for the people, shall not perish from the earth."

"The only thing we have to fear is fear itself."

"Ask not what your country can do for you . . ."

"Mr. Gorbachev—tear down this wall."

To be fair, there are times when the birth of a new political cliché can be fully justified. In the last year or so, it's become common for a Washington staffer to refer to a colleague as "a Jonah"—after Jonah Ryan, the hopelessly self-regarding White House staffer on HBO's wickedly funny *Veep*. And if a brilliant devious member of Congress has not yet been labeled "an Underwood"—after Kevin Spacey's character on Netflix's *House of Cards*—it's only a matter of time.

Still, there are far too many times when political discourse can trigger an impulse to throw a thesaurus at the TV or computer screen: Do we really need the cable bloviators to describe yet another "defining moment"? Do we really need to read a journalist describing another "carefully crafted" political event—especially when a "carelessly crafted" appearance guarantees media ridicule?

In your hands is guide through the thicket, a machete with which to cut your way through the jungle of rhetoric. It is, indeed, a carefully crafted guide that—if employed by enough citizens—may prove a defining moment in the political education of the American people. At the end of the day, though, only time will tell.

Jeff Greenfield

Introduction

o matter what your political beliefs, you probably long ago reached one conclusion about our nation's public servants: They can be confusing as hell.

They've acquired that reputation in part because Washington, D.C., has become spectacularly, even proudly, indecipherable to most outsiders. It has its own political culture, including a specific language. It is a lexicon, a jargon—a code, if you will—that can be alien to those not in the know. (By our estimate, and from our experience, it takes roughly a year of working there to *start* to get in the know.) Insider-y sounding political jargon often makes it into the news media, but seldom with any explanation or in any meaningful context. This helps sow confusion, which in turn is one of the factors that have fueled the searing and seemingly unending contempt for all things Beltway.

But such talk is absolutely not limited to Washington. Like everything else, it's just more magnified there. Many of the same expressions can be heard at local city council and county commission meetings, as well as statehouses—any place, in other words, where it's important to know the lingo to fit in. And those places can spawn their own unique expressions. A few examples:

- At the Idaho capitol in Boise, the phrase "radiator-capping" has been in vogue.[1] It describes the process of totally rewriting a bill on the floor of the legislature in much the same fashion as one would overhaul an old car, leaving intact just one original part—the radiator cap.
- In the Dakotas, a bill that has been completely changed in a similar fashion is described as "hog housed." According to the public radio show *A Way with Words*, the phrase

derives from a century-old bill that was altered at the last moment to obtain money for a hog barn.[2]

- Among Massachusetts political insiders, the verb "spot" is popular. As the *Boston Globe*'s Jim O'Sullivan explains: "If a candidate 'spots' his opponent, he has wedged him into an uncomfortable political position. If a president uses the bully pulpit to 'spot' Congress, he is portraying it in a negative light unless it votes for his bill. 'We got spotted by the guy,' one Massachusetts lawmaker told me after the governor had used his State of the Commonwealth address to champion his municipal financing package."[3]

Complaints about the murkiness of political language aren't new. "In our time, political speech and writing are largely the defense of the indefensible," fulminated George Orwell in a famous 1946 essay, "Politics and the English Language." He inveighed against what he saw as their "euphemism, question-begging and sheer cloudy vagueness" and concluded: "Political language . . . is designed to make lies sound truthful and murder respectable, and to give an appearance of solidity to pure wind."[4] We would argue, however, that the problem has only gotten worse since Orwell wrote this. It's one of the by-products of a polarized political age.

Political slang—like all other forms of jargon—helps its practitioners to develop and maintain a sense of shared identity. British linguist Julie Coleman observed in her 2012 book *The Life of Slang* that such subcultures of language "create in-groups and out-groups and act as an emblem of belonging."[5] And in a town as status conscious as Washington, where it's been often observed that the hunger for power far trumps that for money, belonging to something—such as the Democratic or Republican parties—is a big deal.

This book represents an attempt to defang the slang and crack the code. In writing this, we tried to think back to when we were new to Washington and wishing, like wandering tourists lost in a foreign city, that we had a handy all-in-one-place phrasebook. Some of these are obscure words and phrases; others are broader concepts that we felt we could further explain. We settled on six areas—personalities, expressions, legislation, campaigns/ elections, people/places/things, and media/scandals. These divisions, unlike those in Congress, are not intractable. A number of terms could fit in a different chapter than the one they're in.

We are by no means the first to undertake such a feat—the late *New York Times* columnist William Safire's *Political Dictionary* is the best-known example of a translation of the lexicon, and blogs such as Taegan Goddard's *Political Wire* have compiled impressive lists of definitions. At the same time, the last few years have seen significant peel-back-the-curtain political works such as Mark Leibovich's *This Town* and John Heilemann and Mark Halperin's two *Game Change* books. And others have delved into public attitudes toward political language; University of California–Berkeley linguist Geoffrey Nunberg, in his 2006 book *Talking Right: How Conservatives Turned Liberalism into a Tax-Raising, Latte-Drinking, Sushi-Eating, Volvo-Driving, New York Times–Reading, Body-Piercing, Hollywood-Loving, Left-Wing Freak Show*, noted the paradoxical nature of such language: "Each of us believes that we're inured to manipulation, but that everyone else in the room is susceptible to it."[6]

Other nonpolitically specific linguistic and etymological websites also have made substantive contributions. They include the Free Dictionary and the Global Language Monitor, which has compiled an annual list of political buzzword rankings based on the frequency with which they're used in print, on air, and online. It has noted the disconnection between the phrases that campaigns stress, and their actual importance. In mid-2012, for example, the phrase "Mitt Romney's wealth" was a focus of repeated Democratic attacks, but it ranked dead last in the Monitor's survey. (The winning phrase was "the current U.S. economy," and President Barack Obama's ownership of it.)[7] There's also

Wikipedia, but it has its faults. It once incorrectly asserted that former Democratic congressman Rahm Emanuel, now Chicago's mayor, was in a one-man Klezmer band. When our friend Steve Terrell asked Emanuel about this, he recalled that the lawmaker "looked at me like I was crazy."

We hope that this book will be an even more detailed guide to our *current* political landscape. You won't see, as in other books, explanations for "mugwumps" (a term from the 1880s to characterize Republican activists who bolted from their party) or "boll weevils" (a 1980s-era description of conservative southern Democrats) or "hanging chads" (the main buzzword, along with "lockbox," to emerge from the tumultuous 2000 presidential election). We've also tried to eschew issue-specific words and phrases, such as "amnesty" on immigration or "death panels" on health care. Nor will we revisit political words and phrases that are so popular that they've become part of everyday language, like "spin," "leak" and "wonk." When we do bring up words and concepts that are in common use, we try to provide some context. And we hope to enlighten about some little-noticed phrases and euphemisms, such as "disingenuous" and "We need to have a conversation about . . ."

We have no political agenda. There is certainly merit in arguing that certain kinds of language are inappropriately political, but our purpose—for better or worse—is merely to highlight examples in widespread use. We've concentrated on terms and expressions employed by both Democrats and Republicans, though we do indicate where we make exceptions. Much of our book is focused on Congress, as it's the place where both of us have the most experience—and which, given its moribund public approval ratings, we would argue is the place that is by far the ripest for decoding.

In recent years there's been an increasing realization that all of government needs to be far better explained—witness the emergences of fact-checking sites like the *Tampa Bay Times*' Pulitzer Prize–winning PolitiFact, the popularity of blogs that delve far more deeply into the details of politics than most conventional media, and by-now common observations in media about how the infusion of massive sums of money has irrevocably changed the mechanics of legislating. We'd also like to think that the flood of politics-related TV shows and movies—*Scandal, Veep, Alpha House, House of Cards*, and so on—indicates at least a partial desire among the public to understand what really goes on at the White House, on Capitol Hill, and elsewhere.

We hope—and this hope may be "quixotic," to use a political-journalism cliché we explore—that this book can augment those much-needed services for those of you who are sincerely confused and who aren't obsessive readers of *Politico* or *Real Clear Politics*. As for those who *are*, we would emphasize that our list of terms and expressions is by no means comprehensive. We fully envision it mutating over time, and perhaps one day being able to add to it. And so we fully welcome other suggestions. Visit our website, www.dogwhistlebook.com.

C.M. & D.M.

Dog Whistles, Walk-Backs, and Washington Handshakes

★ ★ ★ ★ ★ ★ ★

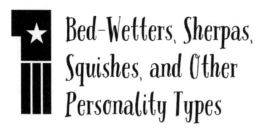

Bed-Wetters, Sherpas, Squishes, and Other Personality Types

You may, like many, be inclined to loathe politicians and the people surrounding them. But they can be entertaining—especially when they open their mouths.

Among our favorites was the late former New Mexico Democratic governor Bruce King, a homespun, handshake-driven guy (Bill Clinton, campaigning in the state in 1992, called him a modern-day Will Rogers) with a penchant for malapropisms. One of his most famous was that a long-forgotten controversy could "open a box of Pandoras."

And then there was Jim Traficant, perhaps the most colorful person ever to serve in Congress. Before being expelled in 2002 after his conviction on bribery and racketeering charges, the Ohio Democrat made an indelible impression for his signature phrase after a speech, an homage to *Star Trek*: "Beam me up," a comment on his wish to escape the bizarreness of Capitol Hill.

Politics brims with overachievers, preeners, and boasters. High-profile politicians often seem narcissistic—attention seeking, grandiose, and ever willing to pass the blame on to someone else. Ego-wallers aim to impress visitors to their office by showing off photos with famous presidents, prime ministers, and others of similar stature—even if the Polaroids are thirty-plus years old.

Mark Leibovich limned some of the less-flattering personalities in his 2013 best seller *This Town: Two Parties and a Funeral—Plus, Plenty of Valet Parking!—in America's Gilded Capital*. He vividly described the jockeying for attention and schmoozing taking place at *Meet the Press* host Tim Russert's funeral. Valerie

Jarrett, perhaps President Barack Obama's closest advisor, took the hardest hit for circulating around the White House a draft memo with thirty-three talking points for people to get their story straight for a *New York Times* profile of her. Its title was "The Magic of Valerie."[1]

Of course, not everyone in Washington behaves so awfully— far from it. There is a wider array of personalities in the political world, as we hope to show.

Appeaser: The opposite of a *hawk*; a dismissive term given to post-9/11 critics of an aggressive foreign policy.

★ Conservatives regularly apply it to President Barack Obama, broadening it to encompass everything he does that they consider weak and counterproductive. As Senate GOP leader Mitch McConnell said in a June 2013 speech about a supposed "war on coal": "The president can simply ignore the will of the representatives sent here by the people because he wants to, because special interests are lobbying him, and because he wants to appease some far-left segment of his base."[2]

Attack dog: A politico who's obviously willing to utter scathingly partisan things—a spokesman, insult comic, and source of blogosphere cacophony rolled into one. This figure can be a bit more mainstream than a *bomb thrower*, whose verbal volleys generally are more indiscriminate. *Surrogates*, for example, are more likely to serve as attack dogs.

★ The attack dog that relished the role more than anyone in recent memory was Sarah Palin. Even after her 2008 turn as John McCain's running mate, she still delivers attack lines such as "How's that 'hopey-changey' stuff working out for you?" with glee. But *all* vice presidential nominees, and vice presidents, play this role. (Witness Joe Biden's campaign-trail sound-bite eruptions in both 2008 and 2012; one of the most heated moments of the latter was when he told a predominantly African American audience that Mitt Romney's plan was to "put y'all back in chains."[3]) So do the chairmen of the Republican and Democratic national committees. And during the 2012 presidential campaign, the dogs often were governors with a potential interest in running someday for the White House, including Maryland Democrat Martin O'Malley and New Jersey Republican Chris Christie.

That kind of negativity turns off voters who don't agree with their views. But people who can serve *red meat* to the base get noticed within party circles.

These days, one of the most prominent attackers is Republican representative Marsha Blackburn of Tennessee, who regularly appears on cable television to blast Obamacare and other topics. She called the administration's response to the 2012 terrorist attack in Benghazi, Libya, "probably more serious than Watergate."[4]

On the Democratic side is Alan Grayson of Florida, who sent a fundraising e-mail in 2013 likening the tea party to the Ku Klux Klan and who made this infamous comment on health care: "If you get sick, America, the Republican health care plan is this: Die quickly."[5] Grayson was beaten in 2010, but won back a seat in a redrawn district two years later.

Backbencher: A lawmaker with little influence—until fairly recently, that is—on the body in which he or she serves.

★ "Backbencher" is derived from the British House of Commons, referring to the majority of parliamentarians that do not hold ministerial office or shadow ministerial office, the would-be government of the opposition. But it wasn't until 1988 that the *New York Times* labeled an American politician as a backbencher. And for that we can thank Newt Gingrich.

The Georgia Republican congressman had just filed ethics charges against Speaker of the House Jim Wright, which would eventually lead to resignation of the Texas political titan. Gingrich was quoted in the *Times* as saying: "If Jim Wright were a backbench member, I probably wouldn't have done anything. . . .

But he's the speaker, and everything he could have done all his life as a backbencher becomes self-destructive when he becomes third in line to be president of the United States."[6]

The term is most often applied to House members. On the other side of the Capitol, even the most junior senators, as one of 100 in the chamber, can wield significant influence. But in the 435-member House there are really only 30 to 40 members that can really affect the fate of legislation.

Backbenchers frequently are members in the "Obscure Caucus," an annual list compiled by the newspaper *Roll Call*. But "obscure" doesn't translate to incompetent; indeed, several of its members, such as New Jersey Republican Leonard Lance and Washington Democrat Rick Larsen, are often admiringly described as *grownups*.

And backbenchers can drive the trains in Congress. Such was the case in 2013 when House Republicans faced off against President Barack Obama and Senate Democrats over efforts to defund Obamacare, by tying it to passing a federal budget and raising the nation's debt ceiling. The *Times* singled out freshman representative Ted Yoho, a Florida Republican and political novice who had knocked off an otherwise conservative and partisan veteran GOP lawmaker in the previous year's primary: "Along with Mr. Yoho, a rotating cast of characters—often backbench newcomers whom few have heard of outside their districts, and who were elected on a Tea Party wave—has emerged to challenge Speaker John A. Boehner's leadership at every turn."[7]

Bed-wetter: A person who expresses doubts; a worrywart.

★ Politics is an exercise in building up confidence among the like-minded. When that isn't achievable, pejorative terms such as this one pop up. The expression has been around for decades, but has come into vogue in recent years. Both parties use it to call out dissenters within their ranks. The *Wall Street Journal*'s editorial section, a reliable bastion of conservatism, sneered in August 2012: "Much as we predicted last week, the Republican Party's Bedwetter Caucus has emerged on schedule to explain why Mitt Romney can't possibly win the election with Paul Ryan on the ticket."[8]

Across the ideological spectrum, Barack Obama's campaign mastermind David Plouffe became known for often castigating doomsayers with this childhood affliction. In a 2010 *Washington Post* opinion piece about what his party had to do to recover in time for the midterm elections, Plouffe listed several prescriptions, among them: "No bed-wetting."[9] (It wasn't enough for his party, which got shellacked that year.)

Blue Dog: An endangered D.C. species. Blue Dogs represent the dwindling band of conservative-leaning House Democrats, particularly on social issues, who can seem more like Republicans than their own party brethren.

★ Though once highly influential, the Blue Dogs' influence in the House has diminished as the chamber has become more polarized, and the post-2012 census redrawing has made their districts more favorable to Republicans. In 2014, their caucus had just nineteen members, down from more than fifty in the mid-1990s.

Although their clout may have waned, Blue Dogs can command serious media attention. They possess two traits that most journalists secretly wish were true of all politicians: They are unafraid to challenge their party's leaders, and they evoke a bygone era of bipartisan aisle-crossing and intraparty fraternization. Consider Tennessee Democratic representative Jim Cooper, currently among the Blue Dogs' leaders (he is a former investment banker, Rhodes Scholar, and Harvard Law grad who describes himself as the group's "nerd"). In 2011 *New York Times* columnist Joseph Nocera wrote an admiring column describing Cooper as "the House's conscience, a lonely voice for civility in this ugly era."[10]

The Blue Dogs' name has been a source of fascination among political junkies. Some suggest it derives from the old saw that voters in Texas would rather vote for a yellow dog than a Republican. Others credit coining of the Blue Dog name to a Texas

Democratic congressman in the early 1990s, Pete Geren. He is said to have opined that members had been "choked blue" by "extreme" Democrats from the left.[11]

Body man: The personal assistant to a prominent elected official or candidate. A body man accompanies the politician or candidate virtually everywhere, arranging lodging, transportation or meals, and providing companionship, snacks, and other assistance. *Body man* is a limiting description, as prominent female politicians' entourages also include female personal assistants.

★ The body-man role gained visibility during Bill Clinton's presidency. The baby-boomer commander in chief regularly had by his side well-groomed, often Ivy League–educated assistants. One body man, Kris Engskov, drew unwanted scrutiny for the position. He was hired one month before the Monica Lewinsky scandal broke and was twice called to testify before a grand jury.

In his later years in the Senate, South Carolina Republican Strom Thurmond—the only member of Congress to reach age 100 while in office—employed a series of body men. "We would walk alongside him and just assist him, give him an arm to lean on when he needed it," recalled one of them, Scott Frick, in *The Centennial Senator: True Stories of Strom Thurmond from the People Who Knew Him Best*. Despite his age, Thurmond had an iron grip, Frick said: "He'd squeeze my arm so hard, I'd have to stop and tell him to let up."[12]

Politicians bond with their body men (and vice versa, as shown by Tony Hale's sycophantic aide on HBO's *Veep*). Barack Obama's aide Reggie Love told CNN that he and the president played cards—about fifteen hands of spades—while watching via satellite link the May 2011 raid that killed Osama bin Laden. (He also told reporters that the commander in chief regularly flossed his teeth in front of him.)[13] And the *New York Times* put it this way in an April 2012 *beat sweetener* about the soon-to-be Republican presidential nominee: "Garrett Jackson and Mitt

Romney are stuck together like the peanut butter and honey sandwiches they both love."[14]

Bomb thrower: A version of *attack dog*. Bomb throwers (also known as flamethrowers) are more prone to act independently of their party's leadership. As such, they're often *wing nuts* or *left-wing loonies*. In November 2013, *National Journal* named what it called "the new Republican flamethrowers," including Colorado congressional candidate Ken Buck, Alaska Senate candidate Joe Miller, and Iowa social-conservative stalwart Bob Vander Plaats.[15]

Boss: The deferential way staffers and campaign workers always refer to the officeholder or candidate for whom they work.

★ When pitching an op-ed article to a news publication a press secretary will routinely say, "The boss wants this to run Tuesday morning, when he introduces his budget bill." Or a campaign staffer will have to check "the boss's schedule" to see if there's time for a requested interview. Referring to a politician as "boss" can provide insulation to staffers if they don't agree with their employer's decision. As in, "It's the boss's call."

Of course "boss," in politics, has traditionally had a different connotation, as in a powerful big-city political-machine leader capable of dispensing patronage and exacting revenge on those who cross him.

Part of a staffer's job is to make the boss sound as important as possible. Staffers—whether press secretaries, chiefs of staff, or someone lower on the political food chain—routinely remind reporters that their boss is late for an interview because "he's still in an intelligence committee briefing." Or "She's at a markup." It's a less-than-subtle signal to reporters that they work for somebody deemed to be important, and that time is short, even when it's not.

Another part of a staffer's job is to put up with the boss's foul moods. One of us once watched the late Pennsylvania senator Arlen Specter launch into a tirade against an aide standing with him—because *Specter* didn't know the answer to a question we had asked. That said, aides to the irascible Republican-turned-Democrat liked to boast that they could get jobs almost anywhere in town once they left his office; future employers knew that if they could work for him, they could handle just about anything.

Bridge builder: A description pinned on politicians—usually *grownups*—who are able to work with the opposing party.

★ Discussing the balance that Senate GOP leader Mitch McConnell had to strike between seeking reelection as a true conservative and as someone who could cut a deal to end the October 2013 government shutdown, the *Wall Street Journal*'s David Wessel noted that the Kentucky Republican faced a primary challenger from the right. "It seems to have influenced his role in this in a way that makes it harder for him to be the bridge builder and the lead consensus person," he said on radio's *Diane Rehm Show*.[16] (As it later happened, McConnell did set aside his primary concerns and did the work of bridge building to help end the shutdown.)

Presidential candidates invariably seek to claim the mantle. George W. Bush was the ultimate self-described bridge builder on the campaign trail in 1999–2000. The then Texas governor nabbed the Republican presidential nomination claiming to be a "uniter, not a divider"—the political rhetorical equivalent of hapless comic Rodney Dangerfield in the 1980s romp *Back to School* declaring himself a "lover, not a fighter." Bush pointed to his bipartisan record in the Texas state capitol, during the Democrats' waning years of control. Once in Washington, though, Bush—at least according to Democratic critics—pushed a highly partisan, tax-cutting agenda that marginalized the other side rather than including them in negotiations.

Bush's successor Barack Obama also claimed to be a bridge builder. But once he arrived in the White House, congressional Republicans complained about a lack of bipartisan outreach. Obama and fellow Democrats argued that too many Republicans had no interest in building any bridges—and in reality wanted to blow them up. But the fact remains that the president has had little luck in forging bipartisan coalitions.

Cable and Sunday show chatterers: The lifeblood of political media. Elected officials and spinners appear in endless loops on cable and Sunday morning news shows, spouting off well-rehearsed and coordinated *talking points*. Journalistic pundits jockey over appearances on the shows, which can provide a boost in visibility as well as potential speaking fees.

★ According to the ratings, old-time evening newscasts on ABC, NBC, and CBS routinely best even the most popular political shows on cable. But the cable shows are beloved by coastal elites and news junkies; in other words, the people who vote consistently, who often contribute to political campaigns—*and* who are attractive to commercial advertisers.

That explains why CNN brought back the conservative-liberal debate show *Crossfire* in fall 2013 after an eight-year hiatus; it went off the air after Jon Stewart of Comedy Central's *The Daily Show* attacked it for "hurting America" by turning every issue into a partisan argument.[17] (Stewart has also trained his guns on Fox News, telling its popular host Bill O'Reilly that he's "the king of Bullshit Mountain."[18])

Guests come and go on the Sunday news shows, but there's always one constant: John McCain.

In 2012, the Arizona senator broke his former Senate colleague Bob Dole's record for the most appearances on NBC's *Meet the Press* (64). He's also appeared on CBS's *Face the Nation* more than any guest in its history. What makes McCain so popular? He's accessible, opinionated, and occasionally in a position to influence debates (most notably on national security, an area in which he's the Senate's leading *hawk*). "I enjoy them," McCain said in 2013, referring to the shows. "I find it is the best way to communicate with the American people."[19] But the former presidential candidate's appearances, week after week, drive liberals apoplectic. "On the Sunday shows, McCain is what passes for 'unpredictable,'" lamented the *American Prospect*'s Paul Waldman, coauthor of the uncomplimentary 2008 book *Free Ride: John McCain and the Media*.[20]

For all of the strides that women have made in politics, white men still dominate the Sunday and cable-show guest lists. Studies have found that women needed to attain leadership positions on committees dealing with national security matters or within the party before being asked to opine on-air, while men have lower fences to climb to get to guest-hood.

Occasionally a sought-after newsmaker will appear on multiple shows the same day. Such a feat is known as the *full Ginsburg* named after Monica Lewinsky's then lawyer William Ginsburg (see separate entry, chapter 3).

Cardinals: A once-powerful group of the House members overseeing the spending of your taxpayer dollars that has seen a steep decline in its status.

★ This term originated back in the 1970s, when the Appropriations Committee was arguably the most powerful place in Congress. A joke circulated on Capitol Hill addressing the difference between its members and those sitting on the authorizing committees, who drafted the legislative language dictating federal agencies' actions without controlling those agencies' pocketbooks. "Authorizers think they are gods," went the joke, "while appropriators *know* they are gods."

To continue the religious theme, the chairs of the Appropriations subcommittees in the House—where revenue-related measures originate—were popularly known as "cardinals" in a Catholic Church–related homage to their immense power over the agencies' budgets they oversaw. But then came the tea party and the successful clamor to ban earmarks, and the cardinals turned into something more closely resembling clerics—they spent more time cutting the federal budget than adding their pet projects to it.

During the heyday of *earmarks* cardinals specialized in something known as "ash and trash," or small, relatively low-cost items tacked onto spending bills, often in coordination with their party's leaders. The chance of being included in this was among the reasons why lobbyists who had pending appropriations projects or programs never left town—or their phones and computers—during last-minute work on the spending bills.

Closer: A person brought in, like a baseball relief pitcher at game's end, to finish a deal.

★ It's often an ex-member of Congress or other powerful figure. Prominent lobbyist Haley Barbour, then governor of Mississippi, was brought in when House and Senate members in 2006 couldn't agree on how much to pay the Hurricane Katrina–ravaged Gulf Coast states. He got the House to agree to the higher Senate amount. "Haley was the closer," a Democratic official involved in negotiations said admiringly.[21]

E-fluentials/poli-fluentials: A subgroup of *influentials* in the marketing world in recent years that has spread to politics, referring to those whose clout is accumulated online. "Poli-fluentials"—a phrase coined by George Washington University's Institute for Politics, Democracy, and the Internet—are opinionated activists with sizeable social networks. Libertarian former representative Ron Paul had numerous poli-fluentials in his ranks; they were instrumental in detonating his *money bombs*.

Elites: A term that once commonly described wealthy Republicans—so-called country-club elites—it has morphed in recent decades into a pejorative description of Democratic intellectuals, including *Acela Corridor* inhabitants, who are portrayed as out of touch and insensitive to average Americans' concerns. As pundit Michael Kinsley once noted, then House Speaker Newt Gingrich "uses the term 'elite' as an all-purpose epithet, meaning little more than someone or something he doesn't like."[22]

★ In the 1950s, Senator Joseph McCarthy inveighed against

elites in his quest to root out Communism: "It has not been the less fortunate, or members of minority groups who have been traitorous to this nation, but rather those who have had all the benefits that the wealthiest nation on earth has had to offer . . . the finest homes, the finest college education and the finest jobs in government we can give."[23]

Over time, a rhetorical distinction within the GOP was made between the business elite, whose wealth was seen as a byproduct of their hard work, and the intellectual elite, who relied on connections among their fellow elites. To voters, "sometimes 'elite' means that they didn't have to hold a job . . . and understand what it's like to pick up a lunch bucket every day," Mary Kate Cary, a former speechwriter for President George H. W. Bush, told National Public Radio in 2010.[24]

That was the thinking of conservative activist Curt Levey when he warned senators to oppose President Barack Obama's nomination of Sonia Sotomayor to the Supreme Court in 2009: "Remember the values of the regular folks who sent you to Washington. Don't vote for a Supreme Court nominee whose values are closer to those of the intellectual elite than to those of your constituents."[25] It didn't work. Sotomayor may have graduated from Princeton and Yale Law School, but she grew up in the Bronx—living in a tenement as a child—and hardly appeared to fit the "elite" mold. She was confirmed easily.

From a progressive perspective, "elite" is part of a class of politically related words that can have two conflated meanings, said Geoffrey Nunberg, a University of California–Berkeley linguist and author of several books on American language. "Elite has the snooty sense. . . . The other sense of 'elite' is that it describes elite fighting forces, elite law schools—where it's the best," he told one of us. "Those are glommed together when the right talks about 'the elites' as a plural. They're the snooty people in the East who have all the power."[26]

Other words that Nunberg contends are used in a similar dual fashion:

- *Exceptionalism*: Used to mean both different from others and extraordinary, as in the oft-used "American exceptionalism."
- *Entitlement*: Programs such as Social Security and Medicare providing benefits not subject to budgetary spending decisions and that imply a moral right to those benefits. He noted President Lyndon Johnson's argument for Medicare: "By God, you can't treat Grandma this way. She's entitled to it." In more recent decades, it also has come to embody self-absorption, superficiality, and selfishness.
- *Values*: Deployed in both a cultural and a moral sense. Nunberg argues in his book *Talking Right* that it's acquired its significance "from stories that dramatize the same underlying theme of liberal decadence and moral decay. . . . It's a safe bet that if you pulled 50 people off a bus and gave them a word-association test, even in San Francisco or on Manhattan's Upper West Side, you'd find that 'values' evoked 'conservative' a lot more often than it did 'liberal.'"[27]

Fixer: A derogatory description of a political consultant of last resort who engages in the more unsavory aspects of campaign or legislative work: Think Olivia Pope, Kerry Washington's resourceful jack-of-all-trades character on ABC's *Scandal*, without all the sex.

★ In an earlier era, the Kennedys employed one of the most notorious political fixers, Paul Corbin, to handle the family's political dirty work. The *New York Times* blandly described his passing in a January 1990 obituary, at seventy-five, as "a political consultant who was an aide to Senator Robert F. Kennedy. . . . Mr. Corbin was active in the Wisconsin and West Virginia primary campaigns and in New York State in the general election of 1960. . . . He became a special assistant to the national Democratic chairman and worked in Robert Kennedy's campaign for the Senate in 1964."[28]

That hardly captures Corbin's real role. During the 1960 presidential campaign, all eyes were on the Wisconsin primary, which was the first test of the political effects of Massachusetts senator John F. Kennedy's Catholicism. The day before the primary, thousands of Catholic families all over Wisconsin received a mailing, postmarked Minneapolis (the home of Senator Hubert Humphrey, Kennedy's opponent), urging them not to vote for an agent of the pope of Rome. Corbin always denied he had anything to do with this exercise in voter turnout. Few believed him.

Corbin played a similar role once JFK was in the White House. According to several authors, Corbin was used to keep an eye on Kennedy aides, even the most trusted ones. He purportedly developed evidence that Kennedy confidante Kenny O'Donnell had skimmed $50,000 in campaign funds. Years later, Corbin was fingered in another political who-done-it—the pilfering and turning over to the 1980 Ronald Reagan campaign of the briefing books that President Jimmy Carter was using to prep for his debate with Reagan. Craig Shirley's 2009 book *Rendezvous with Destiny: Ronald Reagan and the Campaign That Changed America*, fleshed out the dirty tricks involved, and gathered a wealth of evidence pointing to Corbin as the culprit.

Fixers get rewarded with plum jobs. James Baker, the patrician Texas attorney and *wise man*, was a longtime confidant of President George H. W. Bush. After winning the White House in 1988, president-elect Bush's first appointment was Baker as secretary of state. As Bush's 1992 reelection bid faltered against Bill Clinton, Baker was brought back in as White House chief of staff, the same position that he had held from 1981 to 1985 during the first Reagan term. Then, in 2000, George W. Bush's presidential campaign called upon Baker as chief legal adviser during the Florida recount. Although Republicans almost universally respect Baker to this day, the late British prime minister Margaret Thatcher disdainfully wrote in her memoir that she considered him just a political fixer, not a true statesman.

One of President Barack Obama's chief fixers is on the policy side — Jeffrey Zients, who served as acting Office of Management and Budget director as well as director of the National Economic Council. Obama turned to Zients to clean up several messes in which demand outstripped anticipated resources: the Cash for Clunkers car trade-in program, the updated version of the GI Bill, and the glitch-plagued HealthCare.gov website.

Formers: Most people don't return to old workplaces regularly, walking around their old haunts and fraternizing with former colleagues. Yet it's not at all uncommon to see former members of Congress at the Capitol.

★ They're often wearing a former member's lapel pin, almost indistinguishable from a current member's pin. It's as if they had never left the place. Former House majority leader Tom DeLay popped up on Capitol Hill the same day in September 2013 that an appeals court in Texas threw out his controversial conviction on money-laundering charges. "Around the political arena, I'm around," a jubilant DeLay told reporters, somewhat redundantly. "They never got rid of me."[29]

When ex-members of Congress return to Capitol Hill it is often for reasons other than reminiscing. Many have gone *downtown* (see chapter 3) to become lobbyists or consultants, raking in annual paychecks several times higher than their congressional salaries. After the 2006 Jack Abramoff scandal, though, lawmakers sharply cut back on where their ex-colleagues could roam. That led to an incident five years later in which former Louisiana representative Bob Livingston, a well-connected lobbyist, was on the floor of the House for the swearing-in ceremony. "I was under the impression that opening day and the State of the Union were days when I, as a lobbyist, could indeed go on the floor," Livingston later told the *Times-Picayune* of New Orleans. "When I was informed that I was mistaken, I left."[30]

Graybeards: See *wise men.*

Grownups: The description of serious legislators who would rather accomplish something than gain publicity. After the

2013 standoff that led to a government shutdown, the *New York Times* ran an editorial with the headline "In Search of Republican Grownups."[31]

★ The Senate has a smattering of these types. Oft-mentioned lawmakers include Senators Dianne Feinstein (D-CA) and Rob Portman (R-OH). While both generally hew to their party's lines, each has gone his or her own way from time to time. Feinstein supported the Bush-era tax cuts in 2001 and the Iraq war resolution in 2002—though she later said supporting the Iraq mission was a mistake. She also backed renewal of the USA Patriot Act, which beefed up law enforcement against terrorism.

Portman came out in favor of same-sex marriage after his son told him he was gay, something that won him plaudits among Democrats. His intellect and amiable persona made him one of the top 2012 GOP vice presidential prospects. As political analyst Stuart Rothenberg told *Time*: "He's a grownup. Rob is smart and incredibly likable, personable, not mean, not angry."[32] (When one of us asked him how he felt about the label, Portman opted for *comic self-deprecation*: "When your hair starts to turn more gray, as mine has been, people are going to call you a grownup."[33])

It should be noted that examples of what are considered "grownups" often come from the news media. Democratic officeholders are rarely lauded in the same way for moving to the right. In contrast, Republican politicians often are said to "grow in office" if, after several terms, they take more liberal, or at least more moderate positions.

Happy warrior: A politician who takes an unapologetic—and, at least outwardly upbeat—stand based on what he or she believes to be deep principle.

★ Now a cliché, the phrase was made famous in a nineteenth-century William Wordsworth poem. William Safire noted that Franklin Roosevelt used it in a speech nominating New York governor Al Smith for president in 1924. But it has been most closely associated with former Minnesota senator and vice president Hubert Humphrey, who earned the nickname in the 1960s for his adherence to liberal causes and his now-anachronistic embrace of what he called "the politics of joy." (Yes, times were different then.)

Since then, the tag has been applied to politicians of both parties. In his 2012 reelection victory speech, President Obama described his running mate Joe Biden as "America's happy warrior."[34] But in that same election, the *National Review* stuck it on Biden's opponent, Representative Paul Ryan. It can be used derisively, as when Democratic senator Robert Byrd sneered at President George W. Bush's declaration aboard an aircraft carrier that things were going smoothly in Iraq: "President Bush typified the happy warrior when he strutted across the deck of the U.S.S. *Abraham Lincoln* a year ago."[35]

Sometimes politicians use it to describe themselves. "I'm just a happy warrior," House Speaker John Boehner told reporters in September 2013 shortly before the House voted not to fund the federal government unless Obama's Affordable Care Act was delayed or defunded.[36] Needless to say, Boehner was considerably less happy following the battle that took its toll on House Republicans' overall popularity.

Hawks: Traditionally associated with foreign policy right-wingers, the term "hawk" has come to encompass anyone taking conservative stands on some domestic matters.

★ "Hawks vs. doves" was a classic Cold War formulation—those who aimed to counter Soviet aggression at every turn, and rivals who sought accommodation against the West's Russian rivals. Foreign-policy hawk carried over in political parlance after the Soviet Union's demise. People on the opposite spectrum were deemed *appeasers*.

The hawk-versus-dove lines have become somewhat muddled during President Barack Obama's time in office. Many of the same "national greatness conservatism" lawmakers and their cheerleaders in think tanks, academia, and the media grew much more skeptical of military action under a Democratic president. And Edward Snowden's disclosures of the National Security Agency's snooping aligned libertarians with liberals.

That earlier period, immediately after 9/11, spawned an inversion of traditional militaristic hawks. "Chicken hawks" became the favored put-down by Democrats for right-wingers who wanted to wage seemingly endless war, but had shirked military duty themselves. In February 2004, Senator Frank Lautenberg took to the Senate floor to castigate "chicken hawks." Without naming names, Lautenberg, a decorated World War II veteran and liberal who delighted in speaking his mind, took aim at Vice President Dick Cheney and Senator Saxby Chambliss. The latter, a Georgia Republican, had defeated Democratic senator Max Cleland in 2002 in a brutal race that critics said questioned the incumbent's patriotism. "My definition of a chicken hawk is someone who talks tough on national defense and military issues, casts aspersions on others who might disagree on the vote, but when they had a chance to serve, they were not there," Lautenberg said.[37]

Domestically, "deficit hawks" strongly oppose running up more debt on the government credit card. Leaders in both parties have tried to claim the role of deficit hawks, and the roles have at times been reversed. Republicans were once willing to accept tax hikes to cut deficits, even as some Democrats sought tax cuts.

Liberal blogger Ezra Klein, among others, has called for a new breed of bird to address deteriorating roads, bridges, and other public works: the "infrastructure hawk."[38] But media critic Jack Shafer, then with *Slate*, wrote in 2009 that reporters too often give such hawks a platform to make Chicken Little claims about public works: "None of this is to suggest that we needn't worry about repairing or maintaining bridges," he wrote, "only to observe that the state of the nation's bridges ain't as dire as the press makes it out."[39]

Influentials: The age-old shorthand for the people with the ability to get things done—usually those in congressional leadership posts and key positions in the White House, but also prominent activists, lobbyists and anyone else commanding a large following. As such, they push through bills, initiate discussions on blogs, and command media attention with their arguments.

★ Before President Barack Obama's 2011 State of the Union address, former George W. Bush campaign strategist Matthew Dowd wrote: "The key barometers on which to judge the address's effectiveness in the days following it are those men and women who are elected every two or six years, and influentials who help drive the discussion in Washington."

Far more than any other place, Washington is obsessed with identifying influentials. That leads *National Journal*, *Politico*, and other similarly inclined publications to publish lists in such esoteric categories as "The 25 Most Influential Women in Washington Under 35" (Washington GOP representative Jaime Herrera Beutler and Hawaii Democratic representative Tulsi Gabbard joined lobbyists Eugenia Edwards and Kristen Soltis Anderson on the list in 2013), or "The 30 Most Influential Out Washingtonians" (Wisconsin Democratic senator Tammy Baldwin and White House social secretary Jeremy Bernard were on the 2014 list of openly gay power players). Subgroups include *e-fluentials* and *poli-fluentials* (see separate entry).

Left-wing loony: A dismissive conservative way of describing liberal activists.

★ *Weekly Standard* editor Fred Barnes is believed to have coined the phrase during the heat of the 2004 presidential race between President George W. Bush and Democratic challenger John Kerry. Leftist filmmaker Michael Moore played more than a bit part in the campaign, as many Democrats embraced his scathingly anti-Iraq war *Fahrenheit 9/11*.

"Flights of paranoia, far-out analogies, conspiracy theories, and wild charges devoid of evidence are the stock in trade of the Loony Left," Barnes wrote in 2004. "Normally such ideas are ridiculed or ignored by those in the political mainstream.

But these days the fantasies of the Loony Left are increasingly embraced and nearly always tolerated by the Democratic party and its auxiliary groups. The result? The Loony Left now has a toehold on the Democratic party."[40]

Loony left actually has British origins. It's one of the most beloved political slams of the British Right. *Loony left* made its first appearance in the 1980s and has remained a staple of the Tory-supporting press to the present day.

"Mr. Chairman": In the high-school-like atmosphere that prevails in Congress, only a small group of lawmakers have significant power. Along with the elected leadership in the House and Senate, committee chairmen can wield real clout.

★ It's customary to give these powerful barons due deference. Colleagues refer to committee heads as "Mr. Chairman" or, more commonly these days, "Madame Chairwoman." The aforementioned former Ohio representative Jim Traficant was known for calling virtually everyone he encountered "Mr. Chairman," from his colleagues to lowly aides. It was because, as Hill staffer-turned-lobbyist John Feehery remembers, "There were a lot of chairmen around, and it was better to be safe than sorry."[41]

Operative: One of many terms borrowed from the spy world, this is a general term describing any behind-the-scenes figure in a political campaigns—fundraisers, media consultants, *strategists, fixers*, and the like.

★ There's often little in-between with how operatives are portrayed. They can be savvy heroes, like James Carville after engineering Bill Clinton's 1992 election for president. Or they can emerge as hapless scapegoats, as political consultant Stuart Stevens learned after steering Mitt Romney's disastrous 2012 presidential bid. But because there's always another campaign coming up—and politics is a game of second, third, fourth, and fifth chances—they can always change that.

"Operative" is often a derogatory term, as when Representative Mike Coffman (R-CO) lashed out in 2013 against a Department of Veterans Affairs official whom he accused of covering up problems at the agency. "I don't think you're incompetent," Coffman said at a hearing. "I think you're a very smart political operative."[42]

Principal: This can refer to the key leaders involved in a political negotiation or decision, as in "The principals need to sign off on this deal." More often, though, it's the person for which an eponymous lobbying shop or public affairs firm is named. These businesses aim to capitalize on the name recognition of a former official or otherwise prominent figure.

★ D.C. is full of such groups. Often the principal is a genuinely high-ranking, well-connected government official. The Scowcroft Group is named after former national security advisor Brent Scowcroft, who held that position in the administrations of both Presidents Gerald Ford and George H. W. Bush.

Even considerably less prominent former officials can become a principal at their own firm. Consider Michael Patrick Flanagan, a Republican who in 1994 beat a Democratic titan, Representative Dan Rostenkowski. In fall of that year Flanagan was a struggling Chicago lawyer with considerable student debt. But he benefited from a confluence of circumstances—Rostenkowski's indictment months earlier on corruption charges, and the Republican wave that gave the GOP its first House majority in forty years. Flanagan became the first Republican to represent a significant portion of Chicago since 1967, but his political good fortune quickly ran out. The district reverted to its Democratic form, and Flanagan lost his 1996 reelection bid, 64 percent to 36 percent.

He then became principal at Flanagan Consulting LLC. His firm's business plan was less discreet than former top officials like Scowcroft. "Mike Flanagan," it explained, "maintains excellent relations with Capitol Hill, various federal Departments and at the Administration generally."[43]

Progressive: A preferred term among those on the political left to describe themselves, thus avoiding the negative connotations of "liberal."

★ Ironically, *liberal* once traditionally applied to conservativism—"classical liberals" who favored laissez-faire economic policies. Yet around the mid-twentieth century, Democrats adopted the phrase as their own. To them, a liberal was one who accepted the idea of progressive change and looked forward in a rapidly evolving world. In his 1959 inaugural address, California governor Pat Brown used the word *liberal* or *liberalism* seven times in the first eight paragraphs. The catchphrase of his Democratic administration was "responsible liberalism."[44]

President John F. Kennedy, by the same token, defined a liberal as someone who "cares about the welfare of the people—their health, their housing, their schools, their jobs, their civil rights, and their civil liberties." By that definition, he added, "I'm proud to say I'm a liberal."[45]

But over time, conservative politicians, activists, and media outlets shaded the word with an ominous and sinister connotation.

Even the most left-leaning Democratic members of Congress tend to shy away from the definition. According to the Congressional Progressive Caucus's founding statement of purpose the leftie-lawmakers' group was "organized around the principles of social and economic justice, a non-discriminatory society, and national priorities which represent the interests of all people, not just the wealthy and powerful."[46] But nowhere in the document is the word *liberal* found. And the George Soros–funded Media Matters describes itself as "a Web-based, not-for-profit, 501(c)(3) progressive research and information center dedicated to comprehensively monitoring, analyzing, and correcting conservative misinformation in the U.S. media."[47] Again, no use of the term *liberal*.

Some on the left do make a distinction. David Sirota, a well-known blogger and author, wrote in a *Huffington Post* column:

"It seems to me that traditional 'liberals' in our current parlance are those who focus on using taxpayer money to help better society. A 'progressive' is one who focuses on using government power to make large institutions play by a set of rules."[48]

"Reasonable Republicans": A somewhat condescending way in which Democrats and liberal, ostensibly neutral, reporters describe moderate members of the GOP. In this view, *reasonable Republicans* are to be distinguished from their uncouth cousins—*true believer* conservatives who don't accede readily to Democratic demands.

★ The phrase is a favorite of Senate Democratic leader Harry Reid (D-NV), who has used it more than a dozen times in floor speeches in recent years. As he griped during the 2013 government shutdown, "I've had the opportunity to work with many reasonable, thoughtful Republicans, including those serving in this body today." Today's GOP, he said by contrast, is "infected" by "extremists."[49] Or as Reid admonished House Speaker John Boehner a few months earlier on a compromise over a student loan bill: "He should remember that the only way to pass meaningful legislation in either chamber is to do so with votes from both reasonable Democrats and reasonable Republicans."[50]

Conservatives regard them as *RINO*s, but a handful of Republicans will describe themselves this way. When campaigning in the 2012 New Hampshire governor's race, Republican Kevin Smith—an ex-state representative and founder of a conservative advocacy group, Cornerstone Action—told a local reporter: "People who know me not just from Cornerstone, but know me from my time in state government . . . would tell you that I'm a very reasonable Republican and a very thoughtful Republican."[51] Reasonableness, however, was not enough for Smith, who came in second in the GOP primary behind Ovide Lamontagne (who boasts one of the best names in politics).

RINO: Republican in Name Only, one of the most common disparaging epithets hurled at GOPers by conservative critics who complain they have strayed too far from the party's core principles—in other words, become *reasonable Republicans* to the Democratic enemy.

★ As members of the tea party have sought increasing fealty to their antigovernment agenda, many Republicans have rankled at getting branded a RINO. Among them is lobbyist John Feehery, a former aide to House Majority Leader Tom DeLay and Speaker Dennis Hastert, who complained in 2013 during the House GOP-induced government shutdown about the flak he was receiving on Twitter from conservatives who castigated his assertion that the shutdown was a stupid idea and that Texas senator Ted Cruz had gone too far.

"And now the Tea Party twitterers want me to go," he wrote in his "Feehery Theory" column. "Of course, they don't just want me to go. They call John Boehner, [New York representative] Peter King, Mitch McConnell, [Tennessee senator] Bob Corker, and just about every Republican who disagrees tactically with Ted Cruz, RINOs too. So I am in good company."[52]

Wayne Fields, an English professor at St. Louis's Washington University who studies political argument, also dislikes the tag. "Any traditional Republican, any Republican who was recognizable as a Republican during the Reagan era, is disqualified by that kind of language," he said.[53]

But *Pittsburgh Post-Gazette* columnist Reg Henry prefers to look at the bright side. He wrote in 2012 that "the word sounds like rhino, an animal much to be admired. It is thick-skinned, unpredictable and intimidating with a giant horn on its snout. Who wouldn't want to be a rhino—a Republican Highly Intuitive, Not Obtuse?"[54]

Democrats are less likely to use DINOS as an equivalent phrase, at least when it comes to Congress. When they do, it refers to *Blue Dogs* and independent-minded lawmakers such as ex-Nebraska senator Ben Nelson, whose voting patterns put him in the company of Northeastern moderate Republicans. Some use the expression "*going Zell Miller*" (see separate entry).

Sherpa: A Washington *wise man* brought on to ease an administration appointee's path to Senate confirmation. The name takes after the Nepalese people hired by climbers of Mount Everest, K2, and other Himalayan peaks.

★ Sherpas are most prominent in Supreme Court considerations. Indiana GOP senator Dan Coats recalled in a political science journal the time in 2005 when he was lobbying and George W. Bush's political guru, Karl Rove, asked him to guide the nomination of Harriet Miers through the confirmation process. "As a former senator, according to Rove, I was the 'perfect' person to serve as Miers' guide or Sherpa. . . . My task, as he explained, was to help grow the base of support through public and private advocacy, bridge building to the Senate and strategizing with the White House nominating team."[55] Yet no amount of strategizing could help Miers, who withdrew her nomination after even many Republicans expressed doubts about her qualifications.

Because the nomination fight has become so highly charged, part of a sherpa's job is giving the nominee a crash course in politics. "The nominee needs to understand that she is preparing for an overt political event, without many rules and with few express assurances of due process, that is unlike anything that occurs in a court of law," A. B. Culvahouse, who as President Ronald Reagan's White House counsel in the late 1980s worked on the nominations of Robert Bork and eventually Anthony Kennedy, told *Real Clear Politics*.[56]

And just as important as the content of the answers, the sherpa and other advisers also coach the nominee on demeanor. Superlobbyist Tom Korologos, Bork's sherpa, wrote in a 2009 *Washington Post* op-ed that Bork's performance failed in part because he had broken an agreed-on "80-20 rule" to ensure "the senators spoke 80 percent of the time and he answered 20 percent of the time."[57]

A sherpa can also be a lower-level figure doing unglamorous but important behind-the-scenes work in other contexts. Before being nominated in 2013 to the Federal Reserve, the Treasury

Department's undersecretary for international affairs, Lael Brainard, often was described as a sherpa for international economic summit meetings involving President Barack Obama.[58]

Socialist: A term that in the last decade has replaced "liberal" as the favorite conservative epithet for a Democrat considered to have an unnatural fondness for government. It is intended to invoke terrifying images of Soviet-style control and a powerful yet inept bureaucracy doling out handouts to the undeserving.

★ The label is most frequently pinned on the White House's current inhabitant. "Barack Obama is a socialist; he believes in socialism," Sarah Palin declared on Fox News in 2012.[59] It was both an implied and direct theme of Mitt Romney's failed 2012 attempt to unseat Obama; as businessman Kyle Koehler told reporters on a conference call on Romney's behalf: "It seems to me that the Obama America, there's no risk but there's plenty of reward. That's called socialism to me."[60]

It's clearly something that intrigues voters. That same election year, *Merriam-Webster's* online dictionary found that "socialism" and "capitalism" were its two most looked-up words. *Merriam-Webster* defines socialism as "any of various economic and political theories advocating collective or government ownership and administration of the means of production and distribution of goods."

In an infamous and much-criticized move, *Newsweek* magazine ran a cover with the headline, "We Are All Socialists Now," a play on Richard Nixon's observation that "we are all Keynesians now."[61] The cover appeared in February 2009, less than a month into Obama's presidency, as he was pushing a nearly $1 trillion economic stimulus bill—eventually pared back to $787 billion—through a Democratically controlled Congress.

All of this predictably has irritated Obama, who occasionally has sympathized with the conservative belief that government got too big. That, he told the *New Yorker*, "is why it's ironic when I'm accused of being this raging socialist who wants to amass more and more power for their own government."[62] Among those equally peeved are . . . actual socialists. In a 2009 *Washington Post* article headlined "Obama's No Socialist. I Should Know," Billy Wharton—editor of the *Socialist* magazine—opined: "Not only is he not a socialist, he may in fact not even be a liberal. Socialists understand him more as a hedge-fund Democrat—one of a generation of neoliberal politicians firmly committed to free-market policies."[63]

Squish: A derisive term conservative Republicans use to mock moderate or centrist members of their party.

★ "Squish" had been used intermittently during the Reagan years about Republicans who were unreliable in backing the administration's agenda. It became cable fodder in the late 1990s, used by far-right provocateur Ann Coulter as a barb to Republican lawmakers who hemmed and hawed over impeaching President Bill Clinton.

In 2013 the term went *viral* when freshman senator Ted Cruz of Texas used it to knock his fellow Republican senators for insufficient fealty to the conservative faith. Cruz derided colleagues as squishes for opposing a filibuster on a recent gun control vote. They were too concerned with winning popularity among the political intelligentsia like the *New York Times* and Washington think tanks—rather than opposing all gun control, Cruz argued. "There is an alternative—you could just not be a bunch of squishes," Cruz said at a FreedomWorks event in Texas.[64]

"Squish" doesn't always apply to Republicans. It's become a catchall phrase for politicians who avoid taking firm stands on issues. "Clinton," *Newsweek* reported in 1993, "was haunted once more by his old nemesis, the Squish Factor: the impression that he had difficulty making up his mind, that he was too anxious to please, too eager to compromise, too easily rolled."[65]

Strategist/adviser: Broad catchall descriptions for campaign consultants. Television talking heads are often labeled this way, even when the strategist has little or no experience working on an actual campaign.

★ This type of labeling tends to burn up actual strategists, who spent years getting little sleep at Holiday Inns between campaign stops, all the while shepherding their candidates from one rubber-chicken-circuit dinner to another. "What's frustrating for people who worked on campaigns is seeing these folks second-guessing decisions every day," one Republican strategist who has been a veteran of several presidential campaigns told *Politico* in 2008. "It has to be like an astronaut who spent their whole career and life trying to get to space, and you've got somebody who has never been there giving you an opinion of what it's like on the moon."[66]

Presidential-level campaigns have real strategists who handle big-picture strategy rather than day-to-day logistics. In John McCain's presidential bid, longtime Republican lobbyist and strategist Charlie Black was a fixture on his campaign buses and planes. For Mitt Romney, the job went to Stuart Stevens, a veteran political consultant and author.

Such strategists generally are far more big-picture people than "advisers," another functionary that candidates often employ. As Bill Clinton's campaign guru, James Carville, told William Safire in 2007: "Every campaign has 10 advisers, and one in 10 campaigns has a strategist. An adviser says, 'Wear the green necktie or the blue shirt.' A strategist develops a rationale for the campaign."[67]

Surrogate: A person designated to speak on behalf of an officeholder or candidate. The surrogate's remarks are supposed to sound extemporaneous and on-the-spot, but in reality are well-coordinated *talking points*.

★ Spouses are the most consistent campaign surrogates. They're brought out to ooze authenticity and share the "lighter" side of the candidate. Spouses often tell endearingly corny jokes and stories about their first date, weakness for junk food, or other harmless tales.

One of the most unique campaign surrogates was former president Bill Clinton, who traveled extensively to campaign for his wife Hillary during the 2007–8 Democratic primaries. Bill

Clinton was in a unique position for a spousal campaign surrogate, having actually served in the office his wife was running for.

After Hillary Clinton lost the Democratic nomination to Barack Obama, Bill Clinton became a surrogate, if somewhat reluctantly, for her former rival. Four years later, though, Bill Clinton was all-in as an Obama surrogate. The forty-second president cut a campaign ad touting President Obama's authorization of a risky mission to kill 9/11 terrorist mastermind Osama bin Laden. At the Democratic national convention in Charlotte, Clinton's speech was considered superior to President Obama's own argument for reelection.

Team player: The expectation by party leaders that lawmakers will—if only for the sake of political expediency—act as a voting bloc with their colleagues. Party honchos regularly exhort their troops that if they splinter over a vote or procedural move, the opposition will gain the majority.

★ Not being a team player can have dire consequences. Former Republican representative Zach Wamp of Tennessee recalled that his frequent challenges to GOP leaders led to his ostracism. "The staff is all told that 'Zach Wamp's a rebel and he's not always with the team.' . . . It took me a while to recover," he said in 2008.[68]

Being a team player in politics used to be considered a positive. It involved putting aside one's own political ambitions for the greater good of the cause. But in the highly polarized early twenty-first century, team player took on a decidedly negative tint, as one who tossed aside their own ideological principals on a whim.

No less an ideological stalwart than Rick Santorum was hit for having been a self-proclaimed team player during his twelve-year Senate career. Running for the 2012 Republican presidential nomination, the ex-Pennsylvania senator had to fend off criticism from frontrunner Mitt Romney over his support, a decade earlier, for the No Child Left Behind education law. At a Republican primary debate, Santorum openly said his vote was a mistake, but offered a caveat. "It was against the principles I believed in, but, you know, when you're part of the team, sometimes you take one for the team," Santorum said.[69]

Party leaders once had more inducements to keep their members on board as team players—particularly in the House. Earmarks, appropriations, and even Capitol Hill parking spots could ply their minions enough to vote with leadership. But in a decentralized media age, in which lawmakers have their own powerbases on partisan cable shows, Twitter, Facebook, and so on, there's often little leadership types can do to make their own side behave as team players.

In the 2010 and 2012 elections, a new breed of House members came into office with the stated purpose of *not* being team players. In December 2012, several House Republicans were stripped of their committee seats after it was determined by the GOP conference that they were not team players and had publicly spoken against leadership too many times.

Tracker: A campaign staffer sent to record on video every public appearance of the opposition candidate. Trackers are usually young people, fresh out of college, looking for a way into politics.

★ It's often a thankless task, because politicians these days have become so adept at staying so *on-message*. For every gaffe that goes viral, the trackers record hundreds of hours of pure tedium. But occasionally the candidate the tracker is tailing slips up. Take an April 2012 town hall appearance by Republican representative Allen West of Florida. The legislator was asked, "What percentage of the American legislature do you think are card-carrying Marxists or international socialists?" Some in the audience laughed. West, however, responded: "No, that's a good question. I believe there's about 78 to 81 members of the Democrat Party that are members of the Communist Party."[70]

The remark was reported on local news sites. But what gave it legs, propelled by left-leaning sites like *Huffington Post* and overtly liberal *ThinkProgress*—was the fact that it was caught on video. West lost narrowly that November after a single term. The gold standard of political tracking remains the summer 2006 taping of Senator George Allen of Virginia. A telegenic former governor, state legislator, and congressman, Allen had his eye on the 2008 Republican presidential nomination. But Allen got too far ahead of himself in his race against former Navy secretary and author Jim Webb. Allen twice used the word "macaca" to refer to the dark-complexioned S. R. Sidarth, who was filming as a tracker for Webb's campaign and who was of Indian ancestry. Allen's "Macaca moment" quickly went viral online and on television. Webb eked out a narrow victory, effectively ending Allen's political career.

True believer: A term that originated with Eric Hoffer in his 1951 classic book of the same title in reference to people who become deeply, even obsessively committed to a cause. It has become shorthand to refer to the most ideologically driven politicians and their adherents.

★ Ronald Reagan often gets that description, in both a positive and negative connotation. More recently, Texas senator Ted Cruz has received the tag as he has ascended among the political right, with the *New York Times* dubbing him "the true believer's true believer" during his successful 2012 race.[71] True believers who tweet use the hashtag "TCOT," for "Top Conservatives on Twitter," to ensure that the like-minded will be able to easily follow what they're saying. The No. 1 TCOT in fall 2013: former House Speaker Newt Gingrich.

But conservatives also use the term on liberals. When Venezuelan leader Hugo Chavez died in March 2013, a post appeared on conservative Texas representative Steve Stockman's Twitter account before being deleted within a few seconds: "Chavez nationalized oil companies, censored opposition media and banned guns. Democrats lost a true believer."[72]

Vetter: A specialized form of *operative* who does the work of combing the backgrounds of candidates for high office, including the vice presidency and Supreme Court judgeships.

★ The importance of vetting has grown as politics has become both more combative and competitive. Recounting the missed opportunity of picking up a Senate seat in Delaware in 2010, former Bush White House political guru Karl Rove lamented in a speech that Republican Christine O'Donnell—of "dabbled in witchcraft" fame—was a losing candidate who required better vetting.

A successful vetting can be highly discomforting. "You just have to know going in that it's totally invasive," former Indiana Democratic senator Evan Bayh, who was considered as Barack Obama's 2008 running mate, told *GQ* magazine's Jason Zengerle in 2012. "It's like having a colonoscopy, except they use the Hubble telescope on you." Zengerle himself submitted to the process after filling out a fifty-four-part biographical questionnaire. He recounted some of the questions asked by Ted Frank, a Republican attorney: "Have you ever had a homosexual encounter? Could a rogue IT guy have access to a sex tape or anything like that?"[73]

Wacko bird: See *wing nut*.

Whale: Like the highest of high rollers at casinos, these are the biggest of the wealthy campaign donors. Their numbers are small—fewer than 100 on the Democratic and Republican sides earn that classification.

★ Las Vegas casino magnate Sheldon Adelson is the preeminent of the species. The world's twelfth-wealthiest individual, he gave nearly $93 million to GOP candidates and causes during the 2012 election cycle, or three times more than the second-place donor, Texas billionaire Harold Simmons. Adelson typifies most whales in that he has a fairly limited number of interests—in his case, fighting Internet gambling and fiercely supporting Israel. The Koch brothers, the Kansas-based libertarian-leaning tycoons, are a slightly different breed in that they have a wide-ranging ideological agenda.

But Florida-based political consultant Rick Wilson observed that more and more whales are becoming interested in specific issues. "An increasing number of these guys are asking policy-related questions," he said. "It's no longer just, 'I want to be an ambassador.' That was a much more common thing in the past." He contrasts that with smaller-dollar donors, who can be full of demands: "A guy who gives $500 will ask for the most luxurious treatment—'Where's my foot massage?'—versus these types of guys."[74]

Wing nut: A lawmaker or activist known more for his or her proclivity for making outrageous statements than for accomplishing much legislatively. Extreme *left-wing loony* Democrats such as antiwar former presidential candidate Dennis Kucinich occasionally are branded as wing nuts, but *true believer* Republicans get tarred with the description far more often.

★ Because of their outrageousness and quotability, wing nuts are frequent presences in the media, far more so than their less voluble colleagues, and are seen as having been a reason for the free-fall drop in Congress' popularity. "The good news is that wing nuts usually don't matter," former Obama White House official Cass Sunstein wrote. "The bad news is that they influence people who do."[75]

Among the GOP lawmakers who most often have been given the description in news articles, blog posts, and even from their fellow Republicans: Texas representative Louie Gohmert, who made a CNN appearance to discuss "terror babies," an alleged effort to send pregnant women into the United States to give birth to children eligible for U.S. passports who could be trained to carry out terrorist missions, then became outraged when asked for proof; Georgia representative Paul Broun, who called evolution and the big bang theory "lies straight from the pit of hell"; and Iowa representative Steve King, a vituperative critic of illegal immigration who speculated that President Obama's family could have faked his citizenship with "a telegram from Kenya."

A recent variant is *wacko bird*, which Arizona senator John McCain used in March 2013 to disparage his tea-party-driven colleagues Ted Cruz of Texas and Rand Paul of Kentucky, along with Michigan representative Justin Amash. Not only did Cruz embrace the term, his like-minded and entrepreneurial followers began selling bumper stickers and T-shirts. One selling for $15.95 depicted a bald eagle with the inscription "American Wacko Bird and Proud of It!"[76]

Wise men: An expression borrowed from the Bible, it refers to reputable veterans of D.C. who have an intimate knowledge of the town's inner workings. Often synonymous with "graybeards."

★ To qualify, members generally have to have served in or be associated with multiple presidential administrations or campaigns, or had a multi-decade tenure in Congress that preceded a lucrative lobbying career. They generally are pragmatists who shun partisan politics, which makes them something of an anachronism in today's polarized climate.

Lawyer Clark Clifford, who advised four Democratic presidents and served as Lyndon Johnson's secretary of defense, is often held up as the preeminent Washington wise man. Today, former secretary of state Colin Powell is generally acknowledged to hold the post. He and others of the ilk often are called to serve on commissions that spring up whenever politicians want to put off a firm decision on a vexing issue. They also act as campaign advisers, as sherpas for high-profile nominations, and to solve crises. Among others considered the wisest of the wise: former Federal Reserve chairman Paul Volcker, former secretary of state James Baker and veteran lobbyist Vernon Jordan.

Like other exclusive clubs in politics, the group as a whole is overwhelmingly male. But women can belong, too. Former secretary of state Madeleine Albright was named to an international NATO council in 2009 that was dubbed "the Wise Men."

Workhorse/show horse: Age-old expressions describing, in the first case, politicians who dutifully introduce bills and show up to hearings—in other words, the substantive stuff of governing—and, in the second, those who hold incessant news conferences, churn out press releases, and indulge in grandstanding.

★ Hillary Rodham Clinton is among the many who embraces the term: "I believe I am a workhorse," she told NBC News during her 2008 presidential bid.[77] Another Democrat, California representative Brad Sherman, also was quick to describe himself that way even after being asked in 2012 why he had been the original sponsor of just three pieces of legislation. "Well, I'm a workhorse, not a show horse," he told MSNBC. "I never go into a meeting saying my name has to be first on the list [of introduced bills] . . . I cosponsored and worked to pass 140 bills that are now law."[78]

Washingtonian magazine helpfully identifies the top members of Congress in each category with its annual anonymous survey of hundreds of congressional staffers.[79] The "workhorse" winners usually change from year to year, though they often are part of their party leadership, such as Democratic whip Dick Durbin of Illinois, or intellectual leaders of their party, such as GOP House Budget Committee chairman Paul Ryan.

The *Washingtonian*-chosen show horses have been remarkably consistent. In the Senate the winner invariably has been Chuck Schumer (D-NY), who is widely known for his unquenchable thirst for the media spotlight (though in 2012, he also tied with three other senators for "biggest workhorse"). In the House, the crown has belonged almost exclusively for a decade to Sheila Jackson Lee (D-TX), who is infamous for her long-winded speeches (including one at singer Michael Jackson's funeral) and for once saying: "I am a queen, and I demand to be treated like a queen."[80] Jackson Lee has been unapologetic about her activities, saying she tries to work hard on behalf of her constituents. And those constituents appear not to mind; since 1994, she has never gotten less than 70 percent of the vote in any election.

Young gun: An up-and-coming elected official or candidate. The endurance of the term rests in its conflation of two potent political images: youth and power.

★ *Young guns* (the title of a 1988 movie about Billy the Kid starring Emilio Estevez and his brother, Hollywood trouble-maker Charlie Sheen) was popularized by a 2007 *Weekly Standard* story hyping House Republican leaders Eric Cantor (Va.), Kevin McCarthy (Calif.), and Paul Ryan (Wis.). The trio liked the article so much that they soon coauthored a book playing off its title, *Young Guns: A New Generation of Conservative Leaders.* Like most tracts written by sitting officeholders, no matter the party, it was long on partisanship and short on analytical information about policy.

The name Young Guns was then incorporated into the House Republican campaign apparatus. During the 2007–8 election cycle, with House Republicans mired deep in the minority, the Young Guns Program started with the goal of electing GOP candidates, in open-seat and challenger races. The program was opened to all Republican candidates—no matter the candidates' age. By the 2010 election cycle, which saw House Republicans sweep back into the majority by picking up an astonishing sixty-three seats, many office-seekers were more graybeard than young gun, even if they benefited from that youthful moniker.

Cantor, McCarthy, and Ryan also benefited politically. After the fall 2010 elections they became, respectively, House majority leader, House majority whip, and House Budget Committee chairman—with Ryan then picked as the party's 2012 vice presidential nominee.

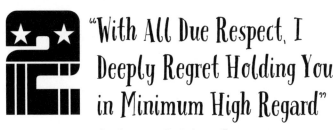

"With All Due Respect, I Deeply Regret Holding You in Minimum High Regard"

Only-in-Politics Expressions

Politicians used to be remembered for sweeping oratory that spoke of inclusion. Think John F. Kennedy's "Ask not what your country can do for you . . ." and Franklin Roosevelt's "The only thing we have to fear is fear itself."

At the risk of sounding like we pine too much for the *good old days*, that's not the case anymore.

"There's no longer the need to speak to a large constituency, so [politicians] develop hybrid political vocabularies that are, in a sense, as much to exclude as include," Wayne Fields, an English professor at St. Louis's Washington University who studies political argument, told one of us. "It goes across the board. It's hard to say which comes first—whether politics corrupted the language, or the language has corrupted the politics."[1]

As a result, the political right speaks of "San Francisco values" and "judicial activism." The left substitutes "progressive" for "liberal" and "investment" for "spending." Both sides talk of "class warfare."

At the same time, when one side does reach out to the other, part of political speech is defined by putting sentiments behind a veneer of false courtesy or blatant euphemism. "My good friend" is the most obvious example. But again, there's a wider array of words doing different work, so here's our attempt to capture some of them.

Accountability: A high-minded, responsible-sounding word used against whichever party holds the White House.

★ The opposition party in Congress routinely demands accountability on any number of perceived misdeeds. Whatever the facts of the situation, calling for it can be enough to win all-important news coverage.

In October 2013 the Obama administration's botched rollout of HealthCare.gov, the website of its signature Affordable Care Act—Obamacare—provided plenty of fodder for congressional Republicans to demand accountability. House Speaker John Boehner said at the time, "Whether it's Obamacare or issues with the Department of Defense, it's our job to hold them accountable. . . . And when it comes to Obamacare, there's a lot to be held accountable."[2]

"As you know": In politics this often means "as you SHOULD know." It's a subtle way of either reminding people of an accomplishment of yours, of pointing out something that someone, in fact, does *not* know, and of conferring the status of truth on what may be only a matter of opinion.

★ For the former, here's Arizona senator John McCain at a November 2013 town-hall meeting on immigration reform: "I've tried very hard, as you know, and worked with seven other senators on a comprehensive reform bill that passed the Senate."[3] And for the latter, White House press secretary Jay Carney a month earlier in response to a question about the House Armed Services Committee's position on the terrorist attack in Benghazi, Libya: "The 'poor' statement is a reflection of an assessment made by Republicans who have, as you know, attempted unfortunately to make this a partisan issue."[4]

Bipartisanship: As we all learned in elementary school, bipartisanship is supposed to mean Republicans and Democrats—*true believers, left-wing loonies,* and the like—setting aside their differences—in other words, going all *squishy* and *Neville Chamberlain*—to team up on legislation for the good of the country. Charges of its absence often serve as a way for partisans to try to shame the other side into going along.

★ Bipartisanship has long been considered a worthy goal. Political science professors routinely lament the decline of opposition party members working together. An entire think tank, the Bipartisan Policy Center, sprouted up in 2007 to promote the notion.

But lawmakers on both sides see it differently. They routinely place their side's policy priorities ahead of bipartisanship for its own sake.

Consider then House Speaker Nancy Pelosi's February 2009 statement about freshly inaugurated President Barack Obama's economic stimulus bill. The California Democrat was trying to stave off Senate attempts to slash up to $100 billion in spending from the $819 billion package, which the House had recently passed. Pelosi dismissed calls from minority Republicans for bipartisanship as "process" arguments. "Washington seems consumed in the process argument of bipartisanship, when the rest of the country says they need this bill," Pelosi said.[5]

More recently, conservative Indiana Senate candidate Richard Mourdock in 2012 declared: "I certainly think bipartisanship ought to consist of Democrats coming to the Republican point of view."[6] Mourdock lost, but not because of that statement—he made an even more controversial remark that pregnancies resulting from rape are "something that God intended to happen," a gaffe of the highest order.

There have been periods of genuine bipartisanship in American politics, though usually when one party dominated and there were simply fewer voices in the political minority to shout down. During the 1930s congressional Republicans, though few in number, regularly crossed the aisle to support President Franklin Roosevelt's New Deal policies.

For a period in the mid-1960s, some Senate Republicans worked with President Lyndon Johnson on Great Society domestic issues. And the war in Vietnam originally had bipartisan support. In the 1980s, a period of more divided government, conservative-leaning Democratic "boll weevils" were key allies for President Ronald Reagan's economic and international initiatives.

Bipartisanship became more difficult because there was little if any crossover between the two sides. And so these days, it is largely confined to *small-bore* issues—naming post offices, hiring more math and science teachers, helping ex-convicts reenter society. To work on a bipartisan basis in an election year, for example, "You've got to find topics with real needs and not a whole lot of political value associated with them," then Kansas Republican senator Sam Brownback, an occasional aisle-crosser before becoming one of the country's most staunchly conservative governors, once told one of us.[7]

Bold: A politician's most common description of their own or their party's proposals. It manages to be a punchy, optimistic-sounding break with conventional thinking and deliberately vague all at once.

★ The much-heralded GOP governor Scott Walker of Wisconsin warned Mitt Romney's campaign several months before the 2012 election that Romney would lose if he didn't "go bold."[8] (Walker's fondness for the word earlier led one critical Badger State blogger to write a post headlined "Bold Ideas Are Politically Shrewd, But Mostly, 'Bold' Is Just a Clothes Detergent."[9])

Newt Gingrich based his entire unsuccessful 2012 White House bid on what he repeatedly termed "bold solutions" (which, given that they included establishing colonies on the moon, may actually have been on the mark). Ralph Nader called one of his books *Seventeen Solutions: Bold Ideas for Our American Future.* And so on.

When a politician does something even a little bit unexpected, "bold" is often the first word heard on-air or read online. Stephen Colbert mocked this on his show after Romney chose the more-conservative Wisconsin representative Paul Ryan as his running mate. Colbert showed a stream of pundits and campaign officials using the word, followed by an ad for the Chili's restaurant chain that promised "the bold flavor you're craving." Then he put in his trademark two cents about Ryan: "Bold! Bold! So daring! White, Christian, *and* male?"[10]

But it's not always political pabulum. One of the most poignant invocations of "bold" came during the January 2013 congressional testimony of former representative Gabby Giffords (D-AZ) two years after she was shot in the head. "You must act. Be bold. Be courageous," Giffords said in advocating new gun-control laws.[11]

Class warfare: A charge thrown around by both parties to suggest political opponents are insensitive to voters' economic concerns.

★ Democrats use "class warfare" to argue that Republican policies favor the upper classes. Republicans, meanwhile, contend that Democrats want to punish society's most successful by redistributing income and limiting opportunities for economic growth.

"Class warfare" became commonplace in American politics during the industrial revolution of the nineteenth century. As America became less of an agrarian society, with cities growing quickly, the richest in society came to control the lion's share of wealth. The results were violent strikes, the rise of unions, and the beginnings of the socialist movement.

In the early 1900s, Republican Theodore Roosevelt fought excesses of the infamous "robber barons" whose greed he contended had undermined economic fairness in America. He pushed for the adoption of an income tax and a federal estate tax on the inheritances of wealthy families. To his critics, Roosevelt was engaging in class warfare. Later, another Roosevelt, Franklin Delano, would engage in similar so-called strife with the New Deal.

According to Bruce Stokes of *National Journal*, "Issues of class are central to American politics, as abhorrent as they may be to Americans' self-image and the narrative they tell themselves about their history and society."[12] As a result, both sides have tried to claim the class warfare mantle as their own. In his 2004 annual letter to his company's shareholders, investor Warren Buffett, one of the world's richest men, observed in a now-famous quote: "If class warfare is being waged in America, my class is clearly winning."[13]

For a time in his 2000 presidential bid, Vice President Al Gore promoted the slogan, "The people versus the powerful," that got him tagged as a class warrior. Twelve years later, Republican presidential nominee Mitt Romney got portrayed as an über-defender of the upper classes when he was surreptitiously taped decrying the "47 percent" of the American electorate who would never vote for him.

But some on the right contend class warfare can be a winning political position. A 2012 Republican presidential primary rival of Romney's, former Pennsylvania senator Rick Santorum, said as much in an August 2013 talk to GOP activists in Iowa. Santorum said his party should reject Democrats' divisive talk of "classes," even if it's the broadly lauded "middle class." "Since when in America are people stuck in areas or defined places called a class?" Santorum asked the crowd. "That's Marxism talk."[14]

Clubhouse turn: See *pivot*.

Common sense: The label politicians apply to policies they're trying to sell that aren't popular with the public. It's a form of rebranding aimed to make the proposals seem like no-brainers.

★ Gun control is the most prominent example of this common-sense political marketing effort. For years, Democrats found themselves on the losing end of this issue. President Bill Clinton blamed the newly enacted 1994 assault weapons ban for his party's devastating congressional losses that year. When his vice president, Al Gore, ran for the White House himself in 2000, his support of gun-control measures likely cost him major votes in states with significant rural populations. West Virginia, for one, went Republican for the first time since 1984—its five electoral votes would have given Gore enough to claim the presidency.

Over the following dozen years, national Democrats largely shelved the gun-control issue. But the tenor changed after a series of mass shootings—Virginia Tech University in 2007, a July 2012 massacre at a Colorado movie theater, and then the December 2012 carnage in Newtown, Connecticut. Backers of firearms restrictions started referring to their proposals as "commonsense gun control." The phrase aimed to draw a distinction from previous efforts to ban all handguns and other popular weapons. Gun-control supporters wanted to be clear that they were only looking to take limited steps. That included requiring instant background checks on all gun purchases, including those at gun shows and online.

This reframing didn't seem to help gun-control's cause, though. Just four months after the Newtown massacre, the Senate rejected a background-check proposal. Then in September 2013, two Colorado state senators—including the chamber's president—ended up on the wrong side of recall efforts for backing gun-control regulations. Voters decided that removing them from office was just common sense.

Constructive: See *cordial.*

Cordial: An age-old diplomatic and political way of describing a relationship, or a private meeting, between two rivals that is distant and/or frosty.

★ When former president George W. Bush was asked in 2013 about the tone of his dealings with Dick Cheney, Bush surprised some observers by giving an extremely tepid response about his highly controversial vice president. "You know, it's been cordial," Bush told c-span, adding, "but he lives in Washington and we live in Dallas."[15]

"Cordial" sometimes is paired with "candid" to describe a situation in which both sides expressed their views without resorting either to political posturing or punching each other in the face. When President Barack Obama met with House Republicans in March 2013, both sides used those same terms, along with the often meaningless-but-polite adjective "substantive." And as Bill Clinton told reporters in September 1995 of his dealings with then House Speaker Newt Gingrich in a prelude to a shutdown of the federal government: "Our personal relationship has basically been candid and cordial."[16]

Two other adjectives in this same family are "useful" and "constructive," generally used to describe a closed-door meeting in which little progress was made, but the two sides are still talking. In his biography of Ohio governor Mike DiSalle, *Call Me Mike*, Richard Zimmerman discusses a meeting between the governor and John F. Kennedy as the latter was seeking to become president in 1960. "Kennedy called their meeting 'useful'; 'DiSalle said the conversation was 'constructive'—political code words meaning little if anything was resolved," Zimmerman wrote.[17]

Deeply concerned/deeply troubled: The stock phrases that invariably get brought out in inaugurating any political clash. When you hear them, consider them the opening bell; plenty more blows stand to be struck.

★ A few recent examples:

- Two weeks after the 2012 presidential election, nearly 100 GOP House members sent President Barack Obama a letter saying they were "deeply troubled" at the prospect of nominating Susan Rice—then at the epicenter of the controversy over the administration's response to terrorist attacks in Benghazi, Libya—as secretary of state.[18] Rice withdrew her name from consideration after other Republicans echoed those concerns in the same way.

- Oklahoma's James Inhofe, the Senate Armed Services Committee's top Republican, opened the confirmation hearing for Chuck Hagel in January 2013 by declaring that Hagel's record "is deeply troubling and out of the mainstream."[19]

- Shortly before Secretary of State John Kerry struck an arms deal with Iran in November 2013, House Speaker John Boehner put out a statement: "Given the Iranian history of obfuscation regarding its nuclear program, I am deeply concerned by reports that the administration is prepared to cut a deal providing sanctions relief for minimal, and reversible, Iranian concessions without requiring a full and complete halt to its nuclear efforts."[20]

Presidents also often use "deeply concerned" to register the intensity of their feelings about an issue. Among the issues on which Obama has publicly expressed deep concern—the political situation in Egypt; reports on the use of nerve gas in Syria; South African leader Nelson Mandela's deteriorating health prior to his death; the nation's unemployment rate.

Will Ferrell mocked this while impersonating a different president—George W. Bush—in a 2005 video on the environment: "Global warming is an issue that my administration is very concerned about—deeply. Deeply, in a deep kind of concerned way."[21]

Deep regret: A classic form of non-apology apology, in which the politician does not actually express contrition.

★ Politicians or officials are frequently in the news for something they said, or did, which was deemed offensive by someone. Depending on the severity of their misstep, after a delay comes a message of deep regret, which if parsed closely isn't much of an apology.

Senate Democratic leader Harry Reid found himself forced into this ritual early in 2010, upon publication of the book *Game Change*. The Nevada lawmaker apologized, in a way, for making racially insensitive remarks about Barack Obama during the 2008 presidential campaign. Authors Mark Halperin and John Heilemann quoted Reid as saying privately that Obama, as a black candidate, could be successful in part to his "light-skinned" appearance and speaking patterns "with no Negro dialect, unless he wanted to have one."

In a statement to CNN, Reid said, "I deeply regret using such a poor choice of words."[22] ("Poor choice of words," incidentally, has become the standard response to "I'm sorry what I said caused such an uproar." So has the passive-voice "mistakes were made" that is often attributed to Nixon's White House during Watergate but actually stems from the Reagan-era Iran-Contra scandal.)

"Deep regret" also pops up in announcements of political resignations. Generally speaking, it means someone that a politician is genuinely sad to see depart. Someone who was forced out or encouraged to step down, on the other hand, often merits a simple "regret." When embarrassing income-tax problems led former Senate majority leader Tom Daschle to withdraw his name in 2009 as the nominee for secretary of Health and Human Services, President Barack Obama gave him the regrets-only treatment.

Disingenuous: This has long been the polite code word for liar, and is used to describe not just a twister of the truth but one who is hopelessly misguided.

★ Though this is slowly no longer becoming the case, it's long been considered bad form—at least in person as opposed to online—for political figures to accuse someone of out-and-out prevarication. (Then-Nebraska Democratic senator Bob Kerrey discovered this in 1996 when he caused an uproar after referring in a magazine interview to then president Bill Clinton as "an unusually good liar"; South Carolina GOP representative Joe Wilson caused an even bigger furor when he shouted "You lie!" at President Barack Obama during a 2009 speech to Congress.) This euphemism lets a politician or surrogate get their point across without having to be so unseemly. (A similar euphemism is "misleading.")

Here's Republican National Committee chairman Reince Priebus, complaining in March 2012 about President Obama's comments on *judicial activism* regarding the 2010 health care law challenge before the Supreme Court: "It's sort of disingenuous and foolish as a lawyer and a former law professor."[23]

When Representative Steve Rothman (D-NJ) found himself in 2012 having to run against fellow New Jersey Democrat Bill Pascrell because of congressional redistricting, he put out a video showing the blustery Pascrell appearing tongue-tied in an interview with MSNBC's Chris Matthews. Pascrell spokesman Sean Darcy retorted: "This video is disingenuous to the point of being laughable."[24]

The word can even transcend lying to encompass a whole category of behavior that is despised, as when Obama visited Oklahoma in 2012 to discuss his administration's record of domestic oil drilling. Far-right senator James Inhofe told a local newspaper: "I welcome President Obama to my home state, but his visit is disingenuous on a number of levels."[25]

"Distraction from the real issues": The phrase politicians invoke to dismiss gripes about their own or their party's actions, or other things they'd prefer not to discuss. It's one of the most common ways for them to seek to regain the rhetorical high ground in any debate.

★ "When your opponents have you painted into the corner, a tried and true way to help yourselves get out of the hole and on the offensive is to accuse them of distracting from the real issues," said lobbyist Jim Manley, a former spokesman for Democratic senators Ted Kennedy and Harry Reid.[26]

When House Republicans released a budget proposal in March 2012 that Democrats called "anti-woman," GOP representative Cathy McMorris Rodgers of Washington—now a member of her party's leadership—went on MSNBC's *Hardball*. "This is a distraction from the real issues," she said. "The reality is that the Republicans won the women's vote in 2010, and the Democrats know they have to win the women's vote and they are scared."[27]

Democrat Cory Booker, then mayor of Newark, New Jersey, and now a U.S. senator, drew plenty of attention a few months later when he careened off message and criticized the Obama reelection campaign's attacks on Mitt Romney's record at Bain Capital. "This stuff has got to stop, because what it does is it undermines, to me, what this country should be focused on," Booker said on *Meet the Press*. "It's a distraction from the real issues."[28]

Double down: Increasing the use of a high-risk, high-reward political strategy, as in a game of blackjack when doubling down boosts your odds of winning.

★ "Double down" is usually used as a pejorative against a political opponent. In his speech at the 2012 Democratic National Convention in Charlotte, North Carolina, former president Bill Clinton slammed Republican nominee Mitt Romney with it. "We simply cannot afford to give the reins of government to someone who will double down on trickle-down," Clinton said to the uproarious crowd of partisan Democrats.[29]

The phrase has become a journalistic favorite over the years and is rapidly becoming a cliché. But politicians do sometimes use "double down" as a positive phrase. In his 2012 State of the Union speech, President Barack Obama, in fact, doubled down on it. In his section on energy policy, Obama said, "It's time to end the taxpayer giveaways to an industry that rarely has been more profitable, and double-down on a clean energy industry that never has been more promising." Later on, when speaking of the need to develop the nation's human capital, Obama said, "At a time when other countries are doubling down on education, tight budgets have forced states to lay off thousands of teachers."[30]

Entitlement: See *elites*, chapter 1.

Exceptional: See *elites*, chapter 1.

Extreme: See *radical*.

"Frankly, . . .": Stressing the truth of a statement, à la Clark Gable's pronouncement in *Gone with the Wind*. In political-speak it signifies, "I'm not going to be like every other politician—I'm going to tell it like it really is."

★ Take this use from Representative Eliot Engel (D-NY) talking in 2011 about ending the dispute between the Israelis and Palestinians: "The only way that you can resolve the issue is if the two adversaries sit down and hammer out the issues—not by going to the United Nations, which is, frankly, a kangaroo court against Israel."[31] Or from New York governor Andrew Cuomo in 2013 after being pressed to discuss a high-profile corruption scandal: "People do stupid things, frankly."[32]

"Frankly" has become the politicians' most popular verbal crutch (though "at the end of the day" appears to swiftly be gaining ground). Appearing on the House floor in February 2011, Representative Glenn "GT" Thompson (R-PA) used "frankly" no less than seven times within the first minute of a speech.[33]

But no politician deploys the adverb with greater gusto than Newt Gingrich. Comedienne Paula Poundstone once observed that the conservative standard-bearer "says 'frankly' enough to make you wonder what he's being when he doesn't declare he's being frank."[34] When Gingrich ended his bitter 2012 White House bid against Mitt Romney and endorsed the former Massachusetts governor whom he had often disparaged, President Obama's reelection campaign put out a tongue-in-cheek web video called "Newt Gingrich: Frankly, Not Romney's Biggest Supporter."[35]

Gingrich has used the f-word in all sorts of situations, including his dismissal of the political class ("I frankly don't care what the Washington establishment thinks of me"[36]); the federal judiciary ("The courts have become grotesquely dictatorial, far too powerful, and . . . I think, frankly, arrogant in their misreading of the American people"[37]); and his anger over CNN's airing an interview with his ex-wife Marianne in which she declared his interest in an open marriage, then questioning him about it at the outset of a January 2012 candidate forum ("I am frankly astounded that CNN would take trash like that and use it to open a presidential debate"[38]).

A different adverb—"fundamentally"—is another Gingrich favorite. *New York* magazine's Dan Amira in 2011 searched Nexis transcripts and news accounts with the goal of plucking out every single phrase in which he uttered it. He made it as far as the beginning of 2007 "before I had to stop, for my own health and sanity, which, according to my editors, was beginning to suffer in noticeable ways." But he came up with 418 entries, such as "fundamentally a falsehood," "fundamentally alien to American tradition" and, for good measure, "fundamentally dishonest and fundamentally dangerous."[39]

Going rogue: A synonym for *off the reservation* that was popularized during Sarah Palin's 2008 vice presidential bid; she even gave her memoir the title. (The liberal rejoinder book, naturally, was *Going Rouge*.)

★ Like so many other expressions, it emanates from the spy world and has survived because of its coolness. To Palin, it was a point of pride in showing her independence. But Republicans have sought to return it to a more sinister context in criticizing what they see as the fecklessness of President Barack Obama. "Instead of working with Congress to fix the problems in current K-12 education law, the Obama administration chose to go rogue, granting temporary waivers in exchange for implementing the president's preferred reforms," said Minnesota Republican John Kline, chairman of the House Education and Workforce Committee, in July 2013.[40]

Going Zell Miller: The Democratic equivalent of a *RINO* (see chapter 1). Named for former Georgia senator Zell Miller, nominally a Democrat, who became such a critic of his party that he delivered the keynote address at the 2004 Republican National Convention.

The good old days: Nostalgia for earlier eras in American politics, which in reality weren't always that great. "Good old days" recollections can take on an old-timers' get-off-my-lawn flavor.

★ In a hyper-partisan age, some lawmakers, journalists, and good-government types regularly yearn for the days when party leaders could cross the aisle and cut a deal for the good of the nation.

The working relationship between President Ronald Reagan

and House Speaker Tip O'Neill is often cited in this regard. A top aide to the Massachusetts Democrat, Chris Matthews, went on to host MSNBC's *Hardball*. His 2013 book, *Tip and the Gipper*, recounted the pair's fights across Pennsylvania Avenue combined with their willingness to get together for a drink after 6 p.m. In a 2011 *Washington Post* article, Matthews similarly reflected that there was "something the American people liked about this test of wills."[41] Yet some consider that revisionist malarkey. Radio host Rush Limbaugh said on-air: "Tip O'Neill called Ronald Reagan 'the most ignorant man who had ever occupied the White House.' . . . O'Neill also said that Reagan was 'Herbert Hoover with a smile, a cheerleader for selfishness.' . . . Now, all this talk about how these guys are good friends and they went out and drank beer after work every day? It's a bunch of poppycock."[42]

The nostalgia regularly finds its way to journalism. Idealists look back to a less cynical age when reporters didn't try to trip up politicians at every turn. Of course, in laying off certain stories of womanizing, boozing, and other bad behavior, the press corps was not providing the fullest picture possible of the country's would-be leaders.

President John F. Kennedy's marital infidelities were no secret to the reporters who covered his administration. And Lewis Gould's excellent *The Most Exclusive Club: A History of the Modern United States Senate* details how lawmakers in the chamber used to routinely show up for work drunk after ingesting three-martini (at least) lunches.

Grow in office: See *grownup*, chapter 1.

High-class problem: A problem that's less a problem than an unanticipated result of something positive occurring. It's the political variation of the phrase "first-world problem," a tongue-in-cheek commentary on the supposed foibles of the well-off—such as, blogger Jessica Hagy observed, being forced to park too far from your house or having too much goat cheese in your salad.[43]

★ Bill Clinton regularly made use of the phrase during his presidency, such as in a 1999 speech in Chicago. "We have a high-class problem in America: we're all living longer," he said.[44] A decade out of office, he used it again in a 2011 speech on technology in reference to the "enormous amount" of Internet-related commerce.[45] Clinton's former strategist Paul Begala said on CNN in October 2013: "Now the left is united. And they've seen the power of unity. . . . When your biggest problem is, 'I might overplay my newfound strength,' that's a high-class problem."[46]

But Barack Obama has pulled it out, too. When he first ran for president, he used it to describe his inability to personally interact with increasingly large crowds. When he ran for reelection in 2012, he spoke in Washington State to hail aircraft giant Boeing's challenge in how to produce planes quickly enough. "That's what you call a high-class problem," he said.[47]

"I'm focused on . . .": The standard polite dodge that every politician, without exception, uses to duck questions about his or her future ambitions. It's yet another maxim that is difficult for anyone beyond a politician's inner circle to disprove. And of course, it helps to demonstrate said candidate's devotion to his or her current duties. A few examples:

- "I'm focused on winning re-election; that's my goal"—then senator Hillary Clinton in 2005, before announcing her subsequent White House intentions.[48]
- "I'm focused on doing my job here as a Wisconsin congressman, as a Budget Committee chairman"— Representative Paul Ryan in 2012, two months before his selection as Mitt Romney's running mate.[49]
- "I'm focused on being the best governor that I can be"— New York governor Andrew Cuomo in 2013, about 2016.[50]
- "To be honest, I'm focused on the land commissioner race in 2014"—former Florida governor Jeb Bush in 2013, also about 2016 (his son George P. was running for the land commissioner job).[51]

- "My focus is 100 percent on the U.S. Senate."—Texas senator Ted Cruz in 2013 after his emergence as the tea party's hero gave rise to 2016 talk.[52]

Athletes and coaches trot it out, too, as a way of indicating that they're not looking ahead to another game, the lavish sums of money they could earn in upcoming free agency, or anything else beyond what's in front of them. But the most memorable nonpolitical use was by Martha Stewart in 2002, when she was the target of insider-trading allegations for which she eventually did jail time. Asked repeatedly about her financial misdeeds on CBS's *Early Show* during her cooking and home-entertainment segment, she curtly responded that she wanted "to focus on my salad."[53]

"I'm just raising the question": A way of bringing up negative, even conspiratorial, information about an opponent without seeming to look like the bad guy.

★ Asking the question gives the critic plausible deniability about actually believing the information. Yet just by engaging in speculation, they're inherently providing legitimacy to what could be a highly fanciful notion. There's a long history of this, with some episodes more bemusing—or serious—than others. Birther conspiracy theories about where President Barack Obama was born provided near-endless "question-asking"—though there was never a shred of evidence suggesting Obama was born anywhere other than a Hawaii hospital, as he had always maintained.

Right-wing provocateur Glenn Beck was known for regularly raising questions about various conspiracy theories on his talk show. More recently, Senator Dean Heller (R-NV) said in 2012 that two two-year-old federal investigations of Las Vegas casino mogul Sheldon Adelson were drawing attention because Adelson was donating millions of dollars to the GOP. When the *Las Vegas Sun* tried to get him to answer whether those investigations were politically motivated, Heller responded: "I think people get very nervous when you have people like Adelson involved." He added: "I'm not saying it's true. I'm just raising the question."

"I'm sorry if I offended anyone": A classic non-apology apology that makes it clear the public figure is sorry for being caught, not for what he or she actually said.

★ Any time "if" is included in an "apology," it's safe to say the person isn't particularly sorry. Adding it "or any other conditional modifier to an apology makes it a non-apology," author John Kador writes in his 2009 book *Effective Apology: Mending Fences, Building Bridges and Restoring Trust.*[54]

One of the most infamous "if I offended" examples was in 1995, when Senator Al D'Amato went on a radio talk show and mocked the accent of Lance Ito, the Japanese-American judge in the O. J. Simpson murder case. D'Amato's first apology was conditional, and the New York Republican drew heavy criticism. A chastened D'Amato went to the Senate floor to try again, this time without any qualifiers: "I offer my sincere apologies." In resigning as president two decades earlier, Richard Nixon was even less contrite: "I would say only that if some of my judgments were wrong, and some were wrong, they were made in what I believed at the time to be the best interest of the nation."[55]

More recently, Pennsylvania governor Tom Corbett got in hot water in October 2013 after a television interview in which he compared gay marriage to the nuptials of a brother and sister. The Republican chief executive said in a statement he was sorry if anyone was offended by the incest comparison. Corbett added his "words were not intended to offend anyone"[56]—and that he was apologizing if they did. Corbett said he was simply trying to provide an example of the categories of people who aren't legally entitled to obtain marriage licenses in Pennsylvania. That same month, in Colorado, Democratic state representative Joe Salazar suggested that women don't need to carry guns on college campuses to feel safe. "It's why we have call boxes, it's why we have safe zones, it's why we have the whistles," he said. When several angry Republican women said that females were entirely capable of handling firearms, Salazar put out a statement: "I'm sorry if I offended anyone. . . . We were having a public policy debate on whether or not guns make people safer on campus. I don't believe they do."[57]

"I want to spend more time with my family": One of the most pervasive euphemisms in the government and business worlds, it's the lame excuse when someone doesn't want to provide the real reason for departing a job.

★ The expression has become a cliché, and as such, an object of regular ridicule. During a rough political patch for President Obama in May 2013, Dana Perino—President George W. Bush's former spokeswoman—tweeted: "I predict that someone soon in the [White House] will be deciding to spend more time with his or her family."[58] After liberal Democrat Dennis Kucinich dropped his bid for the presidency in 2008 to be with his spouse Elizabeth—thirty-one years his junior—the gossip website Gawker.com cracked that it was "the first time in recorded history the 'spend more time with my family' excuse was believable."[59]

That said, some IWTSMTWMFers insist it's the truth. CIA deputy director Michael Morrell, who became embroiled in the controversy over his agency's talking points on the terrorist attack in Benghazi, Libya, said in a 2013 statement announcing his resignation after thirty-three years: "When I say that it is time for my family, nothing could be more real than that."[60] That can be a potent argument, says Wake Forest University professor Allan Louden, who studies political speech. "It's one of those ones you can't argue against—you can't say that it's not true," he said.[61]

Laura Vanderkam, author of two books on balancing work and family life, dislikes the expression for several reasons. "The people who use this phrase tend to be near the top of organizations, which grants them reasonable control of their time," she wrote in a 2013 column. "If you want to come in late because you're bringing your kid to school once or twice a week, you're probably not going to get fired. If you can schedule lunches with donors, you can schedule lunch with your spouse. If you are powerful enough, you can often get people to come to you—meaning travel can be managed as well. Presenting 'demanding job' and 'time with family' as opposing forces contributes to the false choice duality so prevalent in the popular narrative."[62]

"Let me be clear": A frequent expression of exasperation from a politician who believes he or she isn't making a fully understood argument. It's the rhetorical heir to Richard Nixon's famous "Let me make one thing perfectly clear."

★ "Let me be clear" is President Barack Obama's most common verbal tic. "It is his emphatic windup for, well, everything," the Associated Press's Ben Feller wrote in 2009.[63] But House Speaker John Boehner uses it a lot, too: "Let me be clear, tax hikes are off the table," he declared in June 2011.[64] A variation is "Let me tell you," which *Time*'s Katy Steinmetz observed was Mitt Romney's way of emphasizing he held strong positions on areas where he had been accused of flip-flopping. "Let me tell you: I—I want to make it very clear. I have been a champion of protecting traditional marriage," he said at a 2011 debate.[65]

Minimum high regard: A lofty-sounding yet thinly veiled insult by a politician against a colleague. It came into fashion with an older generation of members, but still pops up from time to time.

★ Former Texas Democratic representative Martin Frost recalled "one House member says to another during floor debate: 'I hold the gentleman in minimum high regard.'" Frost, who served as DCCC chairman, chair of the House Democratic Caucus, and in other leadership roles during his 1979–2005 House tenure, helpfully translated the phrase for us: "It means, 'You are an idiot.'"[66]

Former representative Lee Hamilton said House Speakers—third in line in presidential succession—typically hold members of the minority party in minimum high regard over stalling maneuvers, carping about floor procedure, and other annoyances. Hamilton, who represented southern Indiana in Congress from 1965 to 1999, recalled in a 2005 lecture at Kansas State University: "Some years ago we had a speaker of the House of Representatives by the name of John McCormick [D-MA]. He was a great debater. He would step off of the rostrum from time to time and go into the well. Someone on the other side of the aisle would invariably irritate him and he would turn to that person and say, 'I hold the gentleman from Iowa in minimum high regard.'"[67]

And not only House members have been known to use the derisive phrase. In a candid 1996 George Washington University interview, former senator Eugene McCarthy of Minnesota said of his rival for the 1968 Democratic presidential nomination, the late senator Robert F. Kennedy of New York: "Well, I don't have a very high regard for him—as we say, a minimum high regard. But he was a destructive person, very different from Jack. . . . Teddy doesn't destroy anybody but himself, but Bobby would destroy other people."[68]

Sometimes it's legislation, not colleagues, which members hold in minimal high regard. In a 2007 House floor debate over a spending bill, House Appropriations Committee chairman David Obey (D-WI) dismissed arguments in favor of an amendment by Representative Tom Price (R-GA) that would have cut several programs, by saying simply, "I have minimum high regard for it."[69]

Misleading: See *disingenuous*.

Most vulnerable: A rhetorical trick to make it sound as if the opposition is being greedy and mean-spirited by enacting a policy likely to hurt the most defenseless in society.

★ Liberal Democrats use "most vulnerable" most often, to decry proposed cuts to food stamps, welfare, and other social programs they deem essential. Representative Rosa DeLauro of Connecticut, whom conservative journalist Robert Novak once called the "doyenne of the congressional hard left,"[70] slammed the proposed 2013 budget to fund the departments of Labor, Health and Human Services, and Education. The Republican bill, DeLauro warned, "goes on to target the most vulnerable in our society for the deepest cuts. Cuts to programs that improve our schools and combat child abuse, substance abuse, elder abuse, mental health issues, teen pregnancy and domestic violence are all devastating."[71]

But Democrats don't have a monopoly on "most vulnerable." Anti-abortion Republicans regularly decry what they call pro-choicers' assaults on innocent human life. Texas in July 2013 enacted a law to ban abortions after twenty weeks of pregnancy and hold abortion clinics to the same standards as hospital-style surgical centers, among other requirements. GOP governor Rick Perry praised the political acumen of legislators and anti-abortion activists, who, he said, "tirelessly defended our smallest and most vulnerable Texans and future Texans."[72]

My good friend: Politician-speak for somebody they often can't stand. Of all the expressions in this book, most people we interviewed cited this one as the euphemism *they* least could stand.

★ "My good friend" is used most commonly on the House or Senate floors when addressing a colleague. Usually it's a thinly veiled way of showing contempt for the other lawmaker while adhering to congressional rules of decorum. When Democratic representative Gene Green of Texas first arrived on Capitol Hill in the early 1990s, he recalled, "The joke we had was, when someone calls you their good friend, look behind you. I try not to say it unless people really are my good friends."[73]

Sometimes it's not even clear that a lawmaker even *knows* his or her supposedly "good friend." After all, in a chamber of 435 members it's unlikely one House member knows the names of the majority of his or her colleagues, let alone is friends with many of them.

In the Senate, a chamber of just 100, most members are at least on a first-name basis with each other. That doesn't mean they like each other any better, even if they refer to colleagues as friends.

Senate GOP leader Mitch McConnell, who has long had a testy relationship with Democratic leader Harry Reid, demonstrated this in July 2013. If Reid went ahead with a plan to change filibuster rules to subvert Republican objections, McConnell said, "our friend the majority leader is going to be remembered as the worst leader here ever."[74] (Five months later, Reid did force through a rules change over Republican objections, presumably not worried about his friendship with McConnell.)

This American political tradition of hypocrisy over friends likely has British lineage. Parliament has its own version of the English language in which words have meanings different from their use outside. "Liar" can be usefully translated into Parliamentese as "Right honorable Gentleman," or even "My honorable friend."

Washington isn't the only place where the expression can have a negative connotation. In his best-selling book *Kitchen Confidential*, chef-turned-cable-travel-show-star Anthony Bourdain wrote that among restaurant workers, "'My friend' famously means 'asshole' in the worst and most sincere sense of that word."[75]

"Friend," of course, has always been a fungible word in politics. President Harry Truman's remark, "If you want a friend in Washington, get a dog," has become one of the most-quoted maxims of all time. Vito Corleone, head of the fictional Corleone mob family, puts the notion of political friends more plainly in *The Godfather*. He tells an upstart rival who's trying to muscle in on the narcotics business, "It's true I have a lot of friends in politics, but they wouldn't be so friendly if they knew my business was drugs instead of gambling, which they consider a harmless vice. But drugs, that's a dirty business."[76]

Off the reservation: To break sharply from a previous position or established party doctrine, often in an unthinking way. It is the opposite of *on message* and synonymous with *going rogue*, which came into vogue during Sarah Palin's 2008 vice presidential bid.

★ These days, "off the reservation" is most frequently applied to Vice President Joe Biden. "The rap on him is that he talks too long, his speeches don't end and occasionally he goes off the reservation," CNN's John King said in 2008.[77]

But it also has come to mean any deviation whatsoever. Republicans in the House "had a six-vote majority last year and we have a five-vote majority this year, so it hasn't gotten any easier," then House Speaker Dennis Hastert told *National Journal* in 2001. "Any time five people are off the reservation, you can't move the agenda."[78] William Safire traces the first use of the phrase to the *Atlanta Constitution* in 1900 and says it derives from the language of those who traded with Native Americans, who could purportedly get imprisoned or killed for leaving their predesignated lands. It has become less common as people have complained it is hurtful to Indians.[79]

Pivot: Defined as a shift in regular English, it has a more specific meaning to a politician: to move to what *you* want to focus on, as opposed to whatever the focus is on at the moment.

★ In early 2010, when President Obama's party was getting hammered on the economy and some of its members talked of blaming big business for the economy's woes, *National Journal*'s George Condon observed: "For Democrats, this pivot to populism is almost an automatic reflex reaction to bad times."[80] ABC News' Jake Tapper used the word in much the same way in August 2011 to discuss how the administration wanted to concentrate on addressing unemployment: "It feels like every couple of months I am reporting that the White House is announcing that they are pivoting to a jobs agenda, and something else happens."[81] By May 2013, the Republican National Committee had counted fifteen examples of the administration's use of "pivot" "shift" or "focus" to talk about creating more jobs.

A related phrase is *clubhouse turn*, which describes the specific pivot that candidates make while answering questions during a live debate. Northeastern University journalism professor Alan Schroeder, author of several books on presidential debates, traces the origin to Michael Sheehan, a performance coach for Bill Clinton and other Democratic debaters.

"The idea is this: You spend the first 30 seconds or so responding to the question that the moderator or audience member has asked, then devote the remainder of your time to what you would have preferred to talk about in the first place," Schroeder said. "'Clubhouse turn'" strikes me as a particularly appropriate metaphor to apply to debates, since this is a genre with other parallels to horse racing."[82]

Poor choice of words: See *deep regret*.

Radical: An oft-used way to dismiss opponents by casting them as out of the mainstream.

★ The Online Etymology Dictionary says its use as a synonym for "unconventional" dates to 1921, though in the context of political reform it goes back to the early nineteenth century. In the 1960s, it came to describe violently passionate leftists, and this is the context in which it's now used in politics — as someone completely out of control.

Which is too bad, according to Timothy Patrick McCarthy, a Harvard lecturer and co-editor of *The Radical Reader: A Documentary History of the American Radical Tradition*. He told the *Chicago Tribune* in 2011: "To see radicalism as only a bad thing is short-sighted. This nation is filled with examples of people identifying as radicals who moved us forward as a nation. Among our nation's most egalitarian and democratic thinkers are people who've been radicals, and they've pushed the nation to all sorts of progress."[83]

Senate Democratic leader Harry Reid invoked the slam in the September 2013 jostling over the looming government shutdown, calling it a "radical tea party plan."[84] But Republicans also regularly describe as radical such things as environmentalists, bureaucrats, and of course, President Barack Obama. In an October 2013 interview with former vice president Dick Cheney on NBC's *Today Show*, cohost Savannah Guthrie proclaimed a "civil war" in the Republican Party and urged him to blame it on the tea party. Instead, Cheney answered: "I think the most radical operator in Washington today is the president. I think he's trying to take the country in a direction that is fundamentally different than anything we've seen before."[85]

"Radical" is synonymous with "extreme," another word tossed around to depict someone as out of touch. During the 2010 midterm elections, Democrats made especially frequent use of the term in reference to opponents who wanted to eliminate the Federal Reserve and several cabinet agencies. Republicans said the criticism was too broad-brush. "I think when you can't argue on the policies, you start throwing the kitchen sink and name-calling and using this extreme label," Mary Kate Cary, a former speechwriter for President George H. W. Bush, told National Public Radio in October 2010.[86]

Shocked: A favorite ironic and sarcastic way to make a point about official hypocrisy by quoting Captain Renault from the movie *Casablanca*. "I'm shocked, shocked to find that gambling is going on in here!" says Renault, who happens to be a regular at the casino.

★ Senate Judiciary Committee chairman Patrick Leahy invoked the line in a November 2013 interview with C-SPAN's *Newsmakers*. Asked about reports of National Security Agency spying on foreign leaders, the Vermont Democrat said even U.S. allies shouldn't be surprised about such espionage activities. "Hearing these complaints from some of these other countries, it's like the old *Casablanca* movie, 'I'm shocked to find gambling going on here.'"[87]

Leahy was hardly the first to compare NSA activities to the classic 1940s flick. At a congressional hearing weeks earlier, Director of National Intelligence James Clapper used the "shocked" line in dismissing the outcry over the tapping of German chancellor Angela Merkel's cell phone. "Some of this reminds me a lot of the classic movie *Casablanca*: 'My God, there's gambling going on here!'" Clapper said during a public hearing of the House Intelligence Committee.[88]

Slicing the salami: An expression from the business world, where "salami slicing" connotes a financial scam, also known as "penny-shaving," in which a bank collects tiny rounding errors over numerous transactions. It also can mean, in negotiation, seeking concessions in tiny increments. In the political world, "slicing the salami too thin" means emphasizing something too much or reading too much into something.

★ In a 2013 *New York Times Magazine* article about the Obama presidential campaign's voter data-analysis efforts, Obama communications director Dan Pfeiffer said the president warned against getting too deep into the data and "slicing the salami too thin."[89] Earlier that year, State Department spokeswoman Victoria Nuland dismissed repeated follow-up questions about Syria's chemical weapons acquisition after her initial answer by telling a reporter: "We're slicing the salami awful thin."[90]

Sorrow, not anger: A politician's caveat for harsh criticism of their opponents. Politicians saying their slams are done in sorrow, not anger are meant to leave the impression that they're actually nice people and are being forced into uttering such unpleasant words.

★ When Republicans were pulverizing Attorney General Eric Holder in 2012 over the botched Operation Fast and Furious gun-tracing program, GOP senator John Cornyn of Texas told Holder at a hearing: "It's more with sorrow than anger that I would say you leave me with no alternative but to join those who call upon you to resign your office." That led *Washington Post* blogger Chris Cillizza to marvel at its euphemistic power: "Is there a better political phrase than 'more with sorrow than anger'? I don't think so."[91]

Mitt Romney's 2012 presidential campaign was, in some ways, built on a sorrow-not-anger motif. Mindful that most voters don't want candidates to always be *attack dogs*, Romney suggested in his Republican National Convention speech accepting the nomination that he really, really wanted Obama to succeed as president. But since that didn't happen, it was time to hire somebody else—him. Republican insider Ed Rogers noted Romney's rhetorical headshaking, writing in the *Post*, "It appears that the Romney campaign has made the strategic decision that their attacks on Obama will be made more in sorrow than in anger. Given that Obama is well-liked, Romney himself has high negatives, and many voters—particularly some women voters—are turned off by boiling campaign rants, one can understand this decision."[92]

That approach didn't work so well for Romney. But the Republican presidential nominee twelve years earlier, George W. Bush, employed the more-sorrow-than-in-anger theme more effectively. Of outgoing president Bill Clinton—who had vanquished his father from the White House eight years earlier—the GOP nominee said: "Our current president embodied the potential of a generation. So many talents. So much charm. Such great skill. But in the end, to what end? So much promise, to no great purpose."[93]

Straw man: The tendency of politicians to argue against positions that nobody actually holds—in other words, an imaginary opponent. By extension, this mischaracterizes opponents' views, making them easier to argue against. This approach assumes voters are stupid and incapable of critical thinking.

★ The Online Etymology Dictionary dates its figurative use to 1896. Though politicians of all kinds employ it, presidents, naturally, have the loudest megaphone to put forward such fallacies.

Conservatives regularly inveigh against President Barack Obama for constructing too many straw men. In particular they cite his second inaugural speech, in January 2013, for containing a series of straw-man arguments. "We reject the belief that America must choose between caring for the generation that built this country and investing in the generation that will build its future," Obama said. "For we remember the lessons of our past, when twilight years were spent in poverty and parents of a child with a disability had nowhere to turn."

But that was a false verbal construct. Nobody was proposing pushing Granny off a cliff. What *was* at issue in D.C. budget battles was some sort of balance in spending and tax priorities, not a total abolition of programs to help the elderly and disabled, as Obama seemed to be implying. That led Representative Paul Ryan of Wisconsin, the 2012 Republican vice-presidential nominee, to blast Obama's "straw man" attack on the Republican Party over entitlement programs. Ryan told *The Laura Ingraham Show* the next day the speech demonstrated the president did not understand the Republican position on entitlements such as Medicare and Social Security.

Obama's immediate predecessor, George W. Bush, was himself a master of straw-man phony issues. A March 2006 Associated Press article detailed numerous examples of Bush's use of the "straw man argument." The AP noticed that Bush frequently began sentences with "some say" or "some in Washington believe," referring to "Democrats or other White House opponents." By not naming them, Bush was more free to omit "an important nuance or [substitute] an extreme stance that bears little resemblance to their actual position." Bush could then knock "down a straw man of his own making" that nobody would actually defend.[94]

Substantive: See *cordial.*

Throat clearing: The opening stage of a political negotiation. Just as a singer's preconcert warm-up is not his or her best performance, political throat clearing includes opening offers that are far from final.

★ As a "fiscal cliff" approached at the end of 2012 that would hike taxes across the board, the Associated Press reported on opening positions in the negotiations between President Barack Obama and House Speaker John Boehner: "One month before the deadline, negotiations between President Barack Obama and Republicans to save the economy from a plunge over the fiscal cliff are still in the throat-clearing stage. Serious bargaining is on hold while the two sides vie for political leverage."[95] That same year, a House Republican aide told *National Journal* that the White

House wasn't serious about working with the GOP: "Their further comments about wanting to do other things seem more like throat-clearing or checking a box than anything else."[96]

Throat clearing can also refer to long-winded members of Congress during committee hearings. And, of course, real throat clearing can be a tic that draws unwanted notice. During his extremely brief stab at the presidency in 2007, former Tennessee GOP senator Fred Thompson's persistent pauses to harrumph— which he chalked up to a cold—merited an actual story in the *New York Times*,[97] proving once and for all that no detail during campaigns is too trivial for reporters to chronicle.

Throw under the bus: The opposite of loyalty; an all-too-frequent occurrence in which someone ditches or trashes a friend, employee, or associate.

★ Examples of throwing someone under the bus in politics date back to the 1990s and are legion. The *Washington Post*'s David Segal branded it *"the* cliché of the 2008 campaign" and observed it doesn't make logical sense: It ostensibly refers to a campaign bus, and by extension a politician and his or her cause. Because the person being cut loose presumably is aboard the bus, how can they be tossed beneath a vehicle in which they're riding?[98]

It was often used in the run-up to and during the October 2013 government shutdown. Congressional Republicans decided one way to frustrate Senate Democrats—and, by extension, President Barack Obama—was to make lawmakers vote to keep their subsidies for health insurance, as provided by the Affordable Care Act (aka Obamacare). But a Republican bill to kill the subsidies also affected congressional staff. "I understand it politically, and as a talking point," one Republican staffer told *Mother Jones*. "But Congress literally threw staff under the bus on this. . . . You're hurting staff assistants who are sorting your mail."[99]

Useful: See *cordial*.

Values: See *elites*, chapter 1.

"We need to have a conversation about . . .": A favorite that politicians use, closely related to *pivot*, to try to steer a potentially messy debate in an advantageous direction. It's code for, "Let's not jump to conclusions about this; just shut up and listen to *my* view of things."

★ Thus, when mass shootings such as the one in Newtown, Connecticut, have occurred, President Barack Obama talked about the need for a conversation about gun control. Or about federal drug policy, after Colorado and Washington state legalized marijuana use in 2012. Or race, after any number of incidents in which it was a factor. Or about balancing privacy and national security after Edward Snowden revealed the extent of the National Security Agency's domestic snooping.

Not to single out Obama. Former Florida governor Jeb Bush has talked about his party's need to have a conversation with Hispanics. And as the Republican Party's image took a shellacking during the 2013 government shutdown, House Speaker John Boehner proclaimed on the House floor: "We need to sit down and have a conversation about the big challenges that face our country."[100]

"With all due respect . . .": An age-old preface to leveling criticism, with the perfunctory pretense of appearing fair-minded. As humorist Dave Barry once wrote in his mock language column: "It is correctly used to 'soften the blow' when you wish to criticize someone in a diplomatic and nonjudgmental manner, as in: 'With all due respect, you are much worse than Hitler,' or 'No disrespect intended, but you have the intelligence of a macaroon.'"[101]

★ Here's Representative Lois Frankel (D-FL) on the House floor in September 2013: "With all due respect to my friends on the other side of the aisle, this shutdown talk has evolved to ridiculousness."[102] And her colleague Mike Quigley of Illinois a few months earlier addressing House Budget Committee chairman Paul Ryan's budget blueprint: "With all due respect, Mr. Ryan's plan is the wrong way."[103] And another Illinois congressman, Republican Aaron Schock, on Fox News: "The Senate Republicans, with all due respect, are only relevant, I would argue, because we have a House majority."[104]

Journalists often use it in the context of challenging an opponent. When the *Chicago Tribune*'s David Kidwell sat down with Mayor Rahm Emanuel in 2012, the former White House chief of staff began talking about his goals for the city. Kidwell tried to steer the conversation toward his administration's actual performance, particularly on its controversial withholding of public records: "With all due respect, I'm far more interested . . ." The famously combative Emanuel interrupted: "I don't think you have any respect for me, so don't worry about it."[105]

The phrase can sometimes appear as an afterthought to those who don't want to appear *too* brusque. "Some of the president's advisers were on the morning talk shows saying voters don't care about job creation," far-right Minnesota representative Michele Bachmann said in 2011. "I thought, 'What planet are you living on?' With all due respect."[106]

Going Downtown through the Overton Window to Play in the Endgame

People, Places, and Things, Both Real and Imagined

Of the novels that have sought to capture Washington, Jeffrey Frank's *The Columnist* ranks among the most underrated. It's the 2001 comic "memoir" of an imaginary bed-hopping and pompous pundit who, at the outset, listens to former President George H. W. Bush heap praise on him—"Not that you weren't tough, but you always put your country first"—and then implore him to chronicle his life's exploits for history's sake. "Don't hold back," Bush urges.[1]

"Don't hold back" is the unofficial motto of the *score-settling book*, something that's become especially prominent in politics. Of course, athletes, movie stars, and musicians write juicy tell-all memoirs in which they exact revenge on those who slighted them. But in the world of lawmaking and politics, there's an eagerness to twist the knife as quickly as possible that distinguishes the literary output. E-books discussing internal strife or depicting someone as an incompetent bungler now get published during presidential campaigns. Former defense secretary Robert Gates's *Duty* is not a score-settling book per se, but when Gates came out with his 2014 memoir in which he rebuked Barack Obama and Joe Biden, some critics said it was too soon.

As such, we thought it was one of the things—along with people (Neville Chamberlain, the American people) and places (Downtown, the Acela Corridor)—that merited inclusion in this chapter. Some are imaginary or metaphoric, like the "Land" that encompasses a powerful politician's entourage, or "The Pledge" never to raise taxes. Rest assured, though: They're quite real to anyone having anything to do with the nation's capital.

Acela Corridor: The densely populated stretch of the Northeast traversed by pundits, campaign consultants, and other political cognoscenti. Named for the express, pricier Amtrak trains that can shuttle between Washington, D.C., and New York City in under three hours. Vice President Joe Biden is Amtrak's best-known patron; much was made of his daily train commute between D.C. and Delaware when he represented that state in the Senate. (He even half-jokingly once complained to one of us, "When I die, they'll put it on my tombstone: 'He took the train.'"[2])

★ "Acela Corridor" can sometimes be used as a pejorative. This is usually a knock against liberals. Conservative-leaning *New York Times* columnist Ross Douthat wrote in June 2013 that gun control, immigration reform, and climate change are "pillars of Acela Corridor ideology, core elements of [then New York Mayor Michael] Bloombergism, places where Obama-era liberalism overlaps with the views of Davos-goers [a reference to the World Economic Forum, a gathering of political/business elites] and the Wall Street 1 percent."[3] Conservative *RedState* blog founder Erick Erickson is harsher in his assessment of the "Acela Corridor" crowd, suggesting they're mostly acolytes of President Barack Obama. "The New York–Washington bubble remains largely disconnected from the rest of the country. . . . There is a disconnect that I think explains both Congress and the President's falling approval ratings," he wrote in June 2013.[4]

The American people: Every politician, even the ones in complete disagreement, claims to speak for the people. It's invoked often enough to have achieved drinking-game status. Vanderbilt University communication studies professor Paul Stob says "the people" has become "the keyword for all populist discourse."[5]

★ That means that *true believers* can call the agreement that ended the 2013 government shutdown a lousy deal for the American people, while President Obama said the shutdown offered incontrovertible evidence that "the American people are completely fed up with Washington."[6]

But as Stob notes, there are other subsets to describe political audiences: hardworking Americans, American families, the good people of [fill in the blank with any state or city], God-fearing Americans, "real Americans," and so on. And there is "We the people," taken from the first three words of the Constitution. It's become an increasingly popular expression of outrage on both liberal and conservative circles, as in "What about 'We the people?'" Conservatives also talk about "the undeserving," or those deemed unworthy of government benefits that have to rely on "handouts."

A related phrase is "in the national interest," a phrase routinely added to legislation that also is used in speechmaking. In recent years, its use has become widespread in connection with the controversial Keystone XL pipeline project. "Approving this infrastructure project that costs the American taxpayers no money is definitely in the national interest, so what are we waiting for?" said Representative Ann Wagner (R-MO) in May 2013.[7] To which President Barack Obama responded, indirectly, a month later: "Our national interest will be served only if the project does not significantly exacerbate the problem of carbon pollution."[8]

The ask: The whole point of lobbying, obviously, is to seek something; it's known as "the ask."

★ Veteran lobbyist Mark Bloomfield says it's "shocking" to him how many of his colleagues forget or avoid this. "Lobbyists, when they get that rare and valued opportunity, may never make a request," he wrote in a column for the *Hill* newspaper. "Or they talk about issues, mutual friends and hobbies but never make a specific ask. . . . It's a waste of everyone's time, and nothing gets accomplished for your cause."[9]

Chicago politics: Unsavory and even corrupt aspects of politics as practiced in America's third-largest city. In the Chicago machine's heyday that included patronage, nepotism, and activities that routinely drew the attention of federal prosecutors but were often shrugged off by locals.

★ The 1955–76 mayoralty of Mayor Richard J. Daley is often considered Chicago-style politics at its worst. Several of Daley's subordinates were jailed for corruption. Bribes were a routine practice in city politics. City workers had to kick back a portion of their salaries to fund the political operation.

These days, Republican politicians and pundits frequently characterize Democratic officeholders and operatives as engaging in "Chicago-style politics" for arm-twisting and other unseemly acts. The phrase took on new resonance in 2008 when Chicago's own Barack Obama ran for president. GOP rival John McCain's campaign ran ads described Obama as "born of the corrupt Chicago political machine"—though the charge had no basis in fact. As Slate Group editor in chief Jacob Weisberg noted, Obama moved to Chicago in 1985 to be a community organizer in a politically disenfranchised neighborhood on the South Side.[10] Though he had no link to the Chicago machine at all, his first White House chief of staff, the infamously profane and brass-knuckled Rahm Emanuel, is now the Windy City's mayor.

In October 2009, the House minority leader and the soon-to-be speaker, John Boehner, charged at a weekly press briefing, "Chicago-style politics is shutting the American people out and demonizing their opponents."[11] Two years later, Mitt Romney routinely linked Obama to his political home in a negative way. "Chicago-style politics" has become a way to call Obama corrupt without saying it outright.

Comic self-deprecation: The now-familiar ritual in which politicians set aside their ego to poke fun at their foibles and hopefully shore up their public image, often after a newsworthy screwup. It's become an essential part of the tightrope that politicians walk in being both *of* the people and *above* the people, not to mention a crucial media benchmark to judge a politician's character.

★ Comic self-deprecation can take many forms. But one of the most common methods is for officeholders to make a beeline to a late-night comedy talk-show couch. Arkansas governor Bill Clinton set the precedent in August 1988 after his long-winded Democratic National Convention speech. The oration had gone on so long that the friendly crowd cheered and clapped upon hearing Clinton's "In conclusion . . ." near-ending. Clinton, then forty-one and with an eye on national office, quickly accepted an invitation from Johnny Carson to appear on *The Tonight Show* and poke fun at himself. When Clinton sat down, Carson grabbed an hourglass and placed it on the desk. Clinton, showing he could take a joke, laughed along with everyone else.

Chris Christie used a *Late Show with David Letterman* appearance in the same manner in February 2013, sharing a doughnut with the comedian who had joked about the New Jersey governor's portliness. *Washington Post* conservative columnist Jennifer Rubin, in urging other Republicans to be more like Christie, reminded her like-minded readers in a column the following November that "self-deprecating humor is the best way of showing humility and good cheer."[12]

Self-deprecation is now the norm even if there's nothing specifically to repent for. Representative Fred Upton (R-MI) is fond of telling the story of how his colleagues reacted when his niece, supermodel Kate Upton, first appeared on the cover of *Sports Illustrated*'s swimsuit issue: "They said, 'Fred, are you adopted?'"[13]

The most prominent self-deprecation ritual comes each spring at Washington's White House Correspondents' Dinner, aka the *nerd prom*. The president's speech gets scrutinized for *zingers*—

but so also does the president himself. "Humor is a powerful weapon," Democratic speechwriter Jeff Nussbaum told *Slate* in 2010. "But to earn the right to wield it against others, you need to turn it against yourself first."[14]

President Barack Obama seemed to grasp this in his first dinner routine poking fun at his stiff, stubbornly even-keeled image. His 2009 speech was peppered with teleprompter jokes ("Pause for laughter," he said out loud) and predictions about his second 100 days ("I will consider losing my cool"). Yet conservatives, in a sign of how important this quality has become, have added the supposed lack of self-deprecation to the list of things they intensely dislike about the president. Far-right blogger Michelle Malkin wrote in 2009 that Obama is "constitutionally incapable" of it, "because self-deprecation requires sincere humility."[15]

On the opposite end of the ideological spectrum, Texas GOP senator Ted Cruz has sought to incorporate self-deprecation to soften what's been portrayed as a strident, sanctimonious image. A staple of his speeches was a story of hearing a page for actor Tom Cruise while on a plane and thinking it was for him. "You have never seen so many disappointed flight attendants," Cruz would say.[16] Liberals, however, scoff at Cruz's efforts. Stephen Colbert made fun of an ABC News interview in which the Texan mentioned his fondness for a painting in his office of him arguing a case in front of the Supreme Court. Cruz laughed as he recalled losing the case 9–0—something he said was "very good for instilling humility." Colbert noted that the case Cruz was arguing was to permit Texas to withdraw from a settlement agreement that gave health care to poor children.[17]

Democrat Party: A GOP distortion of the Democratic Party's name meant to belittle it. The way members of the Democratic Party see it, the phrase is meant to imply that they are less than fully "democratic." Republicans, in this view, use the "Democrat" term to imply "they are the only true adherents of democracy."

★ The phrase was part of Joe McCarthy's rhetorical arsenal

in the 1950s; *Washington Post* columnist Ruth Marcus wrote in 2006 that Republicans likely continue to employ the term because Democrats dislike it.[18] This Republican pejorative has become such an ingrained part of political discourse that GOP politicians often use it inadvertently, even when they're trying to be respectful. In President George W. Bush's 2007 State of the Union Address, delivered shortly after his opposition swept the 2006 midterm campaigns, Bush spoke of the new "Democrat majority." The advance copy that was given to members of Congress read "Democrat*ic* majority."[19] When National Public Radio's Juan Williams later told Bush that the phrase was like "fingernails on a blackboard" to Democrats, the president responded with a form of the *"I'm sorry if I offended anyone"* apology: "Look, I went into the hall [the House chamber] saying we can work together, and I was very sincere about it. I didn't even know I did it. And if I did, I didn't mean to put fingernails on the board."[20]

Since then, the issue has occasionally come to a head among lawmakers of opposite parties. In 2009, after Representative Jeb Hensarling (R-TX) repeatedly used the phrase "Democrat Party" when questioning Office of Management and Budget director Peter Orszag, Representative Marcy Kaptur (D-OH) intoned, "I'd like to begin by saying to my colleague from Texas that there isn't a single member on this side of the aisle that belongs to the 'Democrat Party.' We belong to the Democratic Party. So the party you were referring to doesn't even exist. And I would just appreciate the courtesy when you're referring to our party, if you're referring to the Democratic Party, to refer to it as such."[21]

For what it's worth, Thailand actually has a "Democrat Party." It's taken plenty of criticism for its "Yellow Shirt" supporters who contributed to the country's political strife in 2013.

Downtown: Shorthand for Washington, D.C.'s, lobbyist shops. K Street—located downtown from the Capitol—was a longtime euphemism for the capital's corridor of influence peddling.

That's not strictly geographically accurate anymore, as many firms have moved to the Virginia suburbs and elsewhere, but the point remains.

★ Former members of Congress and top staffers now routinely move from public positions to lobbying jobs. Since 1998, according to the Center for Responsive Politics, more than 400 former members of Congress have worked as lobbyists or joined such firms for at least some of their time since leaving office.[22] (See also *revolving door*.)

It's easy to see why they get hired. A former member is much more likely to get a call returned or be seen for a meeting than a lesser-known supplicant. Former members can expect to make a starting annual salary of $250,000 to $300,000 at the low end and more than $1 million at the high end, considerably more than the $174,000 they received for their public service on Capitol Hill.

Sitting lawmakers have been known to lament the staggering amounts of money they're supposedly leaving on the table by continuing to engage in public service. Representative Phil Gingrey had to *walk back* a private lament in September 2013 over his comparatively small compensation compared to former staff members. In an argument against a special exemption allowing Hill staffers to buy health insurance, the Georgia Republican said he was "stuck" while aides would go on to make big bucks in lobbying, according to *National Review*. Staffers "may be 33 years old now and not making a lot of money. But in a few years they can just go to K Street . . . and make $500,000 a year. Meanwhile, I'm stuck here making $172,000 a year," said the medical doctor and then Georgia Senate candidate, slightly lowballing his own congressional salary.[23]

The hiring of former officeholders and top staffers is actually just one aspect of the influence game. Former politicians often are brought in as *closers*—part of an integrated services campaign to sway votes in Congress, but also public opinion more broadly.

Ego wall: An age-old expression referring to the portion of an office festooned with photos of the office's occupant posing with prominent politicians as an unspoken indicator of their lofty access as well as status. Such an accouterment is also known as a "me wall" or "glory wall."

★ Tables or other furnishings can perform the same duty. Gore Vidal wrote in his 1967 novel *Washington, D.C.* that a piano's "essential function was to serve as an altar on which to display in silver frames the household gods: photographs of famous people known to the family."

Lobbyists are prone to ego-walling. Before the appendage disgraced was affixed to his name, superlobbyist Jack Abramoff got himself into half a dozen photos with then president George W. Bush. Abramoff also instructed one of his clients, a tribal leader in Louisiana, in a 2001 e-mail how having his own photo could help his reelection chances. "By all means mention [in the tribal newsletter] that the Chief is being asked to confer with the President and is coming to Washington for this purpose in May," Abramoff wrote, according to *Slate*'s John Dickerson. "We'll definitely have a photo from the opportunity, which he can use."[24]

But politicians do it, too. Ex-senator Ben Nighthorse Campbell (r-co) displayed an assemblage of photos of himself with Israeli prime minister Ariel Sharon and celebrities such as Bo Derek. "Part of it is memories. Part of it is maybe what we call name-dropping," said Campbell, a member of the Northern Cheyenne tribe. "From my standpoint, when Indians visit, some of them say, 'By golly, we've arrived.' They say, 'Oh, boy, my senator has some clout.'"[25]

Even journalists are guilty. One of every president's least favorite, most teeth-gritting rituals is the annual White House Christmas party, at which he and his spouse are obliged to pose for hundreds of photos with the people who cover him. Or the people who, in many cases, have never set foot in the briefing room but who've managed to score an invite.

Veteran Senate Democratic staffer Jim Manley, now a lobbyist, has a variation on the ego wall at his Capitol Hill home—a collection of bills that his former liberal boss Ted Kennedy collaborated on with now House Speaker and conservative stalwart John Boehner. "I call it the Wall of Shame," Manley told us.[26]

. . . game: Journalism purists decry reporting on political campaigns and government proceedings as little more than hyped-up sports coverage. And they're basically right. But this is also how politicians, their staffs, and others in decision-making positions discuss routine machinations. Among the preferred terms are *inside game* and *outside game*, along with the single-word *endgame* and the half-century-old favorite *blame game.*

★ "Inside game" refers to lobbying and influence peddling. Lobbyists can represent virtually every conceivable industry and field, from bottled water to more traditional interests like defense contractors. Winning the inside game includes setting up meetings with lawmakers and legislative staff, sometimes testifying in committee and—most crucially—donating the maximum legal limit in campaign contributions.

The "outside game," meanwhile, is a coordinated effort to convince ordinary citizens to apply pressure to officeholders. Sometimes this pressure is organic, more often manufactured. This primarily relies on paid media (online, television, newspaper, and radio ads) and free media (getting news coverage). The outside game works best when the issues are broad and easy to understand.

And there's always got to be an "endgame"—the pursuit of the ultimate outcome. It could be an electoral victory, pushing a bill through Congress, or, just as often, blocking legislation. The term derives from chess; it's the period when only a handful of playing pieces remain on the board. Although William Safire says it was first coined in 1881, it's become more and more popular—in addition to politics, it's been the title of songs (R.E.M.

and others), albums (Megadeth, Rise Against, and others), books, TV shows and movies. Let's face it: It sounds so much cooler than "at the end."

"Endgame" was especially popular during the 2013 government shutdown, when it became clear that Republicans didn't have one to speak of. A CNN.com headline asked: "Government shutdown: Is there an endgame?" *Politico* a few days later tried to get at the House Speaker's strategy: "John Boehner's Endgame." And when it all ended, *Bloomberg View* columnist Albert R. Hunt observed: "In war, football, politics or other pursuits, it's incumbent to fight with an endgame in mind; sometimes the goal isn't achieved and needs adjusting."[27]

Another word that has been in perpetual usage is "blame game," the accusatory exercise that both parties undertake through pointing the finger at each other. The *Oxford English Dictionary* traces it usage to a 1958 review by the famed drama critic Kenneth Tynan, who called it "the worst of domestic rituals."[28]

Investment/revenue/resources: Terms that Democrats use to avoid saying "spending."

★ Like the substitution of *progressive* for liberal, "investment," "revenue," and "resources" are safer for public consumption because they don't smack of a redistribution of wealth.

"Spending" was once a routine part of Democrats' vocabulary. House Speaker Tip O'Neill used the term with pride in the 1980s when doing battle with President Ronald Reagan. But as Democrats neared their fourth decade in the majority, House Republicans pushed back against the notion of spending for public good, contending it was too often accompanied by waste, fraud, and abuse.

"Tax-and-spend Democrat" became a pejorative, used with relish by the likes of Republican House leader Newt Gingrich. House Republicans repeatedly threw out the phrase to scare taxpayers into believing that Democrats wanted to take their hard-earned money and squander it on unnecessary things. "Tax-and-spend Democrats" became such a widespread, effective insult that by the early 1990s it was used virtually every time a Republican ran for office or mentioned a member of the other party.

After losing their four-decade House majority in 1994, Democrats in Washington, and nationally, finally moved away from the term *spending.* The linguistic semantics reached a point that a *Daily Kos* writer, "jillwklausen," gave activists new marching orders. "*Never* say Government Spending. Instead, say we Invest in America," she wrote in March 2012. She explained: "When we hear 'spending,' we automatically think of going shopping and whipping out the credit card"—not the takeaway Democrats want voters to have.[29]

But Republicans, having found a fat target, keep blasting away. "'Investment' has become a Washington code word for more spending," Senate minority leader Mitch McConnell of Kentucky complained in 2013.[30] And the quirky former representative Thad McCotter (R-MI) ever so briefly a 2012 presidential candidate before resigning his seat following a ballot-petition-fraud scandal, once took to the House floor with a series of charts purporting how to "speak Democrat," arguing that the translation of "enhance revenues" was "raise taxes" and that "invest your money" really meant to "waste" it.[31]

More recently, some conservatives also have taken exception to the Democratic demand for a "balanced approach" to developing the federal budget. "When our colleagues across the aisle talk about balance," South Carolina GOP representative Tom Rice complained in 2013, "they use it as a code word for a tax increase."[32] Meanwhile, Democrats have shot back that the Republican call to "freeze" spending levels masks their rivals' true intentions. "We all know that this is a code word for cutting funding," said California Democratic representative George Miller.[33]

Judicial activism: A legal decision or pattern of decisions that you don't like.

★ Claims of judicial activism for decades found a home on

the right. Conservatives likened the 1973 *Roe v. Wade* decision, which decriminalized abortion, to "judicial activism" by unelected judges. In later years critics of the landmark abortion decision, including President George W. Bush, would characterize it as "legislating from the bench."

After years of Republican presidents shifting the federal judiciary to the right, liberals later began using judicial activism when politically convenient. The Supreme Court's December 2000 *Bush v. Gore* case proved a tipping point. The justices voted to halt the recount of ballots in Florida and, in effect, make George W. Bush president. Particularly galling to Democrats was the justices' declaration that the *Bush v. Gore* ruling applied only to the presidential election case before them, with no precedential value.

The notion of judicial activism literally came to a head during President Barack Obama's 2010 State of the Union speech. Obama, a one-time *Harvard Law Review* editor and later University of Chicago constitutional law lecturer, took issue with the Supreme Court's recent *Citizens United* decision, which said that corporations could spend as much as they wanted to sway voters in federal elections. "Last week, the Supreme Court reversed a century of law that I believe will open the floodgates for special interests—including foreign corporations—to spend without limit in our elections." Justice Samuel Alito was seen frowning and mouthing the words "not true."[34]

. . . Land: Staffers and confidantes of an especially prominent politician. The inhabitants of "-land" can also include past advisors, current fundraisers, and assorted hangers-on.

★ Former secretary of state Hillary Clinton has the most extensive entourage. "Hillaryland" originated in the Bill Clinton administration, taking in a core group of advisors that largely stayed with her through the 2008 presidential campaign and beyond. It included personal assistant Huma Abedin, advisor Patti Solis Doyle (who's credited with coining the name Hillaryland), political consultant Mandy Grunwald, and others.

The *New York Times Magazine* in January 2014 did an extensive mapping effort depicting "the inner circle" (including Abedin and loyal spokesman Philippe Reines), the people on "POTUS patrol" (her husband, Bill, and his chief of staff, Tina Flournoy), and daughter Chelsea's "people" (which takes in such minions as Eric Braverman, the Clinton Foundation's CEO).[35]

Hillaryland developed its own tight-knit, proudly kid-friendly subculture. As Hillary put it in her autobiography *Living History*: "While the West Wing had a tendency to leak . . . Hillaryland never did, and every child who ever visited knew exactly where we stashed the cookies."[36] One of its denizens, Eric Woodard, also said Hillaryland's members came up with an unwritten rule: Only they are permitted to refer to their former boss as "HRC," her initials. "It's kind of a term of endearment," he said.[37] It also developed its own language; staffers called people who sent threatening or disturbing letters "red dots," from the round sticker placed on their correspondence to flag them as deserving of attention.

Vice President Joe Biden has, after four-plus decades in politics, a land of his own. One longtime aide, Ted Kaufman, was so tight with Biden that after the 2008 election he was appointed to serve as senator from Delaware for twenty-one months. To Biden, Kaufman is a "stand-up guy," to use one of his favorite expressions. (It derives from the nineteenth century, and refers to someone who will stand up and be counted on in battle.) One of us once stood in a hallway with the infamously loquacious Biden and listened for forty-five minutes as he ran through his list of stand-up guys, and stand-up women, then serving with him in the Senate.

Bidenland has had a black sheep or two. Jeff Connaughton had been a Biden sycophant since seeing the then rising-star politician speak at the University of Alabama in the late 1970s. Connaughton went on to a series of jobs working for Biden over the years, including his failed 1988 Democratic presidential bid.

As recounted in George Packer's *The Unwinding*, Connaughton marketed himself around Washington as a "Biden guy," which led to a lucrative lobbying career.[38] Connaughton went on to serve as chief of staff to Kaufman in 2009 and 2010. He later wrote a bridge-burning memoir about his D.C. experiences, including an unflattering portrayal of Biden himself as a soulless climber who was ungrateful for the dedication of his Bidenland aides—a charge that the vice president's office vehemently denied.

Luntzisms: Maxims by Republican consultant Frank Luntz that deal with the effective framing of political language.

★ Luntz's specialty is testing language and finding words to help clients shift public opinion in their favor. He's written several books dealing with communication strategies and public opinion. Luntz rose to political fame in the early 1990s as pollster for House minority whip Newt Gingrich. In 1990 Luntz helped Gingrich produce a memo by the candidate-training organization GOPAC that encouraged Republicans to "speak like Newt." That included describing Democrats and Democratic policies using words such as "corrupt," "devour," "greed," "hypocrisy," "liberal," "sick," and "traitors."[39]

A dozen or so years later, Luntz contributed Republican talking points on environmental controversies. He pushed for "energy exploration" as a substitute for "oil drilling."[40] And he's credited for popularizing the linguistic rebranding of the estate tax—the levy imposed on the transfer of the property of someone who dies—as "the death tax."[41] The fact-checking website PolitFact in 2010 awarded him its "Lie of the Year" for urging GOP leaders to call health care reform a "government takeover," which numerous news organizations and health care officials called a misleading overstatement. A more recent contribution was *job creators*.

Nazi/Hitler: We'll go out on a limb and say these are the most tiresome insults in politics. But naturally, given the no-holds-barred nature of our current discourse, they get tossed around all the time. They're appallingly effective in that people immediately notice them, and as such attract torrents of news coverage.

★ During the 2013 government shutdown, an obscure Arizona state senator, Republican Brenda Barton, achieved national notoriety for comparing President Obama to the German dictator in a Facebook post, calling him "De Fuhrer [*sic*]" and imploring local sheriffs to arrest National Park Service rangers who were keeping parks closed. Unlike most people, who quickly apologize for making such comments in the heat of the moment, Barton *doubled down*, telling a local publication: "You better read your history. Germany started with national health care and gun control before any of that other stuff happened. And Hitler was elected by a majority of people."[42] Barton thus joined an ignominious group that includes country singer Hank Williams Jr., who in 2011 lost his job singing the opening theme on "Monday Night Football" for his use of the H-word in reference to the president.

The left invoked it during George W. Bush's presidency. Liberal comedienne Janeane Garafolo once referred to his administration as "the 43rd Reich."[43] And MoveOn.org took tremendous heat for an ad that used a tape recording of the Nazi leader speaking followed by a photo of Bush raising his hand to take the oath of office. "A nation warped by lies. Lies fuel fear. Fear fuels aggression. Invasion. Occupation. What were war crimes in 1945 is foreign policy in 2003," the ad said.[44] MoveOn disavowed the spot, saying it was just one of more than 1,500 submissions from the general public submitted as part of an ad campaign and not among the 15 finalists that it put on its website. In recent years, however, most political people have become subtler about Nazi comparisons by bringing up Neville Chamberlain (see separate entry).

Neville Chamberlain: The former British prime minister, history's ultimate appeaser, has become the thinking person's way to tie an opponent to the specter of Nazism and Adolf Hitler.

★ During the 2013 government shutdown, Texas GOP senator Ted Cruz, the hero of the tea party, compared his Republican critics to Chamberlain. Similarly, liberal Harvard professor Alan Dershowitz told NewsMax TV in 2012 that if Iran developed a nuclear weapon that could threaten Israel, it would be "the Neville Chamberlain moment for this administration."[45]

Is this fair? Chamberlain's biographer Robert Self argues that the prime minister was "the leader of a militarily weak and over-stretched empire" who made the best of a bad situation in signing a treaty with Hitler before the Führer set World War II in motion. "In retrospect, the depressing reality is that there was probably no right answer to the crucial problems confronting British policy makers at the time," Self wrote.[46]

Nonessential: An unflattering way of categorizing the 800,000 or so federal workers furloughed during a government shutdown. Every agency has to determine which employees are essential and which ones must stay at home.

★ "Nonessential" as a term peaked dramatically in use during World War II, when quick decisions had to be made over what needed to be done to fight the war. Since then, according to Google Books' Ngram Viewer, its usage has steadily declined.

Federal agencies have sought more benign ways to describe workers who don't have to be on the job. Calling an employee non-essential isn't exactly good for morale. Terms of art now describe federal workers as "exempt" or "not exempt" from furloughs. But as National Public Radio's Alan Greenblatt noted during the October 2013 shutdown, "*exempt* hasn't exactly caught on. Conservative commentators have seized on the fact that the government is doing without 800,000 workers—including most of those at the Environmental Protection Agency—as proof of waste."[47]

And Max Stier, president and CEO of the Partnership for Public Service, a nonprofit group that advocates on behalf of federal workers' contributions to the country, finds the term highly offensive. "Lots of federal employees are being crushed," he told

D.C. radio station WAMU-FM during the shutdown. "They're being crushed because they care about their mission and they're not being allowed to do their job, nor are they being paid. So it's a very challenging world for them. To be called 'nonessential' is taking air out of the balloon ever further."[48]

Overton window: A term that refers to the acceptable range of public discourse. It is named for Joseph Overton, who developed the idea at Michigan's Mackinac Center for Public Policy in the mid-1990s. Far-right provocateur Glenn Beck wrote a 2010 political thriller with the title.

★ Overton noticed that in some policy areas, only a narrow range of potential policies are seen as palatable. "This 'window' of politically acceptable options is primarily defined not by what politicians prefer, but rather by what they believe they can support and still win re-election," the center's website says. "In general, then, the window shifts to include different policy options not when ideas change among politicians, but when ideas change in the society that elects them."[49]

The point is that those who step out of the Overton window are deemed outliers who aren't part of the mainstream. For liberals, this includes advocates of a single-payer health care system. For conservatives, it's those who want to abolish the IRS or replace the income tax with a national sales tax. When Todd Kincannon, former executive director of South Carolina's Republican Party, harshly condemned transgender people on Twitter (he called them "sick freaks") in October 2013, he defended his actions by contending he was trying to widen the Overton window.

Overton window is related to what some on the left deem "Broderism" or "High Broderism." It's a knock at the late *Washington Post* political columnist David Broder, who was long admired by fellow reporters for his fair-mindedness and loathed by liberals for his stubborn commitment to achieving compromise. Critics like the left-leaning website Balloon Juice see Broderism as "a fetishistic attachment to bipartisanship for bipartisanship's sake; reflexive adherence to false equivalencies, regardless of whether what one side says is patently insane."[50]

The package: A presidential motorcade. If you're visiting D.C. or live in a town where the commander in chief is visiting, seeing one can be a thrill. If you live in the District, you're more likely to regard them as a not-infrequent traffic annoyance.

★ *The Atlantic* in 2011 published an excellent graphic illustrating in detail how a motorcade functions, using what the magazine stressed were "open sources and years of watching motorcades" and not classified information.[51] It starts with a "route" police car traveling five minutes ahead to ensure that traffic is clear, with a "pilot" car several minutes behind. The "lead" police car is at the head of the motorcade, often flanked by motorcycles. Following it is the "spare," a vehicle identical to the president's in which VIPs often travel, the "stagecoach" or president's armored car, and the "halfback," an suv holding the president's Secret Service detail. Then come "control" and "support" vehicles carrying key staff, along with the cat vehicle carrying a counterassault team and an id car carrying Secret Service who talk to countersurveillance teams and intelligence specialists.

Also part of the convoy are two vehicles with classified names dealing with electronic countermeasures and hazardous/nuclear materials. At the rear are the press vans; the "roadrunner," a White House communications agency van responsible for secure communications; and an ambulance.

The Pledge: An early-1990s era promise by Republican congressional candidates to conservative activist Grover Norquist's organization binding them to a promise never to raise taxes. The Pledge—a sacrosanct document at Norquist's Americans for Tax Reform—has been signed by all but a handful gop incumbents.

★ The Pledge came into being after President George H. W. Bush reneged on his "no new taxes" campaign promise in the 1990 budget deal, though Norquist once joked on *The Daily Show with Jon Stewart* that he came up with the idea when he was twelve years old.[52] Over the years, The Pledge has taken on a life of its own, with Democrats portraying Norquist as a behind-the-scenes puppeteer of Republican lawmakers, unwilling to let them out of their long-ago promise to never vote for tax hikes—even when the revenue is sorely needed for deficit reduction, domestic spending, or to confront other changed circumstances. Norquist reinforced this notion in a 2011 *60 Minutes* interview with correspondent Steve Kroft.

KROFT: You make it pretty clear. If someone breaks the pledge, you're gonna do everything you can to get rid of them.

NORQUIST: To educate the voters that they raise taxes. And again, we educate people—

KROFT: To get rid of them.

NORQUIST: To encourage them to go into another line of work, like shoplifting or bank robbing, where they have to do their own stealing.

KROFT: You've got them by the short hairs.

NORQUIST: The voters do. Yeah.

KROFT: And they have to march in lockstep with Grover Norquist?

NORQUIST: With the taxpayers of their state. I applaud from the sidelines. I go, "Very good. Yes, yes."[53]

But after Republicans won a House majority in 2010 and engaged in a series of brinksmanship-like standoffs with President Barack Obama over the budget and national debt, some Republicans started to rethink their fealty to the pledge. In May 2012 freshman representative Scott Rigell, increasingly known as a *grownup* or *reasonable Republican*, renounced The Pledge in a congressional website statement. He explained that it would prevent Congress in some cases from eliminating corporate loopholes or government subsidies because those changes would have to be revenue neutral. The math, he said, just didn't make sense.[54]

And a "fiscal cliff" deal enacted shortly after New Year's Day

2013 showed that some Republicans were willing to buck the pledge, as the package allowed tax rates on the highest-earners to rise to levels they had been at twelve years before. The measure passed the House 257–167, with 85 Republican voting in favor.

The precise definition of what constitutes a tax increase can be fungible, and bent to fit the current political situation. In October 2013, Norquist came out in favor of a tax on marijuana dispensaries and other pot-related activities. He told *National Journal*—a Washington news organization that, in confirming his Beltway rock-star status, earlier had a reporter accompany him to a night's worth of parties during the 2012 Republican National Convention[55]—that he believed the move didn't contradict his long-held antitax advocacy. That's because, he said, a tax on pot—namely, in the states where it's been legalized, Colorado and Washington—wouldn't represent a tax hike in the traditional sense.

Red meat: Presidential elections are thought to be won in the middle, through independent voters in key swing states. But they wouldn't matter except for the solid base of support each party begins with.

★ Playing to the base by candidates involves a rather cynical view of the electorate as a pack of slavering dogs. You offer "red-meat" rhetoric to keep them satiated. (William Safire notes that Nixon's vice president, Spiro Agnew, in 1970 regularly asked his speechwriters: "Got some red meat in this to stir 'em up?"[56]) For Republican candidates, this means emphasizing so-called hot-button issues like abortion and gay marriage. Democrats, conversely, are often forced to turn to arguments of *class warfare* and social justice, both animating issues for their base voters.

Arizona senator John McCain learned in October 2008 what can happen when the base is denied its protein. Appearing at a Minnesota rally, McCain tried to reshape the perception of himself as angry and impulsive, describing his presidential rival Barack Obama as a "decent person and a person that you do not have to be scared of as president of the United States." The audience booed.[57]

What does the cattle industry think of the term in a political context? Dan Murphy, a former vice president of the American Meat Institute and frequent media commentator on agriculture-related subjects, raised the question in a 2012 commentary and concluded: "As P. T. Barnum supposedly said, 'There's no such thing as bad publicity.' And as long as 'red meat' stands for something powerful, substantive and well, meaty, that ain't bad."[58]

Revolving door: The classic euphemism for ex-government officials who "swing" between public service and considerably higher-paying jobs downtown in the D.C. lobbying and influence community.

★ Washington is filled with former officials who trade on their former positions in the private sector, only to later return to a government salary. Dick Cheney was hired to head the oil-services giant Halliburton in 1995 in large part owing to his government connections. Cheney had served as chief of staff to Vice President Gerald Ford, was a Republican congressman from Wyoming for a decade, and defense secretary in the George H. W. Bush administration. Cheney, of course, reentered government six years later when he became vice president alongside President George W. Bush. The watchdog group Center for Responsive Politics in 2013 identified more than 400 formers who now work in lobbying.

Indiana Republican Dan Coats has probably had more turns through the revolving door than anyone now in office. He was a congressman for eight years before being appointed to an open Senate seat. He served for ten years and retired after the 1998 elections.

Coats practiced law for a couple of years, then took another turn through the revolving door back into government. Ex-Senator Coats served as ambassador to Germany from 2001 to 2005, during Bush's first term.

When that government gig was done, it was back to the

more lucrative private sector for Coats. In 2007 Coats served as cochairman of a team of lobbyists for Cooper Industries, a Texas corporation that moved its principal place of business to Bermuda, where it would not be liable for U.S. taxes. In that role, he worked to block Senate legislation that would have closed a tax loophole, worth hundreds of millions of dollars to Cooper Industries. The *New York Times* also reported that Coats was cochairman of the Washington government-relations office of King & Spalding, with a salary of $603,609—more than triple what senators were earning at the time.[59]

Coats moved back to Indiana and ran for the Senate in 2010, coaxing Democratic senator Evan Bayh into retirement rather than face a tough race in what was already shaping up as a strong Republican year. Coats won easily. Sticking to the metaphor, Coats told the *Indianapolis Star*: "Throughout my life, whenever a new door has opened, I chose to accept the challenge, instead of playing it safe."[60]

The Center for Responsive Politics, in a 2011 report, highlighted another emerging trend: "reverse revolvers" who went from lobbying to working on Capitol Hill. It found that the number of ex-lobbyists in Congress had more than doubled within a few years, with several major companies' former lobbyists working for the committees that they once lobbied. Topping the list with thirteen ex-employees was AT&T/SBC Communications Inc., followed by defense giant Lockheed Martin and the pharmaceutical titan Roche Group.[61]

San Francisco values: Conservative nomenclature for someone who's even further left and more *radical* than a standard liberal—a pot-smoking, gay/bisexual, hedonistic, Grateful Dead–loving, vegetarian socialist.

★ A version of "San Francisco values" was popularized by Jeanne Kirkpatrick, a onetime Democrat who moved rightward during the Cold War era and served as President Ronald Reagan's ambassador to the United Nations. At the 1984 Republican National Convention, just weeks after Democrats held their confab in San Francisco, Kirkpatrick condemned "San Francisco Democrats" for a "blame America first" mentality.[62]

"San Francisco values" took on new life when the city's congresswoman, Nancy Pelosi, ascended to Speaker of the House after the Democrats' 2006 midterm election romp. Shortly before Election Day, Republican Newt Gingrich sent a fundraising letter to supporters, saying, "Will everything you've worked so hard to accomplish be lost to the San Francisco values of would-be Speaker Nancy Pelosi?"[63] (Gingrich often tells the story of his encounter with a transvestite in the city as emblematic of what it represents to him.) In his unsuccessful 2012 Senate race against Democratic senator Claire McCaskill, Republican Todd Akin's campaign used a McCaskill fundraiser in the Golden City to deride her as "a liberal's liberal."[64]

The reality is that San Francisco is in many ways the opposite of a welfare state. It has long been home to a thriving tech-startup culture. Even those cited as symbolizing its permissiveness, like Pelosi, are in many ways upholders of traditional values. She's an Italian Catholic grandmother who's been married to the same man for fifty years.

And of course, politicians of all stripes hunger for the fundraising cash that comes from there. Democratic political strategist Chris Lehane told the *San Francisco Chronicle* in 2006 that the historic task for candidates has been "to get in and out of San Francisco with a lot of money but no sound bites that could be launched against you in a 30-second commercial."[65]

Score-settling books: The political equivalent of newly minted Godfather Michael Corleone wiping out his rivals. In a business with easily bruised egos and manly (now increasingly womanly) pride, politicos—candidates and operators—are often eager to get past opponents' darkest secrets on the public record.

★ Books are the most familiar form of score settling. The *Game Change* series, covering behind-the-scenes machinations in the 2008 and 2012 presidential races, are arguably 400-plus-page exercises in score settling and backbiting between actors from rival campaigns.

Sometimes an aggrieved party is willing to go on the record with their complaints. Former Reagan White House chief of staff Donald Regan set a vindictive standard with his 1988 memoir *For the Record: From Wall Street to Washington*. Regan's tell-all came a year after being ousted from his White House perch amid the Iran-Contra scandal. The book exposed Regan's disagreements with First Lady Nancy Reagan. He claimed, among other things, that the first lady's personal astrologer helped set President Ronald Reagan's schedule—and even steered some of his policy decisions.

House Speakers, too, can be on the business end of a score-settling memoir. GOP Speaker John Boehner in 2013 came in for dozens of pages of lambasting in an autobiography of a one-time Ohio Republican colleague, Bob Ney. *Sideswiped: Lessons Learned Courtesy of the Hit Men of Capitol Hill* painted Boehner as a lazy, boozed-up, ethically challenged, go-along-to-get-along type. "John Boehner's life in Congress seemed like a maintenance job. I say this because although people thought he was a nice guy, he was considered a bit lazy." But that was only the start of Ney's needling at the person third in line in the presidential succession. "Nevertheless, many felt that his money-raising focus would make up for his lack of concern about legislation—he was considered a man who was all about winning and money. He was a chain-smoking, relentless wine drinker who was more interested in the high life—gold, women, cigarettes, fun, and alcohol."

But Ney had his own baggage. He had served eleven months in prison after pleading guilty to federal charges of corruption and falsification of federal documents in connection with Jack Abramoff, the Washington superlobbyist turned criminal. Before that, in fall 2006, Ney dropped out of his reelection race after serving in the House for nearly a dozen years. Ney wrote that then majority leader Boehner convinced him to go by promising him a high-salary private-sector job, and money to pay the lawyers defending him against the Justice Department's Abramoff investigation. Neither the job nor the money ever materialized, Ney wrote. Not surprisingly, Boehner used Ney's legal troubles to dismiss the score-settling book as a work of fiction. "This is a disgraced congressman who went to jail, who has made a lot of baseless and false accusations in order to try to sell a book," Boehner said at a March 2013 news conference. "It's sad."[66]

Sometimes it's less well-known figures that knife former colleagues in the back and twist the blade with relish. Political campaigns—particularly high-pressure presidential bids—make for some of the juiciest score-settling episodes. A self-described senior advisor on Mitt Romney's 2012 presidential campaign, Gabriel Schoenfeld, wrote a bridge-burning memoir about his experiences in that losing effort.

Slam dunk: The most emphatic of basketball's field goals has long meant a sure thing, a certainty. Of course, in politics, it occasionally isn't.

★ Just ask former CIA director George Tenet, who has come to be most closely associated with the expression. According to journalist Bob Woodward, Tenet originally used it in 2002 in assuring President George W. Bush that chemical and other deadly weapons would be found in Iraq, thus justifying an invasion of that country. It became one of the most remembered expressions of the Bush presidency, along with the president's own "Heck of a job, Brownie." Tenet, however, told *60 Minutes* five years later that he never thought the Iraq intelligence to be a "slam dunk." Rather, he said it applied to how easy it would be to build a public case for war, given Saddam Hussein's past use of chemical weapons. The leaking of the quote to Woodward, Tenet grumbled, was the "most despicable thing that ever happened to me."[67]

In fairness to Tenet, others have tried and missed dunks. In 2004, a group called the Coalition to End Prostitution pushed for a ban on legalized brothels in northern Nevada's Campbell

County. Voters in the heavily conservative area reelected President George W. Bush with 71 percent of the vote—but also decided, by an emphatic 2-to-1 margin, to keep the local hookers employed. "I thought it was going to be a slam dunk," lamented Alan Perazzo, head of the coalition.[68]

Twitter: The microblogging site obviously has revolutionized politics, playing a central role in reporting (journalists are now expected to tweet up to several dozen times a day, seven days a week), scandals (Anthony Weiner—enough said), organizing (it's one of the most invaluable tools for any interest group and campaign), and influencing election outcomes (it played a part in voter certification in Virginia's 2013 attorney general race).

★ Not everyone is a fan of its brevity. Former Republican National Committee chairman Michael Steele lamented to one of us: "Our language has been dumbed-down to a level of idiocy. We barely communicate to each other, with each other, face to face. If we can get it into 140 characters, that's our view of everything. The value of explaining and communicating a particular proposition has been lost."[69]

Like other social networking tools, users unfortunately write online what they would be unlikely to say to another person's face. A *New York Times* political writer in November 2013 found himself on the receiving end of Twitter rants actually meant for Miami Dolphins lineman Jonathan Martin. *That* Jonathan Martin had been in the news for leaving the team after a bullying episode that brought to light clubhouse hazing tactics rarely reported on or heard of in public.

And it has led to the *Twitter war*, a back-and-forth fusillade of nasty comments—almost always between an ardent Democrat and equally provocative Republican—laid bare for all to see. One noteworthy exchange occurred in April 2012 between Eric Fehrnstrom, senior adviser for Mitt Romney, and David Axelrod, his Democratic counterpart for President Barack Obama's reelection campaign. Fehrnstrom initiated the "debate" when he took left-wing comedian and Obama donor Bill Maher to task for a crass comment about Ann Romney, after Democratic strategist Hilary Rosen remarked that the mother of five grown sons had "never worked a day in her life." "Obama SuperPac donor Bill Maher says Ann Romney 'has never gotten her ass out of the house to work,'" and such comments "are not easily dismissed" because Maher is a $1 million donor to the PAC, Fehrnstrom tweeted. That touched off a string of tweets from an aggrieved Axelrod, who countered with: "Texas billionaire Harold Simmons pledges $36m to GOP, and calls Obama 'the most dangerous American alive.' Silence from Mitt." That was followed by a reference to Romney's onetime use of a foreign investment institution that is popular with the extremely wealthy: "So until you have the guts to stand up to one of your own, you can take your studied outrage and stick it in your Swiss bank!"[70]

The service also has spawned the *Twitter bomb*, a strategic way to spread political misinformation that is a form of *astroturfing*. Days before the 2010 special election in Massachusetts to fill the Senate seat that had been held by the late senator Ted Kennedy, an anonymous source launched a blast of smears against Democratic candidate Martha Coakley, the state's attorney general, on Twitter over a 138-minute span. Political scientists Eni Mustafaraj and Panagiotis Metaxas later discovered nine similarly named accounts that sent out more than 900 tweets such as "AG Coakley thinks Catholics shouldn't be in the ER, take action now!" Those messages were retweeted until they potentially reached more than 60,000 people.[71]

Warshington: An alternate pronunciation of the nation's capital, which—depending whom you talk to—is either intended as a slur or is just how some folks naturally say it.

★ The best-known utterers of "WaRshington" are ex-GOP presidential aspirants John McCain and Newt Gingrich. Their use of the word has sparked sporadic debate on message boards about whether they're being deliberate in putting word "war" in the word (which some say is entirely appropriate, given the seemingly unending state of conflict there). Both men say they aren't deliberating denigrating D.C.

Indeed, an argument can be made that it comes down to linguistics. The phenomenon is known as "rhoticization," and occurs when the tip of the tongue curls back slightly at the end of a vowel. It's most common among older people in the Midwest and parts of the South, where people have been known to "warsh" their clothes. But Gingrich and McCain, being savvy politicians, know it doesn't hurt them to poke a little subtle linguistic fun at the town.

Washington handshake: Greeting somebody while looking over his or her shoulder to see if there could be a more important person in the room.

★ During his rise to prominence, and during his heady days as House Speaker, Newt Gingrich was said to be a master of the Washington handshake. Relationships for the Republican bomb thrower were transactional and discardable when a new shiny object appeared that could aid his upward trajectory.

The Washington handshake is only the most visible manifestation of insincerity by many D.C. actors. People who previously held prestigious job titles—members of Congress, journalists at a national news outlet, and others—are often shocked that their *friends* aren't interested in talking to them anymore once they're no longer in a position to help professionally.

Political journalists are often the worst purveyors of the Washington handshake, and insincerity generally. After all, members of Congress have risen to the top of the political ladder by knowing how to fake interest in other people. Reporters and pundits, not so much.

Waste, fraud, and abuse: Something politicians of both parties routinely promise to expose in acting as watchdogs for taxpayers. The term evolved from its nineteenth-century antecedent, "waste, fraud, and peculation." Whatever you call it, it plays well: A 2011 poll of likely voters found that 60 percent of those surveyed said—in an extremely inaccurate assumption—that the federal budget's problems could be solved just by eliminating all three.[72]

★ In a typical example from September 2013, House Republicans pushed through a bill to cut food stamps and other nutrition programs by $40 billion over ten years. After Republicans prevailed narrowly on a 217–210 vote, House Speaker John Boehner praised Majority Leader Eric Cantor and Agriculture Committee Chairman Frank Lucas for putting "together a set of common-sense reforms that strengthen the safety net for our nation's poor, root out waste and fraud in the food stamp program, and save struggling taxpayers billions of dollars."[73]

Make no mistake: The government is hardly WFA-free. But in general, they're not always as pervasive as people think. Consider the Obama administration's $787 billion economic stimulus bill in 2009, which even some Democrats said was a ripe target for malfeasance. A 2010 White House report found just 293 "consequential investigations" out of the nearly 200,000 contracts that were awarded, or less than one-quarter of 1 percent. Both the federal official in charge of the Recovery Accountability and Transparency Board, and an official at the watchdog group Taxpayers for Common Sense, concurred that problems were less than anticipated.[74]

Nevertheless, the errors that did occur drew torrents of news coverage—and congressional criticism. And there were things that critics could easily label "abuse," such as a $72,000 federal study of how primates react to cocaine. Sharron Angle, a Republican who unsuccessfully challenged Senate Democratic leader Harry Reid in 2010, seized on that as an example of "coked-up stimulus monkeys," leading the Obama administration to respond the research was done in the name of fighting human drug addiction.[75]

While Republicans have portrayed themselves as rooters-out of frivolous government spending, Democrats have gotten into the game as well. During the health-care reform debate the

Obama White House website even featured a page, "Policies to Crack Down on Waste, Fraud and Abuse" focused on Medicare cheating and other such issues.[76]

Whack-a-Mole: An arcade game invented in 1976, it has come to commonly represent having to endlessly repeat the same task. In the game, moles pop up from various holes and the player must forcefully pound them on the head with a mallet—a handy metaphor for what political leaders often seek to accomplish on perennially vexing issues.

★ Kentucky's Mitch McConnell, the Senate's Republican leader, drew laughter at a private campaign strategy session in 2013— a secretly recorded tape was obtained by liberal *Mother Jones* magazine—for telling his aides what should be done about actress Ashley Judd, who was then mulling a challenge to McConnell. "This is the Whack-a-Mole period of the campaign . . . when anybody sticks their head up, do them out," he said[77] Other issues for which the phrase has been invoked: gun control, comprehensive immigration reform, the 2012 multicandidate GOP primary, China's trade policy, "Buy American" policies inserted into bills to favor U.S. companies, and removing earmarks from spending bills.

The AFL-CIO used the game in 2002 to have some fun with Enron and some of the other corporations enmeshed in the scandals that were prevalent at the time. The union put a take-off of the game on its website called "Smash Corporate Greed," in which the user could use his or her computer to whack the hands of greedy executives as they disappeared down holes clutching wads of cash.

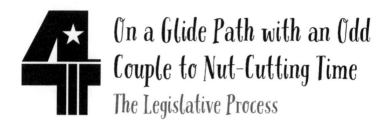

On a Glide Path with an Odd Couple to Nut-Cutting Time
The Legislative Process

Let's start by making clear what this chapter *isn't*—an explanation of parliamentary terms such as "quorum call" and "unanimous consent." That's better left to other books.

We would like to point out, though, that even politicians bemoan how the widespread use of such terms insulates them from their constituents. Missouri Democratic senator Claire McCaskill told us that the question "Can we get cloture?"—the sixty-vote threshold for most legislation to advance in the Senate—best exemplifies to her "the Beltway mentality": "To most people in America," she complained, "it sounds like an improper sexual act."

Instead, we sought more informal terms that you'd hear on Capitol Hill, as well as in many statehouses and city council chambers. Some are euphemistic ("Hope springs eternal"), some are in honor of their originators (Gephardt rule, Hastert rule), and some are just things we thought needed more explanation (hideaways, the lunches).

We're omitting as an official definition one of our favorites: "Roach motel," which describes a circumstance in which senators are all in the chamber voting repeatedly on various bills. As the 1970s commercial for the exterminating insect bait famously boasted, "They can get in, but they can't get out."

Blink first: The eventual—and very often protracted—outcome of *brinkmanship*, as in "Who blinked first?" This cliché comes from the childhood staring-contest game to see who can hold a gaze the longest, and is synonymous with *caving*.

Borking: Refusing to confirm a well-qualified appointee for ideological reasons, often after a well-funded smear campaign.

★ Robert Bork, a federal appeals court judge and conservative legal scholar, was nominated to fill a vacancy on the Supreme Court by President Ronald Reagan in 1987. Within hours of Reagan's announcement, Senator Ted Kennedy took to the Senate floor to denounce "Robert Bork's America," a land of "back-alley abortions" and other potential atrocities. The Senate voted not to confirm Bork, on a 42–58 tally, and a nominee with firmly held views subsequently was seen as a liability.

Now, any time that *any* Supreme Court nominee is perceived as running into the slightest bit of trouble, the headline practically writes itself: "Will (insert name here) Be Borked?" And it extends beyond the court. When Larry Summers' bid to head the Federal Reserve ran into roadblocks that led him to take himself out of the running in September 2013, *Bloomberg Businessweek* ran a headline: "Did Larry Summers Get Borked? Not Really."[1] It explained that he was an unknown figure to most Americans, and thus could not touch off the interest-group rallying that attends a Supreme Court nominee.

Upon Bork's death in December 2012, the *Economist*'s anonymous language column speculated on why "borking" had taken off in political lingo while other similar terms did not. With "no disrespect to the departed intended," the columnist wrote, "while he was alive, many people simply noted that Bork is 'fun to say.'"[2]

Brinkmanship: Once used in the national security realm during the Cold War, to describe moving to the very edge of war in order to force a conciliatory move. It has become yet another phrase that has moved in recent decades into the standard political-combat context to describe virtually any showdown, especially the continued wars between Democrats and Republicans over the budget.

★ As he began his second term in January 2013, President Barack Obama spoke hopefully of future fiscal-related dealings that would include "a little bit less drama, a little bit less brinkmanship, [and] not scare the heck out of folks quite as much."[3] That turned out to be wishful thinking, given the government shutdown that occurred eight months later.

In case you were wondering, the word used is both brinkmanship and brinksmanship, with an added *s*. The version without the *s* is far more common, but both are considered acceptable.

Budgetese: Few languages are more esoteric or confusing than the one dealing with the budget process. We aren't going to fill another book with terms when there are more detailed sources out there (the Government Accountability Office has a particularly handy guide[4]). But we wanted to include some common ones.

- *CBO*: Congressional Budget Office, a nonpartisan agency on Capitol Hill that analyzes or "scores" legislative proposals to see how much they will cost. CBO is often known for issuing dry legislative reports. But from time to time, partisans on both sides use it to argue their fiscal positions are superior to the opposition's. CBO budget estimates are regularly compared to that of the White House's Office of Management and Budget, which oversees the operations of federal departments and agencies.
- *CR*: A continuing resolution. The American public has involuntarily come to learn about continuing resolutions whenever the government is on the verge of running out of money. Continuing resolutions are meant to keep the government running at a previous year's level. It is not an increase in spending, but rather an agreement to continue funding programs and expenditures at the status quo until a new budget can be negotiated—something that rarely happens, meaning that the CR spending levels end up remaining in place for the full year.
- *PAYGO*: Pay-as-you-go, a budget rule requiring new spending

be paid for by making sure that the new costs are balanced by spending cuts, revenue increases, or a combination of the two. Think of it as trying to prevent credit-card holders from racking up any more debt until they've paid off their existing balance.

- *Sequester*: Automatic, across-the-board budget cuts that Congress and the president agreed to in 2011 when Democrats and Republicans couldn't come together on a budget deal. The theory behind the deep cuts in defense, anathema to Republicans, and social programs, which Democrats wanted to preserve, was that the sequester would be so bad neither side would be willing to let it happen. But it didn't turn out that way. With Capitol Hill gridlock rampant, both sides eventually did allow the sequester to happen, allowing for what *Washington Post* columnist Walter Pincus called the "Frankenstein-like budget-cutting monster."

Finally, we would be remiss if we did not note a brilliant piece that ran in the conservative *Weekly Standard* during the 1995 budget wars between congressional Republicans and President Bill Clinton. It parodied budgetese in the form of a *Penthouse* Forum letter, and provoked laughter and knowing nods when it was passed out among staffers at a Senate hearing. "I am a mid-level staffer at the Congressional Budget Office, so I never thought anything would happen to me that I could share with your Forum column," it begins innocently enough.

Naturally, the author encounters two female budget analysts: "I soon could feel Desiree's entitlement caps snuggling against my baseline," he writes. "I love fiscal discipline. Soon Cheri was reconfiguring her CPI calculations, to loosen the pressure on her end, but that only encouraged me to tighten my authorizations. 'I never thought I'd see you in a dynamic scoring posture,' I laughed, pressing my advantage."[5]

Caving: To give in and concede defeat. The all-purpose shorthand to summarize the outcome of any legislative or political debate is "Who caved?"

★ Part of its popularity can be attributed to its vividness as a verb, while part of it is because its brevity makes it handy in headlines. It is most frequently employed by partisans in expressing disappointment with someone in his or her own party. Recounting President Obama's actions on expiring tax cuts first enacted under George W. Bush in 2012, liberal economist Robert Reich fulminated on his blog: "Once again, Obama caved, agreeing to permanently extend the Bush tax cuts for incomes up to $400,000."[6]

Among the faithful, in fact, caving has become synonymous with compromising. It springs from the conflict between what people know, intellectually, and what they want, emotionally. "Basically, people want compromise," National Public Radio's Shankar Vedantam said in a 2012 report on the subject. "But when they see compromise, they see it as caving in."[7]

Codels: One of many perks that members of Congress enjoy, but which the public often finds distasteful when details are revealed. Congressional delegations (codels) are ostensibly to discuss policy issues with foreign leaders. But often the destinations are exotic, beautiful locales that would be pricey if members of Congress had to pay out of their own pockets.

★ The Grand Cayman Islands and Italy are among those frequented by lawmakers. A bipartisan favorite codel has for years been the Paris Air Show. Sometimes, members are even allowed to bring a spouse along.

Sequester spending cuts in 2013—a result of budget impasses between President Barack Obama and the Republican House—led to some limits on codels. Instead, lawmakers seeking all-expenses-paid trips abroad had to rely mostly on private groups, a shift ethics experts said was troubling. Such privately sponsored junkets have been the source of many congressional ethics investigations.

Because lawmakers of both parties enjoy overseas junkets

the trips usually don't become political cudgels. But not always. Representative Jackie Speier made Republican colleagues' travel a prime target during September 2013 House floor debate over a GOP bill to cut $39 billion from the federal food stamps program. On the House floor the California Democrat brought out a cooked steak, a bottle of vodka, and a can of caviar. The props were a pointed reminder that many of the same lawmakers' accusing food stamp recipients of living-off-the-dole had repeatedly taken trips around the world on others' dimes.

"Some of these same members travel to foreign countries under the guise of official business," Speier told the House in righteous indignation. "They dine at lavish restaurants, eating steak, vodka and even caviar. They receive money to do this. That's right, they don't pay out of pocket for these meals." Speier went on, using particular examples of members of Congress who went on sponsored trips and spent large amounts of money on food and lodging. "Let me give you a few examples: One member was given $127.41 a day for food on his trip to Argentina. He probably had a fair amount of steak," she said.

"Another member was given $3,588 for food and lodging during a six-day trip to Russia. He probably drank a fair amount of vodka and probably even had some caviar. That particular member has 21,000 food stamp recipients in his district. One of those people who is on food stamps could live a year on what this congressman spent on food and lodging for six days," she added.[8] But Speier's comparisons ultimately fell on deaf ears. House Republicans prevailed on the vote on a narrow 217–200 margin.

When a lawmaker's aides go on a trip without the *boss* present, it's known as a "staffdel"—a much lower-budget (but more free-spirited, to hear some aides tell it) undertaking.

Complex: Obviously, it refers to something that is not easily solved. But in politics it can double as an excuse not to attack a problem right away.

★ Tart-tongued senator Barbara Boxer, D-Calif., noted this when she upbraided the Environmental Protection Agency in

2007 for not moving fast enough to develop regulations to police the greenhouse gases blamed for global warming. When an EPA official said a court ruling giving EPA that authority was complex and that the agency needed more time to evaluate it, Boxer replied: "'Complex' is sometimes a code word for 'we're going to take our sweet time.'"[9]

To other politicians, "complex" can describe a problem so daunting that anything short of a sweeping comprehensive solution is worthless. The late senator Ted Kennedy invoked this usage in 2006 when talking about a fence across the U.S.-Mexico border. He dismissed the fence as "a bumper-sticker solution for a complex problem. It's a feel-good plan that will have little effect in the real world."[10]

Cooling-off period: A set amount of time that members of Congress have to sit out before lobbying their former colleagues. When House members leave Congress, they are restricted for one year. The Senate has a two-year ban. This also applies to executive branch officials and senior congressional staff.

★ The restrictions aim to prevent those in government from making decisions that could directly benefit them in the private sector months or even weeks later. They're not supposed to be able to trade upon their influence after leaving their government positions—at least not immediately.

Though several laws between 1978 and 2007 have sought to curb immediate influence peddling by ex-members and senior government officials, there are a lot of loopholes. That means the revolving door between government and private industry keeps on swinging.

While former government officials can't directly lobby their former colleagues, they can *oversee* teams of lobbyists who actually carry it out. Hence the creation of lobbyists who aren't officially registered as lobbyists, but who function as "strategic advisers."

It's rare for a former lawmaker or staff member to be prosecuted for violating the cooling-off period, but it does happen. In fact, the rule played a central role in the Jack Abramoff lobbying scandals. In its probe of the once high-flying lobbyist, the Justice Department broke new ground with prosecutions of ex-congressional aides for violating the one-year ban on lobbying their former bosses after departing for K Street.

Coup: Derived from the French *coup d'état* (literally, "a stroke of the state"), an attempt to bring down a major political figure that is engineered by his or onetime supporters. In politics, its exclusive application is now to speakers of the House.

★ House Republicans disillusioned with Newt Gingrich tried one in 1997; though they didn't succeed, they weakened him politically to the point where he resigned in 1998 after the GOP lost the midterm elections. Also removed from leadership at that time was Ohio GOP representative John Boehner, who engineered a political rebound and became speaker himself—and who, of course, became the subject of coup talk after President Obama won a second term in 2012. A group of disaffected conservatives plotted to vote against reelecting Boehner on the first day of the new Congress if they could get at least twenty-five members to go in on the plan. But one member reportedly rescinded his or her participation on the morning of the vote, leaving the group one person short. The *Washington Post* later reported that the Republicans, after praying all night, said that God told them to spare the speaker.[11]

Dilatory tactics: A bit of legalese that has found its way inside the U.S. Capitol (no surprise, given the number of lawyers there), it's the polite parliamentary way of citing the delaying or *slow-walking* of a bill or nomination.

★ Here's New York Democratic senator Chuck Schumer in June 2013, complaining about the pile of Republican amendments offered on a controversial immigration reform bill: "The strategy was, at the last hour, create dilatory tactics so the bill could never be approved."[12] (As it happened, the bill did eventually pass.)

"Don't let the perfect be the enemy of the good": A line from

Voltaire in an eighteenth-century poem (he actually said "the best" instead of perfect), it has become the stock cliché of any lawmaker seeking to hasten compromise.

★ President Barack Obama employs it regularly. "We should do as much as we can, as quickly as we can. And we cannot let the perfect be the enemy of the good," he said in a January 2013 speech pleading for action on gun-violence legislation.[13] And it is a staple of congressional speeches; according to the *Congressional Record*, it had been said more than 400 times by the end of 2013, with slightly more usage in the Senate—where compromises occur more frequently—than the House.

Jim Manley, a former spokesman for Democratic senators Ted Kennedy and Harry Reid who is now a lobbyist, said the phrase can crop up in discussions between a lawmaker's policy specialists and his or her communications team. "If policy staff had their way, the senator would never do anything remotely timely or topical, arguing that they needed more time," Manley recalled. But a press secretary's job "is to get your boss in the news—ergo, don't let the perfect be the enemy of the good."[14]

Earmark: The now-verboten practice of a lawmaker adding money to spending bill solely to benefit his or her district. See *pork*.

Free vote: A vote cast on an issue on which the leadership doesn't exert any pressure or try to influence its members. Also known as "voting your conscience."

★ Such votes often occur on bills that are regarded as having little chance of becoming law or amendments that will get rejected in a House-Senate conference. As a House GOP leadership aide told *National Journal* in 2001: "When you know it's not going through the Senate, it turns out to be a free vote for the House."[15]

Free votes also can occur when opposing nominees that are guaranteed to win Senate confirmation. When Federal Reserve chairman Ben Bernanke was up for a second term in 2010, then senator Christopher Dodd (D-CT) said some of his colleagues saw virtue in opposing the chairman's nomination to look good back home to voters angry about the Fed. "They think it's a free vote. They can be against it, but it will get through. It's the best of all worlds," Dodd told reporters.[16]

Gang: An informal group of lawmakers, usually senators, who try to hammer out an agreement on a contentious issue outside the normal committee process.

★ Gangs of well-intentioned, bipartisan-leaning lawmakers embody the public's vision of how government is supposed to work, and as such, they often get glowing news coverage. Gangs have looked at energy policy, health care, and other gridlock-inducing concerns.

But they have an uneven track record. Gang members can get into trouble with the folks back home for consorting with "the enemy"; the normally conservative Georgia senator Saxby Chambliss (who worked closely with Virginia Democrat Mark Warner on deficit reduction) underwent so much of this rigorous questioning that he eventually decided not to run for another term in 2014. And they can tick off their party's leadership and committee chairmen for not letting *them* tackle the big issues. In 2011, Senate Democratic leader Harry Reid dismissed a Chambliss-Warner "Gang of Six" proposal as "happy talk."[17]

But there are occasional successes. The largest such cluster was the Gang of 14, a bipartisan group of senators who successfully negotiated a compromise in 2005 over stalled judicial nominees. Another gang that included Florida GOP senator Marco Rubio and New York Democratic senator Chuck Schumer got an immigration reform bill through the Senate in 2013.

In journalism, the "Gang of 500" once referred to political insiders who influenced the daily media *narrative* in politics. Gang of 500 was the creation of then ABC political director Mark Halperin, which he called a cluster of "campaign consultants, strategists, pollsters, pundits, and journalists who make up the modern-day political establishment."

Gephardt rule: A now-dormant proposition, between 1979 and 1995 it prevented stalemates over raising the nation's debt limit.

★ Named for then representative Richard Gephardt of Missouri—a future House Democratic leader and two-time presidential candidate—this provision meant that whenever the House passed a budget resolution, the debt ceiling was deemed raised at the same time. But when Newt Gingrich became speaker after the 1994 GOP midterm elections sweep—with Gephardt relegated from majority to House minority leader—the threat of default on the nation's debt began to be used to extort Democratic concessions. The politically painful, but necessary, task of raising the nation's debt increasingly became a political cudgel in the following years. It culminated in the October 2013 government shutdown that led to the nation to the brink of default of its national debt.

Democrats still talk of bringing back the Gephardt rule, and Vermont representative Peter Welch introduced a resolution to that effect in January 2013. But don't look for it to happen until that party regains a majority in the House.

Glide path: Technically it's the final descent route for a landing plane, but in political parlance it has become used with increasing frequency to describe the proper outcome for a bill or a difficult issue.

★ Even before he took office, language lovers took note of Barack Obama's use of the phrase in such contexts as "the glide path that we are on with respect to health care spending" and getting on "a glide path to reducing our forces in Iraq." Since then, other politicians have used it to evoke a sense of comfort and certainty about the course on which something is heading, be it energy independence (former Michigan governor Jennifer Granholm, in a 2012 *Politics Daily* column), immigration legislation (National Public Radio's David Welna in a June 2013 report), or New Jersey governor Chris Christie's reelection (a number of commentators and pundits in 2013).

But when you *parse* the phrase, it falters in every context. "When the glide path metaphor is transferred to economics, I think, it doesn't quite . . . fly," *Wall Street Journal* language columnist Ben Zimmer wrote in a blog post. "Even if the economy is being steered to a 'soft landing,' it's still going down, right? Wouldn't we want to get that plane moving upwards, or at least staying level?"[18]

That sense of a *Titanic*-like move toward disaster was how Utah senator Orrin Hatch deployed it in a 2011 speech: "I have said that if we do not get our spending under control, we are on a glide path to Greece and other Eurozone countries whose credit ratings are destroyed and whose bonds have junk status."[19]

Grand bargain: A comprehensive agreement between the president and opposition congressional leaders in which both sides make politically painful concessions over taxes, spending, and entitlements.

★ The term migrated from the foreign policy realm, where a "grand bargain" represented a deal on trade or other matters struck between the United States and other world powers. The idea of a grand bargain goes back to a 1983 agreement between President Ronald Reagan and House Speaker Tip O'Neill about rescuing Social Security from insolvency. The package included tax increases and benefit cuts, which helped provide the program the $2.7 trillion surplus it would enjoy three decades later. The deal set a standard of bipartisan compromise in the 1980s that has rarely been seen since.

The *Atlantic*'s David A. Graham traced its origin in Barack Obama's administration to a *New Yorker* profile of Peter Orszag, Obama's first Office of Management and Budget director, in a May 2009 article that noted Obama's ambitious young staffers regularly used the phrase to talk about how to achieve their far-reaching agenda.

A grand bargain reportedly nearly materialized in 2011 between Obama and House Speaker John Boehner. Depending on who's retelling the story, the political rivals were tantalizingly close to a deal that would have caused heartburn among their own supporters, but would have been a good deal for the U.S. economy in the long-term. The *Washington Post* reported eight months later that Obama offered to put Social Security, Medicare, and Medicaid cuts on the table in exchange for a tax hike of roughly $100 billion per year over ten years. Meanwhile, government spending would have been cut by roughly three times that amount. But the deal fell apart—at least in the view of Democrats—because Boehner was unwilling to back tax increases in exchange for the massive cuts in federal spending.

Hastert rule: Not an actual rule, but an informal House GOP practice that legislation should only be passed by a "majority of the majority" of Republicans. It basically shuts out minority Democrats in the legislative process.

★ The rule is named for J. Dennis Hastert of Illinois, who was speaker from 1999 to 2007—the longest-tenured Republican in House history. Throughout most of Hastert's tenure, Republicans controlled the House by razor-thin majorities. Even the defection of a few GOP lawmakers could have tanked a bill on the House floor. The Hastert rule came into being in November 2003, during a speech in which Hastert detailed his governing principles this way: "The job of speaker is not to expedite legislation that runs counter to the wishes of the majority of his majority." He explained, "On each piece of legislation, I actively seek to bring our party together. I do not feel comfortable scheduling any controversial legislation unless I know we have the votes on our side first."[20]

Years after leaving office, Hastert occasionally defended this approach. "When you use a majority of the other side, you're not leading; someone else is leading," the former speaker told the *Washington Examiner* in September 2013.[21] At other times, though, Hastert distanced himself from the whole concept. In a subsequent *Daily Beast* interview, he said the Hastert rule "never really existed" and was spawned during an offhand remark at a

2006 press conference, where he was "speaking generally and philosophically."[22]

Whatever the Hastert rule's actual history, it's fair to say the next Republican Speaker after Hastert, Representative John Boehner of Ohio, took a somewhat different approach. Though clearly unhappy at the prospect of doing so, Boehner proved willing to pass legislation with mostly Democrats, including a January 2013 "fiscal cliff" agreement that raised taxes on upper-income households. Boehner departed from the Hastert rule most dramatically in October 2013, when he agreed to bring to a House floor vote a Senate-negotiated agreement to end the sixteen-day federal government shutdown and raise the nation's debt ceiling. The measure passed 285–144, with all 197 voting Democrats supporting it. Only 87 House Republicans backed it.

Not surprisingly, the Hastert rule approach has thoroughly disgusted Democrats. "[W]e just can't wait around [on a bill] for the Hastert rule, which isn't a rule. It's an excuse," Minority Leader Nancy Pelosi told MSNBC in November 2013.[23]

Hideaways: Capitol Building lairs where senior lawmakers can duck out of public sight for meetings. Their doors are unmarked and their locations are unglamorous (a few are on a barren basement hallway linking the House and Senate).

★ Tourists and even Capitol Hill veterans routinely walk by hideaways oblivious to their existence. And the rooms are considered prime real estate. "In an era where nearly every detail of congressional life is documented, scrutinized and dissected, hideaways remain a rare bastion of mystery," *Roll Call* reported in 2011.[24]

Hideaway usage varies. Minnesota senator Al Franken told the online newspaper *MinnPost* in 2010, more than a year into the former *Saturday Night Live* comedian's first term, that his was for staff meetings and that he had never even seen it.[25] West Virginia senator Robert Byrd's hideaway was conveniently located next to the Appropriations Committee he dominated for decades and crammed with tributes to him—including an almost-larger-than-life portrait of him presiding over them all. The late senator Edward Kennedy's office long occupied an elegant third-floor perch, filled with Camelot-era memorabilia and boasting cathedral ceilings, a working fireplace, private bathroom, and well-stocked liquor cabinet. "A lot of legislating took place in that room—and also some good times," Jim Manley, a former Kennedy aide, told *Roll Call*. Ironically, after Kennedy's 2009 death, the office space was assigned to Senator Orrin Hatch, a teetotaling Mormon who was part of a famous *odd couple* with Kennedy.

The House, with more than four times more members than the Senate, simply has less geographic space for lawmaker hideaways. But they do exist. The House Speaker has a suite of offices that are off-limits to the public. Members of the GOP Chowder and Marching Society are known to meet there regularly for fraternal camaraderie.

"Hope springs eternal": A phrase that originated with eighteenth-century English poet Alexander Pope (he said it sprung "in the human breast"), it has become a reliable crutch for politicians who want to avoid sounding pessimistic about an all-but-doomed piece of legislation or political campaign. It's lower down on the hopeful scale than its cousin, "I'm cautiously optimistic."

★ When a reporter asked House Speaker John Boehner in February 2013 about the potential for staving off steep automatic budget cuts that were scheduled to kick in soon, he answered, "Hope springs eternal." That same week, President Barack Obama echoed Boehner, word for word.[26] The cuts, of course, took effect.

A few years earlier, in California, Democratic state assemblyman Gene Mullin introduced a proposed constitutional amendment—a measure that he had pushed twice before—to lower the state's voting age from eighteen to seventeen. "Hope springs eternal; I think I may be wearing them down," Mullin told the Associated Press.[27] Needless to say, his measure did not move.

So if you ever hear the phrase, think of a snowball's chance in hell.

The lunches: Major Washington news often gets made on Tuesdays. That's partly because it's one of the few days in which both the House and Senate are dependably in session. But it also has to do with the fact that all 100 senators get together from 12:30 to 2:00 p.m. for weekly "policy lunches."

★ The lawmakers don't all meet together, as that happens about as frequently as a solar eclipse. Senate Democrats meet behind closed doors in one ornate room; Senate Republicans file into a separate salon down the hall. Before and after they enter, dozens—at times hundreds—of journalists stand outside to grab quotes that form the basis for many of that afternoon's and evening's stories. After the lunches, the majority and minority leaders and their minions step before the microphones, cameras rolling, to expound on the day's floor schedule, their parties' respective themes, and anything else they might be asked.

The lunches are part low-key pep rally, part informal gripe session. When Dick Cheney was vice president he faithfully attended the GOP's events, enabling him to take the temperature of Congress. Perhaps the most infamous closed-door caucus moment occurred in 1999, when New Jersey Democratic senators Frank Lautenberg and Robert Torricelli got into a widely reported quarrel that violated virtually every rule of the chamber's decorum. After Lautenberg chided Torricelli for telling a reporter he felt closer to the Garden State's Republican governor Christie Todd Whitman than he did to Lautenberg, Torricelli— who not for nothing was nicknamed "The Torch"—exploded. "You're a fucking piece of shit," he shouted in front of their astonished colleagues, "and I'm going to cut your balls off!"[28]

Marker: A set of principles that a lawmaker or group of lawmakers introduces (or, in journalese, "lays down") at the outset of a debate or negotiation. The implication is that these principles are something so basic and dear to them that they won't compromise on them.

★ "Since taking the majority," *Politico* reported in October 2013, House Republicans have "typically preferred to lay down a legislative marker at the outset of a fight by passing a bill with only Republican votes." And when Nebraska Democratic senator Bob Kerrey gave a wide-ranging policy address in 1997, he said beforehand that his remarks "may end up being a marker if I decide I want to run for president."[29] (He ended up not running.)

Sometimes, a marker functions as a placeholder before a compromise can be crafted. This often happens late in a legislative session before an issue can be fully debated. In September 2010, a Democratic immigration bill was "largely viewed as a marker to help spur consideration of an overhaul of immigration laws and policy when the new Congress convenes in January," *National Journal* reported.[30]

"Nut-cutting time": A crude description for the period late in a legislative session "when hard decisions have to be made," like which male farm animals are castrated, according to Tim Mathern, a North Dakota Democratic state senator first elected in 1986.

★ "It is ugly and painful—but conclusive," said Mathern, who grew up on a dairy and grain farm.[31]

Elected officials facing tough votes occasionally find themselves in nut-cutting time. The Affordable Care Act—President Barack Obama's signature domestic achievement—was one such difficult issue for House Democrats. Dozens who backed the law, enacted in March 2010, lost their seats less than eight months later.

Three years after that, Representative Bill Foster faced another, if somewhat less dramatic, nut-cutting dilemma upon release of Obama's budget plan. The Illinois Democrat had just clawed his way back to Congress after losing his 2010 reelection bid, in no small part for taking a series of tough votes over Obamacare and other Democratic priorities. But the National Republican Congressional Committee was eager to knock him down a few pegs before he got too entrenched in his swing-ish district. A lengthy National Republican Congressional Committee news release in April 2013 tied Foster to proposed Obama administration tax hikes. A *Chicago Now* column noted, "It's Nut-Cutting Time for Bill Foster."[32] In the end Foster backed the president's budget plan, as did most every other House Democrat.

Libertarian blogger and radio show host Patrick Dorinson adopted the barnyard phrase for his 2012 book *It's Nut Cuttin' Time America!* The pox-on-both-your-houses book takes aim at both parties for what he calls profligate federal spending and insider cronyism.

Obstructionism: What politicians routinely accuse the opposition party leaders of doing when their legislative priorities are blocked. The charges are often deeply hypocritical, depending on the majority or minority status of the politician making the charge.

★ Nowhere is this truer than on the issue of the Senate filibuster, which attempts to kill or at least delay legislation. Beginning in the 1980 elections, Senate majorities shifted several times over the following decades. Minority members who once saw the wisdom of the filibuster have a different view once in the majority.

Here's Nevada senator Harry Reid, then minority leader, in 2005: "The filibuster is the last check we have against the abuse of power in Washington." And here's Reid in 2013 after becoming majority leader: "Time and again, my Republican colleagues have stalled or blocked perfectly good pieces of legislation to score points with the tea party—and they've hurt middle-class Americans in the process."

By the same token, here's Mitch McConnell of Kentucky as a member of the Senate majority in 2005, talking about the need to get President George W. Bush's judicial nominees approved: "It's time to move away from . . . advise and obstruct and get back to advise and consent."[33] And here he is as minority leader two years later, defending his frequent use of the filibuster: "The majority has the majority to set the agenda. If you set an overly partisan agenda, you get . . . what they would argue is an overly partisan response."[34]

Charges of obstructionism on legislation often come when one party controls the Senate and another has the upper hand in the House. Such was the case between 1981 and 1987, when Democrats retained firm control of the House but Republicans held Senate majorities. It happened against for a short time in 2001–3, after moderate senator Jim Jeffords of Vermont defected from his longtime Republican fold to become an independent, handing Democrats a 51–49 majority. And it became the case again in 2010.

Odd couple: Lawmakers of different ideologies who come together on a specific issue or cause. Popularized by the 1970s TV show of the same name that remains one of our favorites (many sportswriters of our acquaintance have more than a little of the slobby Oscar Madison in them).

★ It doesn't happen as often as it used to, but politicians known for being über-partisan or outside the mainstream can enhance their reputations by teaming with ideological opposites. The media *loves* odd-couple stories, as is clear to anyone remembering adulatory coverage of the collaborations between the late Massachusetts liberal Ted Kennedy and conservative Utahan Orrin Hatch (Hatch once wrote a song in tribute to his friend, a man that most of the political right despised).

Oregon Democratic senator Ron Wyden has been a politician perpetually in search of an odd-couple partner. He's worked with Republican representative Paul Ryan on Medicare; with ex-Utah GOP senator Robert Bennett, on health care; and with Kentucky libertarian senator Rand Paul on limiting the Obama administration's use of drones.

Bennett's work with Wyden was a factor in costing him his bid for reelection in 2010; conservatives in his state were suspicious of his collaboration. Being half of an odd couple, Bennett told one of us, "is a very good thing for the country, though it didn't help me on my campaign with the tea party. . . . More people come up to me now in airports and elsewhere who knew about my work with Senator Wyden and say, 'We wish you were still in the Senate' than ever said at the time, 'We're glad you are in the Senate.'"[35]

On the flagpole: A phrase popularized in recent years by Lamar Alexander, a former Tennessee governor who later became U.S. secretary of education and then a Republican senator after two failed presidential bids (his plaid shirt is better remembered than his platform). To Alexander, it means the person or agency responsible for—and thus must be held accountable for—a problem.

★ "My experience in life is that if it's clear who's on the flagpole, the job usually gets done," he told *National Journal*, which observed that some lobbyists and staffers had begun using the expression.[36]

One-minutes/special orders: "One-minutes" are House floor speeches of sixty seconds or less at the beginning of most legislative days that usually include a pithy, sound-bite-ready message aimed at getting picked up by the media.

★ For junior lawmakers, particularly in the minority party, these are sometimes the only time a member can be heard. In his 2004 memoir, then House Speaker Dennis Hastert recalled his early days in Congress when GOP members had virtually no clout: "As a junior member of the minority, you rarely got a chance to speak on the floor or affect legislation. (Oh, sure, you could deliver a one-minute like anyone else, but you never got recognized or given time to say anything substantive.)"[37]

Some of the most memorable—and incendiary—House floor speeches of the early twenty-first century have come during one-minutes. In a June 2003 speech in support of AmeriCorps, Representative Zoe Lofgren (D-CA), referred to President George W. Bush as a liar, saying "the president did not tell the truth to the American people in the State of the Union. He lied to the American people around the country when he promised to expand this program." The speaker pro tempore ruled that Lofgren was out of order and "must refrain from personal criticism of the president."[38]

Congressional observers—and even some members—have tried, unsuccessfully, to curb the use of one-minutes because they start legislative days off in partisan tones. "Special orders," meanwhile, happen at the end of the day when all other legislative business is finished. House members may be recognized to speak on any topic they want for up to sixty minutes. These, too, can be bitingly partisan, and sometimes multiple members will get up to address the same topic.

One of the most frequent special-orderers is Texas Democrat Sheila Jackson Lee, who has consistently been voted the House's biggest *show horse*. The *Houston Press* reported in 2004 that some staffers started a game: A jar of money was distributed among offices, with money deposited every time Lee spoke in a special order or some other widely visible forum. The jar kept circulating until a day arrived in which Lee didn't speak—and whoever had the jar at the time got to keep the money.[39]

Opening statements: Mini-speeches delivered by members of Congress at committee hearings while witnesses are forced to sit by mute.

★ Opening statements ostensibly exist for a substantive introduction to the issue at hand. But they can be long-winded exercises in political grandstanding. At the 2006 Supreme Court confirmation hearing for Samuel Alito, the infamously loquacious Joe Biden—then a Delaware senator—promised that his opening statement would be "brief." It ran for fourteen minutes.

Even some members of Congress contend that opening statements ought to be curtailed. Senator Sherrod Brown, the Ohio Democrat who moved to the Senate in 2006 after fourteen years in the House, published a book in 2000 on his experiences in Washington, *Congress from the Inside: Observations from the Majority and the Minority*.[40]

Opening statements for committee hearings, Brown wrote, "can take up as much time as an hour—a colossal waste of time for all of us. Too often I have seen witnesses—whose time is as important for them as ours is to us—sit for over an hour waiting for opening statements to conclude before they can deliver their testimony."

Like so much else in Congress, however, don't count on it to change. Committee chairmen *will* dispense with opening statements if the chamber is pressed for time—such as facing a looming floor vote—but they're not going to bruise their colleagues' egos in such a direct way. The most time-conscious members will take a pass and simply say, "I ask that my statement be made part of the record"—the written summary of the hearing compiled after it ends.

Adding to the pomposity of the proceedings is the seating arrangement. Members of Congress are high up on the committee dais, witnesses down below looking up. Compare that to committee meetings in the British House of Commons, where lawmakers and witnesses are seated around a table, and opening statements are kept to a bare minimum. The focus is on the presentation of substantive information from panel witnesses, not preening by politicians for the cameras.

Other body: How senators and House members are supposed to refer to the other chamber when speaking on the floor of their own legislative body.

★ The term is part of an elaborate set of rules meant to maintain decorum and dignity in debate while papering over contempt lawmakers often hold for one another. It used to be against House rules to refer to the Senate by name on the House floor. That changed in January 1987, as Texan representative Jim Wright took over as Speaker. Representative Martin Frost (D-TX), said then that the rules change was intended to relieve House members of the burden of referring to the Senate in "an artful and circumlocutious manner," in an era that makes a virtue of straight talk.[41]

Though after that point House members were at liberty to refer directly to the Senate, on the House floor, lawmakers often refrained from doing so for a specific reason. The distant formality of lawmakers continuing to call their legislative counterpart across the Capitol "the other body" broadly reflects the disdain House members and senators often feel for each other—and even toward party colleagues.

It's kind of like a divorced woman calling her former husband "that man"—she doesn't want to dignify her ex by name. Former Speaker Tip O'Neill reportedly once said to a Democratic colleague: "Remember, the House Republicans are merely the opposition. The Senate is the enemy."

P90X: An intense fitness routine that has become popular in Congress. Its literature describes itself as "a revolutionary system of 12 life-changing workouts," which requires only a small space, a set of dumbbells or resistance bands and a pull-up bar.

★ If you think your representative likes to sit around getting drunk all day, you have a seriously outmoded idea of what these people do in their free time. (Some veteran Hill watchers, it must be said, have endorsed a return to the days of boisterous boozing, saying it could induce fraternization and, in turn, some long-overdue cooperation.) Today's members—especially the younger ones swept into power in recent years—would rather gravitate to the gym. And being the hypercompetitive fitness freaks they are, they often are apostles of P90X.

Representative Paul Ryan (R-WI), the 2012 vice presidential nominee who was once a personal trainer, is credited as having been the main instigator of the routine. By 2010, he was leading a P90X class in the House gym every morning, and by 2012, at least twenty-five members were regulars.

And Washington being Washington, the routine briefly became controversial. The watchdog group Citizens for Responsibility and Ethics in Washington (CREW) in 2012 accused Representative Aaron Schock (R-IL)—who has drawn substantial media attention not for his legislative prowess but for his washboard abs—of using campaign funds to buy P90X DVDs. An aide later said the expense was mistakenly reported on Schock's Federal Election Commission report and that the congressman personally paid for the charge.

Pork: That which is tasty only to the person seeking it— the member of Congress trying to add an *earmark* on an appropriations bill for a special project or cause in his or her home state or district.

★ Pork and earmarks are now the dirtiest words in Congress, with interest groups and many lawmakers convinced that they represent legislating at its absolute worst. But their value truly is in the eye of the beholder. A case in point: Former representative Mike Arcuri (D-NY) recalled for us how he once spoke at a senior citizens' center "and a very sweet elderly woman started just hammering me out of the clear blue on earmarks, pork-barrel spending and why the practice needed to end. She was able to get some of the other members wound up, and it took me the rest of the meeting to get them back into in a pleasant and positive mood."

As Arcuri left the center, the woman approached him with an envelope—and a request for grant money to install a new elevator at the senior center. "I looked at her in disbelief and said, 'You realize you are asking me to get you an earmark, the same thing you just railed me on in front of all the people in the meeting?' She answered, 'Oh, honey, that's not what I'm talking about. I'm talking about the other earmarks, you know, the *bad* ones. This is a *good* one, and we need it.' I never submitted the earmark request but kept the envelope to this day."[42]

Regular order: How the House of Representatives is supposed to operate, following a series of elaborate rules and precedents (think "I'm Just a Bill" from *Schoolhouse Rock*)—but rarely does.

★ J. Dennis Hastert said regular order would be a priority after he assumed the House speakership in January 1999. The genial, grandfatherly Illinois Republican had won the esteem of GOP colleagues looking for a calmer period after Newt Gingrich's bombastic crash-and-burn speakership the previous four years. Hastert pledged to move appropriations—spending—bills through the House one at a time, and to allow House committees to deliberate over legislation seriously and give deference to their work. Hastert's former spokesman John Feehery defined "regular order" this way in a January 2013 column: "It means that members of the House are allowed the broadest leeway to offer amendments to legislation. It means that both the House and the Senate complete their budgets on time. It means that federal programs that are not authorized by an authorizing committee are not funded by appropriations bills. It means that the House and the Senate convene in formal conferences to reconcile legislation. It means that the Congress pays for emergency spending requests, or at least doesn't put major spending items (like wars) off-budget,"[43] shorthand for not being counted as part of the regular budget.

Critics contend that's a rather revisionist approach to Hastert-era history. Democrats often cite the November 2003 vote on legislation to add prescription drug benefits to Medicare. Nearly five years into Hastert's regular-order speakership, his Republican leadership team used an all-night session of arm-twisting to finally muster a majority. The roll-call vote, which rarely exceeds twenty minutes, began at 3:00 a.m. and was held open for nearly three hours, as Republican leaders and George W. Bush administration officials scrambled to quell a conservative rebellion.

After Hastert and his House Republicans lost their twelve-year majority in the November 2006 midterms, the next speaker, liberal Democrat Nancy Pelosi, didn't even make much pretense of operating the chamber in regular order. The San Francisco congresswoman, who grew up in the gritty, rough-and-tumble Baltimore political scene, where her father was mayor, took unilateral action in 2008 after her Democrats lost a string of embarrassing votes on the House floor because of Republican procedural maneuvering. House Democrats changed a rule to prevent Republicans from offering a "motion to recommit"—sending legislation back to committee.

Once voters tired of the four-year-old Democratic House majority, the next Republican speaker, John Boehner of Ohio, pledged a return to regular order. Boehner allowed more amendments to be considered on the House floor, even those offered by Democrats. But, facing a fractious Republican caucus, Boehner after a time began ramming compromises with the Obama White House down GOP members' throats. A 2012 year-end fiscal cliff bill was passed with majority Democratic support. So was an October 2013 agreement to reopen to federal government and avoid a national debt default.

Both of these violated the *Hastert rule*, which dictated legislation could only pass the House if it enjoyed a "majority of the majority" of Republican members. House Democrats argued the informal practice was by definition a violation of regular order, since it denied a vote to a majority of members in favor of specific pieces of legislation.

You'll hear peeved members shouting for regular order on the House floor from time to time—something that doesn't exactly convey the highest standard of politeness. "If I hear 'regular order' one more time . . ." an exasperated Pete Visclosky (D-IN) told us, clenching his fist and gritting his teeth. "I would have to say that more than half of my colleagues don't even know what it is."[44]

Slow-walk: To delay something on purpose.

★ When Senate Democrats hoped to bring up climate change legislation in 2009, Republicans insisted on a full reading of the 492-page bill. Liberal senator Barbara Boxer (D-CA) called the move "a slow walk; it's a *dilatory* act on an issue that is most pressing."[45] Three years later, Republicans accused the Obama administration of taking too long to identify spending cuts to avoid a so-called fiscal cliff. "The longer the White House slow-walks this process, the closer our economy gets to the fiscal cliff," charged House Speaker John Boehner.[46]

William Safire said the term might have originated with the Tennessee walking horse, a popular riding and show horse. The animal has three gaits—a flat or slow walk, a running walk, and a canter (which is faster than a trot, but slower than a gallop).[47]

Small-bore/small ball: Small-bore initiatives are those seen as minor and trivial. As such, it's not a compliment in legislatures where the tendency is to think big.

★ When President Barack Obama was stymied in his attempts to advance gun legislation through a hostile Congress, he settled in August 2013 for putting out two executive orders. One of them closed a loophole allowing people who are ineligible to buy guns to register firearms to a corporation or trust. The other stopped private entities from reimporting military-grade weapons that had been donated to U.S. allies back into the United States. Robert Spitzer, a State University of New York political scientist, told Al-Jazeera America that such moves were "small bore" but the best that could be done in a Congress "that is not disposed to enact anything on anything, and certainly not anything that is endorsed by President Obama."[48]

"Small ball," a related term, is derived from baseball and refers to scoring runs through walks, stolen bases, and/or sacrifice bunts instead of hitting homers. When Obama's campaign in 2012 ripped rival Mitt Romney for his record at Bain Capital, one of Romney's *surrogates*, New Hampshire senator Kelly Ayotte, responded that Obama was "running on small-ball politics" instead of tackling the big issues facing the country.[49] Obama, it should be noted, also came into office with a massive disdain for what he considered Bill Clinton's small-ball politics, such as requiring children to wear school uniforms.

Smelling jet fumes: The long-standing phrase for lawmakers' perpetual yearning to hop on planes and rush back to their home states.

★ As much as it's become a cliché, the perceived odor of idling aircraft before a scheduled recess often does serve as a powerful motivator for getting something passed. One example was a bill in April 2013 to put in—coincidentally enough—funding for air traffic controllers who had been furloughed by the automatic budget cuts known as the "sequester" just before Congress winged it out of town for a week.

But the all-consuming itch to travel also can be a hindrance to greater progress. Former senator Olympia Snowe of Maine, a leading centrist, complained in a 2013 interview with National Public Radio that Congress needed to put in a five-day work week like most other Americans instead of its more typical three-day schedule. "By Thursday, you know, jet fumes, the smell of jet fumes," she said. "Everybody's heading home, wanting to know when they can adjourn on Thursday so they can leave."[50]

Thread the needle: To achieve a difficult compromise.

★ In pushing a measure into law aimed at revolutionizing the air-traffic control system in 2011, Senator Jay Rockefeller (D-WV) thanked several senators who "did so much to help us thread the needle that would be a balanced bill."[51] Two years later, with the chamber gridlocked on even the most routine measures, Senator Ron Wyden (D-OR) took to the floor to say: "I know the popular wisdom is, you cannot thread the needle on legislation."[52]

Train wreck: The common mixed metaphor for an epic governmental disaster. It's effective because it's punchy and it connotes a chaotic mess that can't easily be cleaned up.

★ Usage of the phrase zoomed in the 1990s, according to Google Books' Ngram Viewer. In politics, "train wreck" most often was used to describe the events that led to the 1995 disagreements over spending that led to a government shutdown. Subsequently, during George W. Bush's administration, the response to Hurricane Katrina often was described as a train wreck. And liberal bloggers and pundits have used it with regularity to describe the dysfunctionality of Congress itself.

More recently, Republicans have made it their signature

phrase in describing the Affordable Care Act (aka Obamacare). "Tried signing up for #ObamaCare today. How'd it go? Hint: #trainwreck,"[53] House Speaker John Boehner tweeted in November 2013. It also was often described that way on conservative Fox News: "The best thing, actually, for the party is that these crises are temporarily over and now the real attention can shift to the slow-motion, jaw dropping, train wreck that is the president's health care law," radio host Guy Benson told Fox's Megyn Kelly.[54]

Voting your conscience: See *free vote.*

Dead Money, Dog Whistles, and Droppin' the G's
The Lingo of Campaigns and Elections

Know your caucuses from your primaries? Your superdelegates from your super PACs? If you got this right, and can differentiate between a funder and a finance event, you're plugged into the bewildering lingo of American elections. Political campaigns have a jargon all their own. In a sense, it's not surprising or unique. Health-care-supply salespeople have their own specialized terms to discuss their wares with doctors and hospital administrators. The military has so many acronyms that the Pentagon publishes a 489-page guide.[1] Steve Martin used to tell a joke aimed at the plumbers he thought were in his audience using (made-up) insider-ish terms: "This lawn supervisor was out on a sprinkler-maintenance job, and he started working on a Findlay sprinkler head with a Langstrom seven-inch gangly wrench." When the rest of the bit would fall flat, he would pause, look pained, then ask, "Were those plumbers supposed to be here *this* show?"[2]

Still, campaign pros often speak in what seems like an indecipherable patois. *Crosstabs*, *grasstops*, and *GOTV* are just a few of the terms that get uttered frequently in campaign planning sessions—and sometimes make their way into public discourse. Reporters and bloggers pick up and spread them, along with terms such as *grassroots* and *dog whistle*.

Knowing the meanings of such specialized political terms can help cut through spin meant to obscure what's really going on in a campaign. When politicians use the cliché, "The only poll that counts is the one on Election Day," they really mean, "I wouldn't win if the election were held today." Or when an office seeker says,

"'I don't want to go negative,'" it means he or she is preparing to go negative.

Terms uttered frequently and repeatedly aren't used by accident. Republican consultant Brian Donahue says framing, through specific terms, is key to winning over voters. Changing just a word or two in a campaign can be the difference between winning and losing, says Donahue, a founder and partner of Washington, D.C.–based CRAFT Media/Digital.

Donahue likens it to two single women sitting at a bar, seemingly available. One guy who comes over seems rather cocky. That's not necessarily good, but the gals can live with it and get past it. Another guy comes over who oozes creepiness. Game over for him. "Both are negative, but creepy means something so much deeper, putting you at greater unease. Similarly in politics words have an incredible impact on how people think and feel," said Donahue, who, among other achievements, managed the 2004 Bush-Cheney reelection victory in West Virginia.

He notes that on the right, "freedom" is a staple of successful campaign vocabulary. On the left, it's "justice." "Both parties have always fed off those terms and principles. The way parties lose is when parties lose control of those principles. That allows opponents to then define them."[3]

Astroturfing: Masking rich sponsors of a political message to make it appear as if it's coming from a grassroots participant. The common format is for such groups to take innocuous-sounding names with whom no one could quibble, such as "Americans" (or "Citizens," or "People") for [insert issue here, whether it's "Clean Energy," "Fairness" or "Safe Streets"].

★ Senator Lloyd Bentsen coined the phrase in 1985, in response to an influx of mailers promoting insurance company interests in his state. "A fellow from Texas can tell the difference between grassroots and Astroturf," the longtime Texas senator—and 1988 Democratic vice presidential nominee—said at the time.[4]

It's a common tactic to tie a point of view you're fighting

against to alleged Astroturf efforts. Early tea party critics, in 2009 and 2010, often drew a direct line between the limited-government groups, many of which did rise organically, and past Democratic foes. They included 1990s-era pro-tobacco groups who fought proposed Clinton administration cigarette tax proposals, along with the Environmental Protection Agency's findings regarding the dangers of secondhand smoke.

But Democratic-aligned groups are just as capable of creating supposedly grassroots campaigns that aren't exactly upfront about financial backers. Creating stealth lobbying campaigns, known as grass-tops, is a technique pioneered and perfected by the Democratic firm Dewey Square Group (DSG). The website Word Spy dates its earliest citation to a 1992 article quoting lobbyist Ed Gabriel in *Public Relations Quarterly*: "A better way to influence legislation is what we call the 'grassTOPS' approach—mobilizing influential leaders in each community who can reach lawmakers at the federal, state and local levels, with facts tailored to their district's interests."[5]

Boomlet: A short-lived surge in something; in this case, a candidate's popularity. It started coming into general usage in the 1930s and has been cyclically applied in election years.

★ During the 2012 Republican presidential primaries, it was most often applied to Herman Cain, he of the "9-9-9" plan, and Minnesota representative Michele Bachmann before that. When MSNBC's Chuck Todd interviewed Newt Gingrich in December 2011, the ex-House Speaker was experiencing a boomlet of his own. "It was inconceivable; if we'd gone around in July and said, 'I'll wait until the end of December,' none of you would have believed it," Gingrich said. Todd replied, "You'd have missed the Herman Cain boomlet, too." Gingrich answered, "I'd have missed the Herman Cain boomlet; maybe the Bachmann boomlet, and maybe—so start with that."[6]

Bounce: A candidate's rise in the polls over a short period of time. Bounce is used most often for presidential candidates coming out of national conventions, though sometimes for statewide and other candidates after debates and other potentially *game-changing* events.

★ A presidential candidate's bounce comes from a smoothly run convention. That's what happened in 1992, when Arkansas governor Bill Clinton, the Democratic presidential nominee-to-be, went into the Democratic National Convention in New York City trailing President George H. W. Bush. With a near-flawless convention, and closing his acceptance speech with the now-iconic phrase "I still believe in a place called Hope," Clinton left the event with a 16-percentage-point bounce, according to Gallup. Skeptics scoffed, calling it momentary. But it lasted. Clinton never trailed from the close of the Democratic convention until Election Day.

The University of California–Santa Barbara's American Presidency Project has tracked every postconvention bounce since 1964.[7] Clinton's was the biggest overall; George W. Bush in 2000 and Ronald Reagan in 1980 had the largest GOP bounces with 8 percentage points each. Barack Obama's bounces were smaller — 4 percentage points in 2008 and 2 percentage points four years later.

Bradley effect: Refers to a tendency of voters to tell interviewers or pollsters that they are undecided or likely to vote for a black candidate, but then actually vote for a white opponent. The term comes from Los Angeles mayor Tom Bradley's 1982 gubernatorial bid in California.

★ A pioneering political figure in California, Bradley was the first (and to date only) black mayor of the nation's second-largest city. In 1982 he faced Republican attorney general George Deukmejian, a bland yet durable political figure who inspired little excitement among voters. Bradley led in the polls going into Election Day, and in the initial hours after the polls closed, some news organizations projected him as the winner. Ultimately, Bradley lost by about 100,000 votes, about 1.2 percent of the 7.5 million votes cast. These circumstances gave rise to the term, which over the years has grown to cover other minority candidates.

It has dimmed in recent years, due in no small part to Barack Obama's 2008 victory, making him the nation's first black president. But Stanford University PhD candidate Nuri Kim described an unusual variation of the Bradley effect in a research paper: In 2008, Kim found, presidential poll respondents were more likely to say they would vote for Obama if the person conducting the interview *was thought to be* African American.[8]

Campaigning for a post: The art of trying to win a position over which you have no control.

★ It's usually considered gauche to openly lobby for an appointed political job—*openly* being the key word. "It's like how people courted in the Victorian era, where you're doing everything possible—in public—to show you're not interested, while feverishly working behind the scenes to make it happen," said Democratic political consultant Chris Lehane.[9]

The public part of the task is generally left to *surrogates*; the Congressional Black Caucus, for example, often will call for its members to be included in the mix of those under consideration. In early 2013, the Black Caucus chair, Ohio representative Marcia Fudge, publicly suggested fellow Democrats Barbara Lee of California and Mel Watt of North Carolina to head Labor and Commerce, respectively. Neither got the jobs, though Watt drew a subcabinet nomination to head the less-prestigious Federal Housing Finance Agency (he was confirmed by the Senate nearly a year later).

When a vice presidential candidate slot, Senate seat, or cabinet position becomes available, openly campaigning for the slot usually means you don't get the job. Former Massachusetts representative Barney Frank startled people in early 2013 when he openly implored Governor Deval Patrick—"Coach, put me in," Frank said in an MSNBC interview[10]—to name him to the Senate seat that was vacated when Senator John Kerry was named secretary of state. But Patrick chose his own chief of staff, Mo Cowan.

There are rare exceptions to the don't-openly-jockey-for-a-post rule. After Kerry locked up the 2004 Democratic presidential nomination, his vanquished primary rival, Senator John Edwards of North Carolina, went after the vice presidential slot with gusto. He instantly became Kerry's most energetic surrogate, speaking at any event the nominee could not attend. "It had all the earmarks of a very carefully planned campaign," a longtime adviser to Edwards told the *Washington Post*.[11]

Edwards, as it happened, had far less luck later persuading Barack Obama to find him a job. After losing the Iowa Democratic caucuses in January 2008, it was later discovered that he had privately beseeched Obama to appoint him vice president, attorney general, or to his dream job, the Supreme Court—all while keeping secret about his pregnant mistress and their love child.

Crosstabs: Considered the "meat" of political polling, *crosstabs* are meant to provide fine-grained results about the electorate. That way campaigns can target by demographic group, along the lines of *how do men versus women feel about a given issue?* Or *how is gun control playing among suburban women?*

★ Crosstabs are not as sexy as topline results that report simply and starkly who is winning and losing ahead of Election Day. Crosstabs, as detailed statistical/numeric analyses of a survey, offer a trove of raw, unfinished data. This information is then used by pollsters and other strategists to create for the campaign a strategic guide and tactical playbook.

Crosstabs used to be closely guarded secrets among pollsters. Divulging these massive data sets to the public was like a popular barbecue joint disclosing its secret sauce. But with a proliferation of polling outlets and swarms of bloggers to dissect dense political data—bringing more attention and potentially business to a polling firm—crosstabs are now increasingly being made public. Atlanta-based InsiderAdvantage CEO Matt Towery said he now releases background data with every survey. Otherwise, it just won't be believable. "You have to. If you can't show crosstabs, you can't prove that you've got a poll," said Towery, a former state lawmaker in Georgia and the 1990 Republican lieutenant governor nominee.[12]

Dark money: Shadowy sources of funds that don't conform to the strictures of campaign finance laws. The term was coined by Bill Allison of the Sunlight Foundation, a Washington watchdog group.

★ Dark money goes back to the early days of American politics. In fact it wasn't until well into the twentieth century that formalized campaign finance restrictions existed. In 1952, Republican vice presidential nominee Richard Nixon had to fend off charges that he was maintaining a slush fund from the beneficence of wealthy donors.

In races for the presidency and Congress, strict donation limits—and the watchful eye of federal prosecutors—make it at least somewhat challenging to steer money to candidates that they're not supposed to receive. At the state level, though, it's a different story. Many states have no donation limits at all, and elected officials can even accept unlimited gifts.

In November 2013, Washington State voters considered Initiative 522, to label genetically engineered food. Of the $22 million raised to oppose the proposal exactly $550 came from individuals and companies based in the state, according to the Public Disclosure Commission. The initiative's proponents, although more locally funded, received $5.8 million of their $8.4 million from outside Washington, the *Seattle Times* reported.[13] It turns out the opponents spent their money more wisely, as Washington voters narrowly defeated the measure.

Occasionally, though, dark money is exposed, and the givers punished. In October 2013 California's Fair Political Practices Commission announced a settlement in its probe into an $11 million contribution made by a "dark money" nonprofit group in the 2012 elections. The settlement involved an $11 million contribution from the previously unknown Arizona-based nonprofit Americans for Responsible Leadership to the Small Business Action Committee, which opposed Democratic governor Jerry Brown's tax-increase initiative in the November 2012 elections. A judge forced Americans for Responsible Leadership to reveal the original source of the money. But that disclosure showed that the money came from the Center to Protect Patient Rights, another Arizona nonprofit, which received the money from Americans for Job Security, a Virginia-based nonprofit. Both of these groups were connected to the political money network operated by the billionaire Koch brothers. The Fair Political Practices Commission called the money "the largest contribution ever disclosed as campaign money-laundering in California history."[14]

Dead-cat bounce: Taken from stock market analysis, it's a colorful and vivid description of a brief recovery in otherwise declining poll ratings. Mitt Romney, the 2012 Republican presidential nominee, briefly experienced such a dead-cat bounce when he beat President Barack Obama in the first debate. But Romney's comeback was fleeting, and he lost soundly a month later.

★ Sarah Palin is often referred to by political pros as the ultimate dead-cat bounce candidate. When Republican presidential candidate John McCain picked the largely unknown Alaska governor as his running mate in summer 2008, she provided a shot of political adrenaline. Her lack of knowledge about international affairs, antagonistic relations with the media, and a general sense that she wasn't ready for prime time meant that she didn't help McCain all that much in the end.

As *Huffington Post* writer David Latt noted less than a month before Barack Obama's Election Day triumph, "Governor Sarah Palin gave the McCain campaign a shot in the arm but it proved to be a short term fix. With the polls continuing to trend toward Obama, Republican pundits find themselves in an uncomfortable position."[15]

Dog whistle: Political messaging using coded language that seems to mean one thing to the general population, but which to a targeted subgroup means something else entirely.

★ Conservatives are more frequently accused of using political dog whistles to talk past the general public. In his 2003 State of the Union speech, President George W. Bush spoke of "power, wonder-working power, in the goodness and idealism and faith of the American people." Evangelical Christians recognized the phrase "wonder-working power" as a line from the hymn "There is Power in the Blood."[16]

Political scientist Bethany Albertson examined the impact of that phrase in a study for the University of Chicago and Princeton University's Center for the Study of Democratic Politics. She tested a group of Princeton students and found that just 9 percent were familiar with it, compared to 84 percent of Pentecostals that were sampled. "Amongst this group that was familiar with the coded language, they preferred the religious appeal when it was not made explicit," Albertson wrote. Her conclusion: "For religious appeals, coded communication is particularly persuasive in politics."[17]

Another group of alleged code words is supposedly meant to appeal to some voters' inherent racism. The late Republican Party strategist Lee Atwater put the issue bluntly, describing the GOP's Southern Strategy in a 1981 interview: "You start[ed] out in 1954 by saying, 'N----r, n----r, n----r.' By 1968, you can't say 'n----r'—that hurts you. Backfires. So you say stuff like 'forced busing,' 'states' rights' and all that stuff."[18]

More recently, Democrats attributed Newt Gingrich's resounding primary victory in South Carolina in 2012 to what they said was his dog-whistling depiction of Barack Obama as "the food-stamp president." Republicans, naturally, said Democrats read too much into such messages, and blasted Obama for what they called his own masked messaging. "When he says 'pay your fair share,' that's dog whistle, code for redistribution," Fox News talk show host Eric Bolling said in September 2012. "Redistribution is a code word, dog whistle for socialism."[19]

Donor maintenance: The need for elected officials to maintain ties to big financial contributors, which usually involves stroking egos.

★ Donor maintenance can involve spending "quality" time with big givers, providing the impression that their ideas on issues are being taken seriously. For some rich folks it's enough to get a picture taken with the president, or a senator, congressman, governor, or other official.

Even a quick phone call can suffice. Florida-based Republican political consultant Rick Wilson recalls his days working for Connie Mack, a GOP senator who was assiduous about dialing his donors even if he wasn't directly asking for money. "It was often, 'I heard from so-and-so that your big development got approved.' Or, 'Hey, your son got into Harvard!'" Wilson said. "The donors were happy with the two minutes."

More recently, Wilson said, donor maintenance has come to encompass an increasing amount of "hand-holding"—reassuring your backers about poor poll numbers or the repercussions of a given incident. "It's definitely become a necessity in this business to keep these guys happy. . . . In these days, rumor and e-mail spread panic faster than anything I've ever seen," he said.[20]

President Bill Clinton saw maintaining ties to big Democratic contributors as an essential part of his job, one even to look forward to. Clinton was so enthusiastic it led to embarrassing—and law-bending—excesses. The president's thirst for campaign cash was so ravenous that during his 1996 reelection bid big DNC donors were allowed to spend the night in the White House Lincoln bedroom for a contribution of $150,000. The White House also hosted more than 100 coffee visits for donors giving $50,000 each.

The next president, Republican George W. Bush, took a similar, if more subtle approach to donor relations. Having won the presidency in 2000 on a platform of restoring "honor" and "integrity" to the Oval Office after years of Clinton scandals, Bush continued to rake in the bucks. Four months after taking office, Bush hosted a fundraiser that pulled in a cool $23 million. Individual donors paid a minimum of $1,500 a person and corporate contributors paid at least $2,000 each to attend the dinner, the maximum donations then legal under current campaign law (caps have since risen modestly to reflect inflation). A few days later, Vice President Dick Cheney invited 400 top Republican contributors, most of whom had given or pledged at least $100,000 to GOP causes, to a lawn party on the grounds of the vice president's mansion at the Naval Observatory.

President Barack Obama has been less enthusiastic about donor maintenance, but his administration has been successful at it. He campaigned as if he were above politics, but early in the administration came news reports that the Democratic National Committee was rewarding its top contributors with small-group briefings with senior administration officials, conference calls, and other exclusive access to policymakers. When documents surfaced about these perks, the *Washington Post* reported in 2009, "Democratic and White House officials shrugged off the documents as part of normal 'donor maintenance' that does not provide contributors with any quid pro quo."[21]

Droppin' the *g*'s: An abrupt change in politicians' speech patterns in front of friendly crowds to sound informal.

★ The normally well-spoken President Barack Obama said in an April 2011 speech that without a new energy policy, "Folks will keep on makin' conventional cars." Better vehicles already exist, he added: "We don't have to create somethin' new."[22] A year later, Mitt Romney wished one Southern audience "a fine Alabama mornin'."[23]

When this happens, jokes abound and people wince. *Inside the Actor's Studio* host James Lipton—himself a parody target by comedian Will Farrell for his uptightness—lashed out at Obama and his predecessor, George W. Bush. Lipton told conservative radio host Laura Ingraham about the Columbia- and Harvard Law–educated Obama, and Bush, who graduated from Yale and Harvard Business School: "I wanted to write a piece some time ago . . . called 'The Disappearing G.' It was inspired more by George W. Bush than by anybody else, where suddenly this man who comes from an upper-class family and comes from an upper-class world, but the 'g' in '-ing' vanished—'I'm goin',' 'We're talkin'.' And other politicians have taken it on. Obama does it there. I don't like it anywhere."[24]

With the exception of Sarah Palin, the politician who has taken the most grief for dropping *g*'s is Hillary Clinton. Her speech patterns became an issue early in her 2008 Democratic presidential bid. During an appearance with Al Sharpton at a 2007 civil rights commemoration in Selma, Ala., Clinton laid on a rather transparently southern accent. But the criticism may have been unfair because in her case, the semi-drawl had something of an air of authenticity. Though reared in Chicago, Hillary spent nearly twenty years in Arkansas, where husband Bill Clinton was a rising political force. Early interviews from the 1992 election cycle feature Hillary speaking in a form of Southern drawl.

Even one of her most famous quotes drops some *g*'s: "You know, I'm not sittin' here like some little woman standing by my man, like Tammy Wynette. I'm sittin' here because I love him, and I respect him, and I honor what he's been through and what we've been through together."[25]

"Elections have consequences": The political way for a winner to tell a loser, "Tough luck, you lost. Get over it."

★ President Barack Obama famously espoused this view shortly after his 2009 inauguration, during a widely reported meeting with congressional Republicans about economic proposals. Obama was quoted telling the GOP leaders that "elections have consequences," and, in case there was any doubt, "I won."[26] Two years earlier, firebrand liberal Barbara Boxer of California upbraided fiery conservative James Inhofe of Oklahoma— her predecessor as chair of the Senate Environment and Public Works Committee—at a hearing about how ex-vice president Al Gore should respond to Inhofe's questions. Inhofe told her that

Gore could respond when he was done talking, but Boxer bluntly retorted: "No, that isn't the rule. You're not making the rules. You used to, when you did this [chaired the committee]. Elections have consequences. So I make the rules."[27]

It also was Senator Tom Harkin's view, if stated more elegantly, about the November 2013 curtailing of Senate filibusters. By that point the Iowa Democrat had been pushing to limit the filibuster for almost nineteen years. Harkin considered the filibuster an undemocratic abuse by the Senate minority. He was among the few lawmakers with the moral authority to make such a claim, having espoused the same argument for years even as the Senate majority seesawed back and forth. In an NPR interview, Harkin argued that Democrats, if back in the Senate minority, at some point, should have to live under the same rules. "If people vote for a Republican president that's going to nominate someone to the Supreme Court to overturn *Roe v. Wade*, listen, elections should have consequences. People should know, if they're going to vote that way, they better expect the results."[28]

Of course, being on the losing end of an election often changes the view of politicos about how determinative elections should be. During the four-year tenure of Nancy Pelosi as the first female House Speaker, her Democrats didn't seem particularly interested in taking into account the viewpoints of minority Republicans. The Democrats' routinely pushed through legislation with little, if any, support from Republicans. President Barack Obama's signature Affordable Care Act was only the most prominent example, along with a 2009 economic stimulus law and a cap-and-trade climate change bill that failed to become law. "Yes, we wrote the bill. Yes, we won the election," Pelosi said at one point in early 2009 as the stimulus bill ping-ponged between the Democratic-controlled House and Senate.[29]

That was no different than her Republican predecessors as speaker, who approached their House majorities with *elections have consequences* confidence and bluster. But after House

Democrats lost their majority in the 2010 midterm elections Pelosi, back on Capitol Hill in an encore performance as minority leader, seemed to take a different view. In April 2011, after a few months back in the minority, Pelosi told a Tufts University audience in Massachusetts that elections "shouldn't matter as much as they do."[30] Pelosi seemed to urge Republicans to moderate their views so that the space between the parties is not so vast. Then, she imagined, elections wouldn't be so determinative.

Exploratory campaign: The early stages of a political campaign in which a candidate who has already decided to run doesn't yet go all the way. It's usually a rhetorical fig leaf to allow for better fundraising.

★ An exploratory committee technically creates a legal shell for a candidate who expects to spend more than $5,000 while contemplating an actual run. Under campaign finance rules, *exploratory* money may be raised without the full disclosure of sources required of true candidates. Those donors must only be revealed when the candidate drops the exploratory phase and jumps fully into the race.

Most major presidential candidates form exploratory committees before entering the fray. In April 2011, a determined-looking Mitt Romney looked straight into the camera in a YouTube video recorded at a New Hampshire college football stadium and proclaimed: "I am announcing my exploratory committee for the presidency of the United States."[31] The former Massachusetts governor, of course, had every intention of seeking the GOP nomination again in 2012, a prize that had eluded him in 2008. But forming an exploratory committee first allowed for more media attention, which helped in his ultimately successful race for the GOP nod, though he lost the general election.

False flag: Yet another term borrowed from the military and spy world. It originally connoted flying a flag other than one's own on a ship to deceive an enemy ship. In campaigns, it connotes a negative attack that a campaign deliberately launches to generate sympathy for its candidate while assigning blame to one of its rivals.

★ In a California Assembly race in 2012, Democrat Mike Gatto denied his campaign had intentionally misled voters about his opponent, Republican Greg Krikorian, in phone calls and mailers. "I think this is a false flag. This is something they're doing to try to motivate Mr. Krikorian's perceived base," Gatto told the *Glendale News-Press*.[32]

False flag also is a popular term in conspiracy theorist circles. It often is used to imply that incidents such as the 9/11 attacks or the Boston Marathon bombing were the work of the U.S. government. Announcing his support for an assault weapons ban in 2013, Senate Democratic leader Harry Reid said, "I'll vote for the ban because maintaining the law and order is more important than satisfying conspiracy theorists who believe in black helicopters and false flags."[33]

Finance event: See *funder*.

Funder: The life's blood of elected officials. Though many lawmakers disdain dialing for dollars and appearing at dinners with big donors, they're willing to go through such indignities to hold on to their seats.

★ When freshmen arrive on Capitol Hill for orientation, party leaders impress upon new members of their own caucuses the importance of fundraising. Walt Minnick, a Democrat swept into the House by the 2008 wave so big it enveloped his conservative home state of Idaho, was instructed to raise $10,000 to $15,000 *every day*.[34] He eventually exceeded his goal of $2.5 million — but still lost two years later in the subsequent GOP landslide of 2010 to Republican Raul Labrador, who hauled in less than one-third of Minnick's take.

Mitt Romney's 2012 campaign briefly ran into the trouble with the *optics* of funders. Romney's running mate, Representative Paul Ryan, traveled to Las Vegas for a meeting that wasn't on his official schedule. The gathering was hosted by casino magnate Sheldon Adelson, who was generously bankrolling Republicans via his super PAC. To abide by laws that bar elected officials from directly asking donors for super PAC money, Romney aides said the meeting wasn't a funder; it was a "finance event." After reporters besieged the campaign with questions about the difference, it sought to clarify: Unlike fundraisers, people attending finance events don't need to buy tickets.[35]

Lawmakers are unabashed about their need for big bucks to stay in office. Consider Representative Jeff Denham, a California Republican from a swing-ish Central Valley district elected in 2010. In early 2011, with the nation still emerging from recession, Denham defied new Republican Speaker John Boehner's admonition to keep GOP inaugural celebrations austere. Instead, Denham threw a $2,500-a-person fundraiser featuring country sing LeAnn Rimes.[36]

Elected officials rarely miss an opportunity to raise campaign dough, no matter how tacky the *optics*. During the October 2013 government shutdown, in which federal employees were furloughed without paychecks, lawmakers dove into fundraising activities. Party committees and outside groups on both sides of the aisle latched on to the (latest) Washington budget crisis, using the moment to rile their bases and fill their coffers for the 2014 campaign.

That said, many are resigned to it. As Representative Jim Himes (D-CT) lamented to the *New York Times*: "I won't dispute for one second the problems of a system that demands immense amount of fund-raisers by its legislators. It's appalling, it's disgusting, it's wasteful and it opens the possibility of conflicts of interest and corruption. It's unfortunately the world we live in."[37]

Future: It's become a cliché to say that campaigns are all about the future, but that doesn't mean politicians have stopped saying it. It connotes hope and forward-thinking optimism. Both Barack Obama and, earlier, Newt Gingrich tried to claim ownership of the term "winning the future."

★ A few other examples plucked from a totally random Google search of political news in April 2013:

- This campaign is about the future we can create for our families and our community," declared Linda Dorcena Forry, a Democratic candidate for the Massachusetts Senate.[38]
- "This campaign is about the future, not the past, and I'm the right person to bring Arlington Heights into that future," said Ron Drake, a Republican running for president of the village council in Arlington Heights, Illinois.[39]
- "This campaign is about the future of a place we call home," Democrat Thomas Suozzi vowed at an appearance when running for executive of New York's Nassau County.[40]

Apart from the stump, it's been interesting to see just how far politicians take that word these days, especially when it comes to naming their fundraising apparatuses. Republicans in 2012 used the word in several prominent super PACs—Restore Our Future (unsuccessful nominee Mitt Romney's PAC); Winning Our Future (which backed Gingrich); the Brighter Future Fund (a general conservative group). Its use was so prevalent that former Obama aide Bill Burton complained, tongue-in-cheek, that it took him weeks to come up with the name Priorities USA Action for his super PAC because Republicans had trademarked every other slogan. "You can't come up with a name that has the word 'future' in it that Republicans don't control," Burton told the *New York Times* in 2012.[41]

He's actually wrong. Among the Democratic super PACs with the name were the Freedom Fund for America's Future (which opposed Republican U.S. Senate nominee Tom Smith) and the Campaign for Our Future (which backed Democrat Clyde Williams in his unsuccessful primary bid against New York representative Charles Rangel).

Game changer: An event in a campaign or legislative battle portrayed as so momentous that it has the potential to alter the outcome. Its importance was evident in the best-selling book *Game Change*, which depicted the backstage drama of the 2008 presidential campaign and was turned into an HBO movie.

★ The phrase is a heavy favorite of political operatives, journalists, and pundits. Stuart Rothenberg, among Washington's most esteemed analysts, wrote in May 2013, "Forget background checks and gun control, divisions within the GOP on immigration, and Republican intransigence on negotiating a budget deal with the president. The current triple play of Benghazi, the IRS and now the Justice Department's seizure of journalists' phone records has the potential to be a political game changer for 2014."[42]

But its increasingly common usage irks academics looking for less simplistic and less dramatic explanations of how elections are decided. "I think 'game change' is typically used tautologically—'What does (losing candidate) need at this point? He needs a game changer; it's basically, he needs something that will cause him to win,'" said Bethany Albertson, a University of Texas–Austin political scientist who studies political attitudes and persuasion. "When it's used to label events, it's used very freely, generally with no empirical basis. . . . I guess pundits are incentivized to use the language because it makes whatever happened sound hugely important, but there's no check on its use."[43]

The 2013 book *The Gamble* by George Washington University's John Sides and UCLA's Lynn Vavreck took a similarly critical stance: "The search for 'game-changers' may make for grabby headlines, but it does not really help us understand presidential elections in general and the 2012 presidential election in particular."[44] The pair crunched numbers to argue that more basic factors, such as the uptick of the ailing economy's recovery, played a far more crucial role in determining the election's outcome.

Sometimes events *do* live up to their hype as game changers. Often, it's a debate. Even more than a half century later, a fresh viewing of the 1960 debates shows Senator John F. Kennedy of Massachusetts a superior performer to his Republican rival, Vice President Richard Nixon. And while Nixon certainly held his own, speaking fluidly and fluently about a range of public policy issues, Kennedy's cool performance and telegenic appearance, helped seal many voters' decisions. And then there was Texas governor Rick Perry's gaffe at a 2012 primary debate in which he couldn't remember the three cabinet agencies he wanted to abolish.

Get primaried: With the political rise of the tea party, this warning that an incumbent will face a challenger in his or her primary election has become increasingly common.

★ "We're not going to do something in the dark, late at night where no one knows what the practical effect and outcome is," Texas GOP representative Pete Sessions, former chairman of the Republican Congressional Campaign Committee, told Bloomberg Television during the "fiscal cliff" negotiations in December 2012.[45] "If we do that, we do get primaried." A year later, Sarah Palin told Fox News: "Those who can't stand strong to defend our republic, to defend our Constitution—heck yeah, they should be primaried, otherwise we are going down."[46]

Such usage is highly dismaying to those facing just such a situation. "When did 'primary' become a verb?" asked an exasperated Senator Lisa Murkowski (R-AK). "Good heavens, it used to be that a primary was a process; now it's a verbal threat. It's maddening."[47]

Murkowski survived a primary-ing in one of the most unusual ways in political history. A moderate on some social issues, she lost in the 2010 GOP contest to tea party favorite Joe Miller. But with the slogan "Let's Make History," she decided to run in the general election as a write-in candidate. She ended up getting 39 percent of the vote to Miller's 35 percent and Democrat Scott McAdams' 23 percent.

The tea party's emergence has changed how Republicans prepare for, as well as guard against, primaries. "It used to be that [candidates] had to go to the state party people, and county party executive director X was important and you had to kiss their ring," Florida Republican political consultant Rick Wilson said. "Now you need to see the organizers of the local tea party to make sure you're on their 'good' list. It's just become a fact of life. You always had to win the money primary and political primary, and now it's the tea party primary."[48]

GOTV: *Get out the vote* operations are among the most important activities campaigns engage in. While television and polls dominate news coverage about a candidate, it's the campaign's ability to actually make sure voters cast ballots on Election Day—or before, depending on states' early voting rules—that really matters.

★ Tactics used in GOTV include telephoning or sending personalized audio messages (*robocalls*) to known supporters on the days leading up to an election (or on Election Day itself). GOTV can also include providing transportation to and from polling stations for supporters, and canvassing known supporters.

Voter turnout took on increased importance in the hyperpartisan years of the early twenty-first century. Campaigns used to spend massive amounts of resources trying to persuade independent and politically unaligned citizens to cast ballots in their favor. But with Americans' attitudes about politics hardening in one direction or the other, there simply weren't that many people who could be persuaded.

That's made voter turnout vital. For the Bush-Cheney 2004 reelection campaign, political advisor Karl Rove and his team mobilized armies of people to get their neighbors out to vote for the president, despite his deep unpopularity in many quarters. The campaign used sophisticated data crunching to identify likely arm-twisters for the cause. Barack Obama's campaign then turned these GOTV techniques into a high art form in its 2008 and 2012 victories, making sure to throw in some old-fashioned rallying from the candidate for good measure. Two weeks before the latter contest, Obama would, on five or six separate occasions at his rallies, address the catcalls each time he criticized Mitt Romney. "Don't boo—vote," he would respond.[49]

The AARP took a counterintuitive approach to GOTV in 2006. The powerful senior citizen's lobby told its supporters, "Don't vote"—at least not until they actually understood what they were doing. It set up a website, www.dontvote.com, that included links to voter guides and explanations of issues.

Grassroots campaign: A candidate campaign driven by organic support from the community, rather than one tapped by party leaders. Politicians like to refer to grassroots support for their candidacies as a way of distancing themselves from special interests. But as the *Rothenberg Political Report*'s Nathan L. Gonzales observed in a column, "This translates to, 'I'm not going to raise any money.'"

★ The phrase "grassroots and boots" was thought to have been coined by Senator Albert Beveridge (R-IN), who said of the Progressive Party in 1912, "This party has come from the grass roots. It has grown from the soil of people's hard necessities." Over the years the term came to mean underdog campaigns.

Some grassroots campaigns were successful; others weren't. Take Howard Dean's 2004 bid for the Democratic presidential nomination. The former Vermont governor, a doctor himself, initially premised his longshot presidential bid on what he called the importance of universal health care. But months after the Iraq war, with President George W. Bush still riding high in the polls and maintaining his post-9/11 glow, Dean shifted his focus to opposing the president on foreign policy, emphasizing an issue important to his party's grassroots elements. Dean took the politically risky stand of criticizing the nation's recent Middle East adventure. Dean moved his party sharply to the left on foreign policy, and showed Democrats a more pugilistic and confrontational approach against Republicans could be good politics.

Several members of Congress have also gotten into office through grassroots campaigns. Once such challenger was Florida Republican Ted Yoho, a north Florida veterinarian who in 2012 challenged veteran representative Cliff Stearns in the GOP primary. The district had recently been redrawn, and Stearns seemed to take the race for granted after winning easily for nearly a quarter century. Yoho had just one paid employee—his twenty-four-year-old campaign manager. His opponent, the sitting congressman, had exponentially more in campaign cash and a large staff. But Yoho embraced his tea party backing and railed against "career politicians." Yoho narrowly claimed victory in one of the biggest political upsets of the year. (Also see *astroturfing*.)

Hardship porn: A term coined by *New York Times* columnist Frank Bruni in 2013 to describe the tendency of candidates to repeatedly stress how their overcoming of past adversities makes them worthy for office.

★ Bruni saw it as an overused technique politicians use to portray themselves as "one of us." "The economy's stubborn funk has ratcheted up our suspicion of perks and privileges and our support for underdogs," he wrote, "to a point where we're less taken with what people have achieved than with what they've endured." Among the hardships he cited:

- New York mayoral candidate Christine Quinn's disclosure that she had struggled with bulimia and alcoholism.
- Ann Romney's reminiscences along the campaign trail of the basement apartment and tuna casseroles that she and her husband Mitt shared in their early days together.
- North Dakota Democratic Senate candidate Heidi Heitkamp's ordeal with breast cancer.
- GOP representative Paul Ryan's references to the death of his father when he was a teenager.

"Those aren't just anecdotes that flit by," Bruni observed. "They're foundational ordeals, mentioned incessantly . . . its insinuation [is] that surmounting obstacles equals acquiring real character, which is ostensibly impossible without tough times."[50]

"I endorse . . .": Does it really matter how much backing a candidate gets from other politicians or from newspapers? Sometimes.

★ In theory, political candidates can increase name recognition and establish credibility—not to mention get campaign fund-raising help—by winning endorsements. There's some historical precedent for this. As University of Virginia political scientist Larry Sabato noted in a January 2012 *Wall Street Journal* op-ed, "Throughout American history, presidencies have been created by the laying on of incumbent hands." Sabato elaborated: "Thomas Jefferson effectively passed the presidency to his friend and confidant, James Madison. Andrew Jackson handed his populist democracy off to an unlikely dandy, Martin Van Buren, in 1836. . . . Madison, Van Buren, Taft and [George H. W.] Bush all got their predecessor's third term—when popular, presidents have extraordinary powers."[51]

However, legions of campaigns have promoted their backing from prominent politicians and newspapers, only to see them fall flat. The 2012 Republican presidential primary contest alone showed the sometime futility of political endorsements. South Carolina governor Nikki Haley flopped mightily in trying to deliver her state for Mitt Romney. Evangelical leaders held a summit to get the Palmetto State to back their choice, Rick Santorum, but he fared much worse than Romney.

Newspapers, which are under attack for their alleged liberal bias, are slowly getting out of the presidential endorsement business, or choosing not to give an editorial blessing to either aspirant. (Editorial boards—sometimes with a nudge from the publisher—make endorsement decisions, *not* reporters and editors. All politicians know this, but conveniently don't mention it when they publicly accuse the people who cover them on a daily basis of media bias.)

The University of California–Santa Barbara's American Presidency Project found that in 2012, 23 of the nation's top 100 newspapers did not endorse Romney or Obama, up from the 8 papers four years earlier that didn't give the nod to Obama or Senator John McCain. (Of the papers that *did* endorse, Obama topped Romney, 41 to 35; against McCain he ran up a more lopsided 65 to 25 margin.[52]) Earlier, before the New Hampshire GOP primary, the Granite State's once-dominant *Manchester Union Leader* backed Newt Gingrich. But the former House speaker earned less than 10 percent of the vote.

All that said, endorsements occasionally make a decisive difference. Such was the case in the 2004 Pennsylvania Senate primary. Fellow Republicans long considered Senator Arlen Specter a *squish*. Among other moves, he opposed conviction and removal from office in President Bill Clinton's impeachment trial, issuing a mercurial "not proven" verdict based on his interpretation of "Scottish law." By 2004, Republican voters seemed fed up with Specter's antics. The senator faced a primary challenge from the right by Representative Pat Toomey.

However, most of the state and national Republican establishment closed ranks behind Specter. That included the state's other senator at the time, Rick Santorum, a member of the Senate GOP leadership. Specter was also supported by President George W. Bush, a popular figure among Pennsylvania Republicans who himself was seeking a second term. Specter narrowly avoided a major upset. His very public endorsements by Bush and Santorum clearly made a difference. (Toomey got a measure of comeuppance, winning the very same Senate seat six years later.)

To assess their meaningfulness, *Washington Post* political blogger Chris Cillizza has developed an "Endorsement Hierarchy." At the bottom is "The Pariah Endorsement," which comes from damaged goods (the scandal-plagued Rev. Jeremiah Wright backing Barack Obama in 2008). Slightly higher is the "Me for Me Endorsement," which is more about boosting the endorsee's career (New York Mayor Michael Bloomberg supported Obama in 2012, but only after writing an op-ed in which he castigated the president and Mitt Romney for not doing things the Bloomberg way). The progression continues up to the most influential, the "Symbolic Endorsement," a valuable embrace (think extremely popular ex-Florida governor Jeb Bush backing Romney in the 2012 primary—it helped beat back a surging Newt Gingrich, though it wasn't enough to help Romney carry the Sunshine State).[53]

Some political science research suggests endorsements are more important than commonly understood. Thad Kousser, Eric McGhee, and Seth Masket presented a paper at the April 2013 Midwest Political Science Association conference that measured the impact of party endorsements on voters. California had decided to have a top-two open-primary system. It included the parties' endorsements in the ballot booklet it mailed out to voters. The party-endorsed candidates, McGhee and Masket found, tended to get the lion's share of the votes.

"In cycle": The status of a candidate, usually a senator, who is coming up for reelection, something that can exert a strong pull on their legislative behavior.

★ "The most important calculation to a member of Congress (who has to run for reelection every two years) or to a senator who is 'in cycle' (up for election in 2014) is: How will these Shut-Down, Obamacare, Syria, debt limit, Food Stamp, Student Loan, Medicare, Medicaid, and similar votes be greeted by the 'Folks Back Home'?" veteran Republican strategist Rich Galen wrote in a September 2013 column.[54]

In March 2013, then Senate Finance Committee chairman Max Baucus, a Montana Democrat whose home state has become increasingly Republican and whose term was due to expire at the end of the following year, broke from his colleagues to oppose his party's budget blueprint calling for tax increases. The reason was evident to many observers. "He is in cycle," Bill Hoagland, a former top Senate GOP budget staffer, told the *Hill* newspaper.[55] "Voting for raising revenues would definitely be used against him, even if nothing happened on tax reform." (As it happened, Baucus later decided to get off the cycle by announcing he wouldn't run again. He later was named U.S. ambassador to China.)

A related phrase among political insiders is "up," as in "Is he up?" "That means, are you up for election this cycle?" said former senator Byron Dorgan (D-ND).[56]

Internals: Nonpublic polling data that sound more like a medical school anatomy class than campaign parlance for valuable insider survey information. Internal polls, guarded closely by campaigns, often show different results than publicly released surveys.

★ That's because questions are sometimes asked in different ways, based on factors only the campaign is privy to. But when internal poll results show a campaign's candidate winning—or within striking distance if he or she is considered an underdog—the information often gets released.

Of course, internal polls can be wrong. The Mitt Romney campaign's internal numbers in the waning days of the 2012 contest reportedly showed the Republican nominee in a decent position to beat President Barack Obama. "Team Romney's internal polling showed North Carolina, Florida, and Virginia moving safely into his column and that it put him ahead in a few other swing states," wrote the *New Republic*'s Noam Scheiber three weeks later. "When combined with Ohio, where the internal polling had him close, Romney was on track to secure all the electoral votes he needed to win the White House."

But the writer's deeper-dive analysis in to the operation's polling numbers—provided by a "Romney aide"—showed that the polling was less than accurate. It was providing false hope to Team Romney—to the point that the losing candidate didn't even have a concession speech ready on Election Night.[57]

Job creators: A *Luntzism* intended to portray large businesses or wealthy individuals as bestowers of employment instead of greedy and profit-centric.

★ "Job creators" came into vogue in 2011 as Republicans sought to tamp down any populist anger over rich people, including eventual presidential candidate Mitt Romney. The phrase drew plenty of attention, but in the end it may have failed to achieve its desired effect.

The conservative advocacy group American Principles in Action said in a 2013 report: "It was a clever neologism, intended to suggest that policies benefiting business, especially small business, would help the middle class. But it may have been too clever by half. We believe that one of the reasons the Romney economic message failed is that positioning oneself as an experienced 'job creator' working for other 'job creators,' albeit to increase jobs, can backfire. Republicans say 'job creators' but voters correctly hear 'my boss.' And voters increasingly hate their bosses."[58]

Micro-targeting: Political data-mining techniques meant to target the right set of potential voters come election time. Under this increasingly elaborate and detailed targeting method, sophisticated computer modeling groups individual voters into clusters such as "Downscale Union Independents" and "Older Suburban Newshounds"—yes, those are the actual names political consultants came up with. And that's only the beginning of political pros' slicing-and-dicing categories. Other high-target groups include "Flag and Family Republicans" and "Education-Focused Democrats."

★ Micro-targeting took off as a campaign art form in 2004, when Bush-Cheney strategist Karl Rove and his political team used it to reach voters in eighteen targeted states that could have gone either way in the Electoral College. The results were greater contacts with likely Bush voters. In Iowa, the campaign was able to reach 92 percent of eventual Bush voters, compared to 50 percent in 2000.

Barack Obama's campaign took micro-targeting to a new level in 2012. Its strategists knew some enthusiasm for Obama would fall off, so they went about creating new voters. That included people who had turned eighteen since Election Day four years before, and new citizens. The technologists devised hundreds of sub-voter groups to which surrogates could appeal.

One such heavily targeted group was professional single women in Colorado, clustered in specific Denver suburbs. That may sound like a relatively small group of people on which to expend significant resources. But Obama campaign strategists—like their opponents in the Mitt Romney camp—found an Electoral College victory hinging on only eight or nine states. And even within a swing state, like Colorado, not every vote was equal. Rural territories in the eastern and northern parts of the state were largely Republicans. Inner-city Denver was already strongly for Obama, as were Hispanic suburbs, to a lesser extent. So upscale single women were deemed to be a deciding factor in keeping Colorado in Obama's column for the second straight presidential election. Sure enough, the president won the Centennial State.

Money bomb/money blurt: A *money bomb* is an online fundraising technique of recent origin to pull in a lot of campaign cash in a short period to maximize publicity.

★ The unconventional strategy goes completely against the grain of the big-dollar donor dinners most candidates favor; it combines web-based fundraising appeals (that's the "bomb" part of it) with traditional fundraising methods.

The term was first used to pull in campaign cash for the 2008 Republican presidential bid of Texas representative Ron Paul. As Paul's campaign showed, it works best when appealing to a broad range of people who are extremely passionate about a cause or candidate, who can only contribute a small amount of money, but who are all too eager to spread the word via Facebook and Twitter. Paul pulled in $4.2 million in one day, making it at that time the largest one-day Internet political fundraiser ever. That kind of money causes political professionals and the media to sit up and take notice.

A related technique, coined by the *Washington Post* in 2011, is the *money blurt*. This is when an *attack dog* makes a highly provocative statement that plays to *the base* and uses it to bring in money.

Far-right Minnesota representative Michele Bachmann was seen as a master of this technique—in the summer of 2010, she raked in $5 million after several appearances in which she accused President Barack Obama of "turning our country into a nation of slaves"—and some predict it will persist as online fundraising occupies an even more significant place in politics. As Tom Serres, founder and CEO of Rally.org, an online fundraising platform, wrote in a 2012 op-ed column: "I believe the most important axiom in online fundraising is that traditional media-driven events are the rocket fuel for online fundraising."[59]

Monty Python and politics: As anyone who's ever heard of the Silly Party knows, Monty Python has never shied away from politics. But the beloved British comedy troupe's classic skits increasingly have been used to explain events—and even personalities—on the campaign trail.

★ Maybe it's just that a number of pundits are fans of Python's TV show and movies. Or maybe it's that John Cleese, Michael Palin, and the rest of the group were keen anticipators of the absurd. In any event, here are some examples from 2012:

- Two of the Republican candidates who stayed in the presidential race the longest, Newt Gingrich and Rick Santorum, often were compared to *Monty Python and the Holy Grail*'s ever-persistent Black Knight, who exemplifies the meaning of not knowing when to quit—even after losing all of his arms and legs in a swordfight.
- Mitt Romney's personal fortune made him a target for accusations that he was out of touch. Even the *American Conservative*'s Philip Giraldi wondered if the ex-Massachusetts governor could have been cast in one of Python's sketches skewering the wealthy, such as one

in which the self-described "very, very, very rich" Cleese appeared mystified by the notion of donating money to help orphans.

- When the *Wall Street Journal*'s Robert Frank sought to explain what he dubbed "the new politics of wealth denial" involving President Barack Obama, he invoked Python's "Four Yorkshiremen" sketch featuring a group of cigar-smoking rich men boasting about how poor they all once were. After one of them talks of being forced to grow up in a hall corridor, Palin's character says dismissively, "We used to dream of living in a corridor. It would have been a palace to us."
- Opining on what he called the Republicans' steadfast rejection of Obama's agenda, the *Washington Post*'s Jonathan Bernstein cited the "Argument Clinic" sketch, in which Cleese finds a way to disagree with absolutely everything Palin says.[60]

October surprise: An earth-shattering political event late in election season that can change the trajectory of a race.

★ Presidential campaign history is littered with October surprises. One of the most impactful was the late October 2000 revelation that Texas governor George W. Bush, the Republican presidential nominee, had been arrested for drunk driving a quarter century earlier. This might not have been such a big deal except that Bush's campaign and personal appeal was premised on his "redemption" story. Bush said earlier in the campaign that he gave up drinking after waking up with a hangover after his fortieth-birthday celebration.

It wasn't a case of outright hypocrisy when Erin Fehlau of Maine FOX affiliate WPXT-TV reported that on September 4, 1976, Bush had been arrested for driving under the influence of alcohol near his family's summer home in Kennebunkport, Maine. Bush, then thirty, admitted his guilt, was fined $150, and had his driving license in the state suspended for two years. Yet because the Bush campaign hadn't revealed the incident, the case reeked of concealment. Bush's chief political strategist Karl Rove later admitted the political damage, estimating that it cost Bush nearly four million votes from evangelical Christians. Add in those votes and the wrenching thirty-six-day Florida recount spectacle likely wouldn't have been necessary.

October surprises can be acts of God. Take Hurricane Sandy, the 2012 superstorm that took an unusual path through the Northeast, devastating large swaths of New Jersey and even parts of New York City. The storm hit land one week before Election Day. New Jersey governor Chris Christie, one of Republican nominee Mitt Romney's leading supporters, praised President Barack Obama and his reaction to the hurricane. Many Republicans afterward remained livid at Christie for hugging the president so closely politically, but the governor maintained he was just doing his job. (See also *Master of Disaster.*)

Some alleged October surprises are simply the stuff of legend. One such story had George H. W. Bush, the 1980 Republican vice presidential nominee, making a clandestine late October trip to Paris to stave off release of American hostages being held in Iran. After the release of the hostages on January 20, 1981, mere minutes after Ronald Reagan's inauguration, some charged that the Republican campaign had made a secret deal with the Iranian government whereby the Iranians would hold the hostages until after Reagan was elected and inaugurated.

Gary Sick, member of the National Security Council under Presidents Gerald Ford and Jimmy Carter (before being relieved of his duties a mere weeks into Reagan's term) made the accusation in a *New York Times* editorial in the run-up to the 1992 election. But two separate congressional investigations looked into the charges, both concluding that there was no plan to seek to delay the hostages' release.

"Operate government like a business": A frequent campaign-trail pledge by candidates, most often Republicans. Nearly all who have tried to actually implement this in practice bump up against a series of tough political realities.

★ Governments do not actually operate like businesses, for a variety of reasons. First, the employees, for the most part, cannot be fired, and thus have little reason to hit performance metrics, let alone respond to the views of management. And governments aren't guided by the same profit motive as private-sector businesses. The lack of a single, clear metric—earning as much money as possible—makes managing government, and assessing how the whole enterprise is doing, a lot more difficult.

Harvard Business School alum Mitt Romney centered his 2012 Republican presidential campaign on the notion of operating government more like a business. This Romney government-as-business theme went so far that in the months before the 2012 election, a group of high-powered consultants and political operatives prepared a secret report for the candidate. The plan detailed how Romney should take over and restructure the federal government should he win the presidency. "The White House staff is similar to a holding company," read one PowerPoint slide, which would have been presented to president-elect Romney as part of an expansive briefing on the morning after Election Day. It went on to list three main divisions of the metaphorical firm: "Care & Feeding Offices," such as speechwriting; "Policy Offices," such as the National Security Council; and "Packaging & Selling Offices," including the office of the press secretary.[61] In short, very businesslike.

Oppo: Short for opposition research, the underside of political campaigns that dredge up long-buried and embarrassing facts about opponents.

★ Sometimes unflattering information is used as a brushback pitch to keep a potential opponent out of a race. Other times, negative scoops are held back until late in a campaign when they can be deployed to maximum effect.

The full effect of a good opposition-research operation often isn't clear until after Election Day. In the 2008 cycle, researchers for Democratic presidential candidate Barack Obama unearthed evidence of John Edwards's $400 haircuts, billed at his campaign's expense. Campaign manager David Plouffe wrote in his memoir *The Audacity to Win* that he supplied the tip to a reporter.[62] The planted information reinforced the image of Edwards as a preening narcissist, and the North Carolinian was soon out of the race.

Digging up dirt and highlighting unflattering aspects of the opposition's life have a long political history. In the 1828 presidential election, Andrew Jackson's opponents unearthed his marriage records, seeking to imply that the hero of the Battle of New Orleans was an adulterer for marrying Rachel Robards in 1791 before she was legally divorced from her first husband. Jackson won the White House over President John Quincy Adams anyway, avenging a bitter loss four years earlier. But the opposition researchers' work may have taken a toll: Rachel died shortly before Jackson took office—a result, he contended, of the stress of having her honor called into question.

Even Abraham Lincoln wasn't above engaging in oppo research. In preparation for Lincoln's 1860 presidential campaign against Stephen A. Douglas, Lincoln's law partner, William Herndon, combed the Illinois State Library to collect "all the ammunition Mr. Lincoln saw fit to gather" against his Democratic rival.

The art of opposition research came into its own during the 1988 presidential election when Massachusetts criminal Willie Horton was turned into a household name by the campaign of Republican nominee George H. W. Bush. But the idea originated with a primary rival to eventual Democratic nominee Michael Dukakis: Senator Al Gore of Tennessee.

Opposition research used to be considered more of a "dark art" with its practitioners hiding far underground. In the early years of the twenty-first century, more campaigns than ever were admitting to, and in some cases bragging about, their opposition-research handiwork.

While journalists are usually reluctant to admit they've received opposition research on a politician from a rival camp, sometimes they say so openly. In September 2013, *Fox News Sunday* host Chris Wallace said on-air that he'd received opposition research from other Republicans about Senator Ted Cruz, in advance of the Texas Republican's appearance on that show. Wallace's admission reflected just how upset many Republicans were with Cruz leading a legislative charge to defund Obamacare, aka the Affordable Care Act. "This has been one of the strangest weeks I've ever had in Washington," Wallace said. "As soon as we listed Ted Cruz as our featured guest this week, I got unsolicited research and questions, not from Democrats but from top Republicans, to hammer Cruz."[63]

Optics: How voters and the media perceive something. In politics, it often is an event, phrase, or policy that is pushed front and center because of the belief that it will help win the politician more votes.

★ On Super Tuesday 2012, as Republicans in ten states voted in key primaries, President Obama unveiled several new efforts to reduce refinancing costs and bring justice to service members who lost their homes through wrongful foreclosures. Housing industry experts noted the timing. "This is more about optics than it is about substance," said Brian Gardner, an analyst with KBW Inc. "We are in campaign season. There is no accident that this is happening on Super Tuesday."[64]

The *New York Times'* Ben Zimmer said the political use of the word dates to 1978, when the *Wall Street Journal* quoted a Jimmy Carter aide, Robert Strauss, as saying that business leaders who went along with Carter's anti-inflation measures might be invited to the White House as a token of appreciation. "It would be a nice optical step," Strauss said. In an editorial, the *Journal* dismissed the idea: "Optics will not cure inflation."[65]

Packing: In drawing House seats for partisan advantage, a gerrymandering form of vote dilution in which a minority group is over-concentrated in a small number of districts, thus confining its voting strength to those districts.

★ Packing can happen when, say, the African American population is concentrated into one district where it makes up 90 percent of the district, instead of spread across two districts where it could be roughly half of each district. Former representative Martin Frost of Texas called it a strategy "to convince some southern black leaders to create a handful of new packed black districts and thus bleach the surrounding districts, making them Republican."[66]

Frost has firsthand experience being on the business end of House district-packing. A former Democratic Congressional Campaign Committee chairman and House Democratic Caucus chair, among other roles, Frost's twenty-six-year House career ended after the 2004 elections when state Republicans—at the behest of GOP House majority leader Tom DeLay—redrew the lines. Frost was among a wave of white Texas Democrats washed out that cycle, with the state congressional delegation flipping from 17 to 15 Democratic to 21 to 11 Republican. Lost amid the hubbub of Republican gains was the fact that the state's minority members—African American and Hispanic, were made considerably safer in their own districts for years to come.

After the 2012 elections, Democrats saw a more broadly nefarious plan to pack their members into a smaller amount of districts to maintain the GOP's hold on the House it had won in the 2010 midterm elections. Though Republican congressional candidates received nearly 1.4 million fewer votes than Democratic candidates in November 2012, the Republicans lost only eight seats, allowing them to preserve a thirty-three-seat edge in the House.

Gerrymandering, and particularly packing, had played a big role in this. In Pennsylvania, Democratic candidates took 51 percent of the vote across the state's eighteen districts, but only five of the seats. Similar imbalances occurred in Ohio, Michigan, and, to a lesser extent, North Carolina.

"Politics ain't beanbag": The archaic and polite way of saying "life is rough; get over it" to a politician who complains about his or her treatment in the media or by opponents. A beanbag, obviously, doesn't hurt when you throw it at someone.

★ It dates back to 1895, when writer Finley Peter Dunne used it as a quote from his fictional character Mr. Dooley, an Irishman who pontificated on the day's issues from a Chicago pub. "Sure, politics ain't bean-bag," Dooley proclaimed. "'Tis a man's game, an' women, childer, cripples an' prohybitionists 'd do well to keep out iv it."

When Fox News' Sean Hannity asked Texas senator Ted Cruz about the characterization of him and Utah senator Mike Lee as *wacko birds* in 2013, Cruz responded: "You know, listen, at the end of the day, you know, the old saying is politics ain't beanbag. And fortunately, neither Mike nor I have thin skins."[67]

It's often mistakenly pluralized, as Mitt Romney did in 2012 in talking about his then presidential primary rival Newt Gingrich: "There's no question that politics ain't beanbags. . . . The speaker has been attacking me all over the state in ways that are really extraordinary, in some respects painful to watch because it's so revealing of him."[68]

Push poll: Negative campaigning disguised as a political poll. Push polls are actually political telemarketing—telephone calls disguised as research that aim to persuade large numbers of voters and affect election outcomes, rather than measure opinions.

★ Push pollers used to be able to get away with it because the calls were short and tough to track. In the age of Twitter, Facebook, cell-phone recorders, and other devices it's gotten increasingly more difficult. But it does happen. In the spring 2013 House special election in South Carolina's First District, former Republican governor Mark Sanford was seeking a political comeback. His national image had been sullied by an extramarital affair that exposed a prolonged 2009 absence from the state—the infamous "hiking the Appalachian trail"—for a rendezvous with his Argentine paramour. Sanford sought election to his old House seat against Democratic businesswoman Elizabeth Colbert Busch. Shortly before Election Day, a mysterious conservative group placed calls to South Carolina voters. As various media outlets reported, the questions included:

- "What would you think of Elizabeth Colbert Busch if I told you she had had an abortion?"
- "What would you think of Elizabeth Colbert Busch if I told you a judge held her in contempt of court at her divorce proceedings?"
- "What would you think of Elizabeth Colbert Busch if she had done jail time?"[69]

None of this was true, but the ideas had still been communicated to potential voters. Sanford won going away.

In our highly cynical age, researchers have found that push polling doesn't just damage the intended target; it hurts *all* office-seekers. "If I introduce someone to new, hypothetical information about a certain politician being crooked, even though the information isn't true, the question will influence them over time because it matches their existing, negative beliefs about politicians," said the University of Alberta's Sarah Moore, who studies how hypothetical information influences people. "They'll become more negative about that politician and less likely to vote for him, and their attitude about politicians in general will become more negative."[70]

Robocalls: Those highly annoying automated phone calls sent out in an election's final days. The targeted calls can serve the legitimate purpose of reminding potential voters to cast a ballot. Or, more ominously, robocalls often dish negative information on an opposing candidate.

★ In fall 2013 Virginia Republican gubernatorial candidate Ken Cuccinelli took the latter route. Then state attorney general Cuccinelli's campaign blanketed the Old Dominion with robocalls accusing his Democratic opponent, Terry McAuliffe, of profiting off a dying man in a business insurance scam and favoring "abortion on demand."[71] Not that it helped much. The robocalls' target, former Democratic National Committee Chairman McAuliffe, eked out a narrow victory, despite his support for abortion rights in a state with a strong socially conservative voting bloc, and lingering questions about past business dealings.

That year McAuliffe had his close friend, former president Bill Clinton, campaigning for him personally. But even those without such a presidential tie-in—as in most Americans—could still hear from Clinton, at least via robocalls. The forty-second president has become a go-to voice for Democratic candidates up and down the ballot seeking to maximize voter turnout.

You'll be pleased to know that elected officials—including some who used robocalls to win their own campaigns—periodically target the technique in criticism and legislation. It's an easy issue on which to demagogue—stopping annoying, recorded calls, often captured in a monotone voice, from coming in right during dinner or some other annoying time. Ambitious pols have tried to liken robocalls to the federal Do Not Call List blocking telemarketers—though campaign calls enjoy broader First Amendment protections.

Blocking, or at least limiting robocalls, became a national crusade for Virginia resident Shaun Dakin. In 2007 Dakin the founded the nonprofit National Political Do Not Contact Registry. During the next year's election cycle he launched a new initiative to push California regulators to enforce its little-noted robocall rule. "What we're trying to do is to make politicians understand that there is a law on the books against these kinds of automated robocalls without a live person—it's $500 per incident per violation," Dakin told *Wired*. "We want to make them realize that someone's paying attention to this." He noted that with few exceptions, California's public utilities code says that robocalls are only legal when they're introduced by a live person.

But Dakin said that the rules are never enforced, and pointed to the spate of robocalls conducted by the presidential candidates during that year's primaries.[72]

"Significant" special elections: Special elections usually are triggered when someone dies, resigns, or gets elected or appointed to another office, leaving the seat vacant. Both parties reflexively spin such wins as significant harbingers of future campaigns.

★ When Republican Scott Brown came out of nowhere to win a special election for the late Massachusetts senator Ted Kennedy's seat in early 2010, the GOP heralded it as a powerful warning sign of wider discontent with Democrats. (It was; the party recaptured control of the House that fall and picked up seats in the Senate, though it didn't win a majority there.) And when Democrat Kathy Hochul captured a seat in a special House election in May 2011 in a Republican-dominated upstate New York district, Democratic National Committee Chair Debbie Wasserman Schultz told reporters that the win "had far-reaching consequences" for her party in 2012.[73] (It didn't; Democrats picked up House seats, but not enough to regain control, and Hochul lost her reelection bid to Republican Chris Collins.)

So is the spin true? University of Texas–Dallas political scientists David Smith and Thomas L. Brunell examined every House special election between 1900 and 2008 and concluded that they often are reliable barometers. "To the extent that when one party takes seats away from the other party in these elections, they generally fare reasonably well in the general [election]," they said in a 2010 article in Legislative Studies Quarterly. What's more, they said, special elections have greater predictive power if you look at the actual margin of victory, not just the result. Given how random special elections are, they added, "it is somewhat surprising that these elections have predictive power at all."[74]

But there are exceptions. Before those 2010 elections in which they were completely shellacked, Democrats had won seven of the nine special-election races.

Sister Souljah moment: A clichéd term about taking on one's own party base, which continues to have resonance more than twenty years after presidential candidate Bill Clinton made it famous.

★ The term originated from a May 1992 *Washington Post* interview in which rapper Sister Souljah was quoted as saying of black-on-white violence in the 1992 Los Angeles riots that if "black people kill black people every day, why not have a week and kill white people?" That led then Arkansas governor Clinton to say in a speech to Jesse Jackson's Rainbow Coalition, "If you took the words 'white' and 'black,' and you reversed them, you might think [former Ku Klux Klan leader] David Duke was giving that speech."

A "Sister Souljah moment" is designed to signal that the politician is not beholden to traditional, and sometimes unpopular, interest groups associated with the party. We would argue it's endured because it's so malleable; you can apply it to countless situations apart from its original context of race. Also, even though—news flash—it is really, really difficult for politicians to talk about race in America, "Sister Souljah" is in such common usage that its user can feel comfortable that he or she won't be accused of racism.

Not even Sister Souljah, aka rapper/activist Lisa Williamson, cares any more. "For me, 'Sister Souljah moment' is just when you meet a powerful and intelligent and beautiful woman, and you just can't seem to forget her," she told a North Carolina newspaper in 2009. "People talk about it like it was yesterday. So apparently they cannot forget me, and I take it as a compliment."[75]

It's now become *expected* among many quarters of the Washington media and pundit class that a candidate will pull a Souljah. Such was the case in a September 2013 *Politico* article about potential White House aspirants' unwillingness to break with tea partiers in a federal budget standoff—"GOP 2016ers: Government Shutdown No 'Souljah' Moment." And that same Capitol Hill standoff led CNBC political analyst John Harwood to tweet a couple of weeks later, "If Congressional Rs keep this up, '16 nominee will have to pull a Sister Souljah, Uncle Souljah and Grandma Souljah just to stay in the game."[76]

"Suspending my campaign": A technicality that means ending a campaign without actually ending it.

★ When Republican presidential candidates Rick Santorum, Newt Gingrich, Rick Perry, and Herman Cain quit the presidential race in 2012, they "suspended" their campaigns—a technicality that means they could continue to raise money to pay off their accumulated debts. The Federal Election Commission doesn't consider a campaign to be done until all of those debts have been covered. Even four years after her unsuccessful White House bid, Hillary Rodham Clinton's website (www .hillaryclinton.com) was still taking donations—as well as orders for T-shirts that it touted as "campaign memorabilia."

Another advantage to suspending is that it offers a candidate political cover, should circumstances change and he or she chooses to reenter a race. Not that this happens very often.

Swift-boating: An unfair or untrue political attack, and yet another term we would say has carried over beyond its original use because it sounds cooler than "unfair or untrue attack" or "red herring." Witness its application in these contexts: "Swift Boating the Planet" (*New York Times* liberal columnist Paul Krugman, on climate-change denial) and "Swift-Boating Darwin" (a research paper about challenges to theories of evolution).

★ Swift-boating comes from the name of the organization Swift Boat Veterans for Truth (SBVT, later the Swift Vets and POWs for Truth) because of their widely publicized—then discredited—campaign against 2004 Democratic presidential nominee John Kerry.

The attacks came from a group of Vietnam veterans who patrolled the Mekong Delta in Swift Boats similar to those that Kerry piloted. Kerry had tried to inoculate himself on national security issues by making his heroism in Vietnam the center-piece of his nominating convention and the reason he was fit to be commander in chief. To critics, that strategy opened Kerry up to the torrent of criticism about his military service that followed.

The Swift Vets commercials were a milestone in negative campaigning, marking the first time a candidate's active duty military service had been used *against* him, rather than in his own favor. The name stuck, and became a staple of political campaigns.

In 2012 Republican strategists compared Democratic attacks on Mitt Romney's tenure at Bain Capital to swift-boating. The term was also used by a representative of President Barack Obama's reelection campaign, in denouncing the documentary film "Dishonorable Disclosures" and an associated ad campaign released by the Special Operations OPSEC Education Fund, relating to the handling of classified material in the killing of Osama bin Laden.

"The most important election of our lifetime": A cliché that partisans from both sides trot out before each presidential election, warning ominously of effects if the other side were to win.

★ Typical in this regard was conservative talk-radio host and columnist Dennis Prager, who wrote in May 2012, "The usual description of presidential elections—'the most important in our lifetime'—is true this time. In fact, it may be the most important election since the Civil War, and possibly since America's founding." Prager continued, "If Americans reelect the Democrat, Barack Obama, they will have announced that America should be like Western European countries—governed by left-wing values. Americans will have decided that America's value system—'Liberty,' 'In God We Trust,' 'E Pluribus Unum'—should be replaced. The election in November is therefore a plebiscite on the American Revolution."[77]

Democrats are equally prone to such hyperbole. Liberal

writer Jonathan Cohn, on the eve of the 2012 presidential race, argued in the *New Republic*: "The differences between Obama and Romney are not ambiguous—not even now, after Romney's post-convention attempt to act like the more moderate, more sensible Republican many of us once thought he could be. The gap between what Obama and Romney believe—and between what each man proposes to do—is larger than it has been for any election I can remember."[78]

"The only poll that matters is the one on Election Day": The standard spin move of the candidate who trails in polls. As the *Rothenberg Report*'s Nathan L. Gonzales wrote in a 2012 column, "This doesn't guarantee defeat in the upcoming election, but it means you are losing the race at the time and have no empirical evidence to the contrary."[79]

★ Among those who've recently said or tweeted some variation on the expression is Republican Ken Cuccinelli, who lost his bid for Virginia's governorship in 2013 after polls showed him consistently trailing Democrat Terry McAuliffe in the race's concluding months. So did Toronto Mayor Rob Ford, after he was caught on video smoking crack and his approval ratings took a nosedive.

But *winning* candidates increasingly say it, too—just to ensure their supporters don't get complacent and decide to stay home on Election Day. A spokesman for Democratic Massachusetts state representative Martin Walsh said it on the eve of the election in which Walsh won Boston's mayorship. And in New York, a spokeswoman for Democrat Bill de Blasio was saying it two months before de Blasio's even more resounding vote to become that city's mayor.

Good polls do more than reporting who's leading in a particular race. Political pros and serious journalists dive into cross-tabulation tables, or *crosstabs*, as they're known in the trade.

Polling used to be the province of a small group of campaign pros, journalists, and political junkies. But polling drew a popular following early in the twenty-first century as the Internet rapidly democratized access to political information. *Real Clear Politics* gained a measure of fame in the mid-2000s by being the first to aggregate polling results. The thinking was that while no one survey was likely to be precisely accurate, combining the results of several would yield a fairly genuine snapshot of where a race stood. Years later statistician Nate Silver, previously best known for analyzing baseball statistics, introduced polling to elite audiences.

Topline reports: Polling numbers released to the public showing who is winning and losing a race. This data is easy for political journalists to digest and often shapes how stories are written about a campaign.

★ Topline reports are like a steaming-hot, just-delivered meal at a top-notch restaurant. The final product is delicious and looks great when set down on the table—but a lot of unseen work went into the dish. Those proverbial polling chefs are *crosstabs*—detailed background material—that usually only get reviewed by political junkies.

Up: See *in cycle*.

Having to Explain Blowback on the Tick-Tock
The Media and Scandals

Spend time with reporters at a Washington bar and you'll hear references to *tick-tocks*, *hit pieces*, and other journalistic terms. The people they cover in the White House, Congress, and in campaigns have their own trade terms in pushing their agenda, including pushing back against the reporters: *walk back* and *gotcha journalism*, to name a couple.

Knowing that the media won't pliantly take a campaign's vocabulary, operatives go to great lengths to find terms likely to get around the press filter. "The way you deal with the media in messaging is to craft language that's easy to repeat," said David Rosen, founder of the consulting firm First Person Politics, in Washington, D.C. "Everything from 'don't cut and run' to 'tax relief' rather than 'tax cut.'" Rosen recalls coining the phrase "Don't double down on trickle down" in 2011 while working at liberal interest group Media Matters. "That memo was the first time that device appeared anywhere on the Internet. Then it went silent for about a year. Then all of a sudden Bill Clinton was saying it, President Obama was saying it."

The proliferation of scandal coverage is clear from the mushrooming list of "gates" that have joined the political lexicon in recent years, and are covered in this chapter. Any list of gates is an impressive compendium of hype and folly, newsprint and book deals, litigation and vexation. The term has traveled far, precisely because of the press's preference for scandal. It has gone from Watergate, named for the site of a botched attempt by President Richard Nixon to bug his Democratic rivals, to Nipplegate, the name given Janet Jackson's famous "wardrobe malfunction" during the 2004 Super Bowl halftime show. A decade later came Bridgegate, over efforts by staffers for New Jersey governor Chris Christie to cause a traffic jam in Fort Lee as a measure of political payback against local Democratic officials.

This specific sort of scandal packaging may be one of American politics' chief exports. Take a cursory glance at how far the gate name has penetrated the foreign press. Recently, we've seen the international scandals of Climategate, Cablegate (over Wikileaks), and Dopegate (over Lance Armstrong) and well as highly country-specific gates. The UK gave us Murdochgate and Bigotgate; Canada, NAFTAgate and Robogate; from Ireland, Brothelgate; and India gave us Slapgate and Porngate.

Blowback: A term that has migrated from the spy world, where it was coined in the 1950s to represent unpleasant and unexpected surprises resulting from covert operations (such as the CIA helping international rebels who later turn out to be terrorists). In politics it means any unwanted backlash or harsh criticism. Like other national-security-derived terms, we would posit that it's common because it sounds cool.

★ After Vice President Joe Biden blurted out his support of gay marriage before President Barack Obama could do so in 2012, Biden told *Rolling Stone*: "I got blowback from everybody but the president. I walked in that Monday, he had a big grin on his face, he put his arms around me and said, 'Well, Joe, God love you, you say what you think.'"[1] And when Fox News asked Kid Rock if he had gotten any criticism for supporting Mitt Romney that same year, the rebel rock star laughed. "Of course there's blowback," he said. "I'm like the only righty in the lefty industry."[2]

The *Hotline*, an online publication that was once an indispensable source for political information, used to call its reader-response section "Blowback."

Broderism: See *Overton window*, chapter 2.

Committing candor: To speak the unvarnished truth, usually inadvertently, and thus spark a controversy.

★ When Army General Eric Shinseki told the Senate Armed Services Committee in 2003 that it would take "something on the order of several hundred thousand soldiers" to stabilize Iraq, it outraged Bush administration officials, who believed the job could be done with far fewer troops. Shinseki, former president Bill Clinton observed later, "committed candor."[3] And when several 2012 candidates for various offices refused to provide direct answers to questions on tough issues, the Associated Press's Henry C. Jackson wrote that the reason was "the fear of committing candor that's both damaging and hard to take back in the age of fast and lasting social media."[4]

It's quite rare, but at times politicians will do it intentionally. "I'm going to commit some candor now," a chagrined Representative Tom Massie (R-KY), told the *Washington Post* after he and other conservatives lost the bitter battle over the 2013 government shutdown. "I think that we have less leverage in the next [continuing resolution], and the next debt limit, than we have now."[5]

Crisis management: Often politicians' first instinct after running into potentially career-ending trouble. Like PR fixers for the stars in New York and Hollywood, Washington, D.C. hosts a bunch of crisis-management firms whose client lists are often secret, and their tactics not exactly what we read about in civics textbooks.

★ A few of the most common tactics:

- *Dismiss the revelation as "old news."* New York Times columnist Maureen Dowd noted how, on the ABC show *Scandal*, a presidential aide quoted the proper way to do damage control: "It's not true . . . it's not true . . . it's not true . . . it's old news."[6] Conservatives regularly accuse the mainstream media of dismissing what they consider to be valid stories as old news. In 2013, *National Review* raised questions about an oft-told story by Newark, New Jersey, mayor Cory Booker, of a local drug dealer, "T-Bone," who supposedly befriended the Democratic rising star after threatening to kill him. *National Review*'s reporting suggested the story by Booker, then seeking an open New Jersey Senate seat in a special election, was imaginary. In response, Booker campaign spokesman Kevin Griffis tried to put the burden of proof back on the conservative outlet. "This is a national, partisan, right-wing publication that's trying to make a fake controversy from 2008 into a fake controversy from today. That's essentially what it is," Griffis told *Business Insider*. "It's just not—it's old news."[7] Griffis cited a 2008 *Esquire* article that dealt with the subject; Booker told the magazine that T-Bone was real, though he might not have that name. Not exactly an ironclad, I-stand-by-my-story-100-percent, affirmation. But good enough for the campaign trail. Booker won the Senate seat easily a few months later.

- *Take responsibility.* Lawmakers themselves show considerably more acumen in tending their own self-inflicted wounds than keeping out of trouble in the first place. Take Representative Trey Radel, who in November 2013—just ten months after taking office—pled guilty to a misdemeanor count of possession of cocaine. The Florida Republican's arrest, in a D.C. police sting operation, actually happened on October 29. But Radel, who campaigned as a staunch social conservative, managed to keep it concealed for several weeks. When the jaw-dropping news did emerge, it was largely—though not entirely—on Radel's terms. The first news reports came the night before the congressman's D.C. Superior Court guilty plea. At a news conference in his Gulf Coast Florida district later that day, Radel announced he was taking a leave of absence from Congress to undergo drug rehab. Radel followed the classic crisis management moves—acknowledge and admit you have a problem, and take responsibility for it. Radel's only deviation was blaming his cocaine use, at least partly, on an alcohol addiction. That, he suggested, was a legacy of his mother's own battles with the bottle. Adding to his tales of woe was the morbidly bizarre death of his mom nearly four years before, when she choked to death at his own wedding reception.

But even the most aggressive efforts to "take responsibility" have limits. After quietly returning to work in Congress early in January 2014, Radel quit at the end of the month. The Florida Republican governor and several other prominent GOP officials had called for his resignation. The House Ethics Committee had opened an investigation of Radel, and several GOP primary challengers were licking their chops at the prospect of challenging the scandal-ridden congressman.

- *Deploy your spouse.* An on-the-verge-of-disgraced pol's most commonly deployed weapon is often the person who has the most reason to be angry—his spouse. Officeholders caught in sex scandals have planted their wives—yes, always female—next to them in bids to create public sympathy. Hillary Clinton was at her husband's side from his own, 1992 *60 Minutes* admission of having "caused pain in my marriage" through his December 1998 impeachment by the Republican controlled House of Representatives. Senator David Vitter's wife Wendy stood stoically by in 2007 when the socially conservative Louisiana Republican was implicated as a patron of the "D.C. Madam" prostitution ring. (Never mind that seven years earlier, she told Newhouse News Service: "I'm a lot more like Lorena Bobbitt than Hillary."[8]) But when ex-representative Anthony Weiner, of Twitter infamy, ran for New York City mayor less than two years after resigning in disgrace, his wife, Huma Abedin, broke her usual public silence to speak up on his behalf. Weiner's wife's advocacy did little good—he lost the Democratic mayoral primary in a romp. Hillary Clinton and Wendy Vitter proved better crisis-management helpers. The impeachment saga arguably damaged House Republicans more than it did her presidential husband. And in 2010, David Vitter easily won a second Senate term.

Disgraced: Common media shorthand for a pariah, someone who has done something so awful that the adjective is permanently affixed to his or her name. But it doesn't mean they disappear from the news—in fact, quite the contrary.

★ Among those recently receiving the scarlet letter *D* are Jesse Jackson Jr., the son of the civil rights icon whose promising career was cut short when he was convicted of using $750,000 in campaign money to buy presents for himself (including one of singer Michael Jackson's hats); California representative Gary Condit, whose time in office was ruined by an affair with an intern who was murdered (the actual perpetrator was caught, but the thunderous speculation forced Condit out of Congress and led him to start selling Baskin-Robbins ice cream); and Kwame Kilpatrick, Detroit's high-flying mayor before corruption charges drew him a twenty-eight-year prison sentence.

Atop the D-list, though, is Jack Abramoff. Years after he pleaded guilty to defrauding clients and other crimes, the former superlobbyist continues to annoy and provoke Washington's *downtown* like no other figure. Since his release from prison in December 2010, Abramoff has published a book, *Capitol Punishment: The Hard Truth about Corruption from America's Most Notorious Lobbyist*, and was the subject of the movie *Casino Jack* starring Kevin Spacey. More recently, he has made the rounds of the news media and public forums talking about his criminal past as well as his prescriptions to fix all that he considers wrong with his former profession.

Veteran lobbyists lament that too much attention is lavished on someone whom they accuse of being wholly unrepresentative of the state of today's business. "It's amazing that the media are using this ex-con as an expert on what's wrong with our system and what changes need to be made," said Howard

Marlowe, former president of the American League of Lobby-ists. Paul Miller of Miller/Wenhold Capital Strategies, who was ALL's president when the Abramoff scandal broke, said Abram-off has no sincere interest in bettering the profession—and that if he did, he would donate some of his "newfound wealth" to the group's lobbying certification program. "For a guy who screwed the entire profession, he should consider an apology to all of us following the rules," Miller said.

A defiant Abramoff told one of us that lobbyists are guilty of "Orwellian doublespeak" if they think he should donate to their program. Miller's suggestion "that the true path to reform is through donations to his organization would be funny if he were not serious," he said. "His problem does not lie only with Jack Abramoff, but rather with a nation which will no longer condone special-interest money buying legislative results."[9]

Document dump: The time-tested practice of meeting a political adversary's and the news media's demand for information with an avalanche of documents, trying to overwhelm them.

★ Presidential administrations generally employ the practice in the midst of congressional investigations. Those documents that are delivered often are unsorted and contain large quantities of information that are extraneous to the issue under inquiry. "Document dumps" often take place on Friday nights, after many reporters either have gone home or are about to leave the office, meaning the news likely will be diminished and under-played.

Document dumping has a long history in Washington, but was raised to a new art form during the Clinton administration during the many 1990s-era scandals. President Obama's admin-istration has done it as well—even with disclosures it makes vol-untarily, such as the millions of visitor appointment records for the White House complex.

There's another form of document dump. It involves using the public-comment period for agency reviews of highly contro-versial development projects to try to slow down or stop them.

Opponents will submit hundreds of pages of legal files and case studies at the last moment, something that can lead to expensive lawsuits or consulting fees. In California, labor unions and other groups have done this so often that it led to a legislative effort to reform the California Environmental Quality Act that would ban the practice. Despite a strong push from business interests, however, Governor Jerry Brown in 2013 signed only a drastically scaled-back reform law that didn't call for any curtailment.

Drudge hits: Highly coveted links to stories on the *Drudge Report*, which can boost web traffic exponentially. If you're a reporter or blogger and you've been "Drudged," it's a good day— although your e-mail in-box may overflow with vitriol from readers who otherwise wouldn't have seen your work.

★ It's easy to see why news organizations, individual bloggers and others try so hard for *Drudge* links—the site has drawn one billion page views in a month. True, that was in September 2012, with the presidential campaign at fever pitch. And even if those numbers, provided by the *Drudge Report*'s ad sales representative, were somewhat inflated, as liberal detractors claimed, the site still claims monster web traffic.

But how seriously can it be taken? A 2012 study by three State University of New York researchers tried to gauge this. It surveyed college students—a group it warned was an argument against drawing any sweeping conclusions—about the site's merits against several other outlets. It found that the *New York Times* and *USA Today* scored higher than Drudge on "trustworthiness," though not by all that much, statistically speaking. The two newspapers ranked much higher against the website— as did the news sites of Yahoo and Google—on "expertise" and "credibility."[10]

The site has long been popular among conservatives, and Matt Rhoades, who managed Mitt Romney's 2012 campaign, was particularly tight with *Drudge Report* editors, something that won his candidate continued favorable coverage. It also broke exclusives, such as one that the ex-Massachusetts governor was seriously considering popular ex-secretary of state Condoleezza Rice as his running mate (a *pivot* during a rough patch in his campaign). When he won Puerto Rico's GOP primary in March 2012, Romney proudly held up to reporters an iPad showing the site leading with the headline: "Romney Wins 51st State."[11]

Embeds: Off-air television reporters attached to presidential campaigns. They are particularly active through the primary process, before the on-air talents start covering the major-party presidential nominees.

★ Each embed is assigned to a candidate or a geographic region such as the Iowa caucuses or the New Hampshire primary. Duties include reporting, occasional on-air updates, writing, producing, near-constant tweeting, interviewing, shooting, and lugging a camera crew's worth of equipment in zigzag trips across the country.

With news budgets shrinking, embeds have come to play an increasingly important role in campaign coverage, often to the dismay of campaign strategists. A 2013 paper by CNN reporter Peter Hamby, for Harvard's Joan Shorenstein Center on the Press, Politics and Public Policy, called the embeds "anthropomorphic satellite trucks." Hamby noted that 2012 embeds were a source of major irritation for high-level campaign staffers. "If I had to pick three words to characterize the embeds, it would be young, inexperienced and angry," an unnamed Romney adviser told Hamby.[12]

Familiar with the thinking: See *senior administration official/ United States official.*

Full Ginsburg: The impressive-for-Washington feat of a cable chatterer appearing on all five Sunday talk shows in one day. Monica Lewinsky's then lawyer William Ginsburg appeared the same February 1998 Sunday on ABC's *This Week, Fox News Sunday,* CBS's *Face the Nation, Meet the Press,* and *Late Edition* on CNN. Like a perfect game in baseball, the Full Ginsburg is a rare feat in punditry; fewer than two dozen people have accomplished it. Florida GOP senator Marco Rubio pulled off a version of this in 2013 that also included appearances on Univision and Telemundo, something quickly dubbed the "Full Marco." For more, see *cable and Sunday show chatterers,* chapter 1.

Gotcha journalism: What politicians frequently accuse reporters of when doing they're jobs of trying to uncover information. The expression "gotcha" dates to the 1930s, but "gotcha journalism" didn't come into vogue until the mid-1990s.

★ Supposed "gotcha journalism" usually involves trying to get interview subjects to say things that could hurt their cause, character, integrity, or reputation. Candidates and their staffs often suggest that journalists are engaged in gotcha journalism if they move from the agreed-upon topic of the interview and switch to an embarrassing subject that was thought to be out-of-bounds.

In 2008, Sarah Palin contended that interviewer Katie Couric was engaging in gotcha journalism by asking about her reading habits. Far-right representative Michele Bachmann (R-MN) broadened it in an interview with Larry King that year to include "the gotcha media . . . that are looking for a leftist candidate."[13] Four years later, a prominent financial backer of ex-Pennsylvania senator Rick Santorum, Foster Friess, joked that in his day, "they used Bayer aspirin for contraceptives. The gals put it between their knees, and it wasn't that costly." When CBS's Charlie Rose asked Santorum about Friess' remark, he was immediately accused of "gotcha journalism."[14]

Office seekers have long confused gotcha journalism with legitimate questioning. The late *Meet the Press* host Tim Russert fell on the side of tough, but fair, interrogations. Russert was known as an interviewer who demanded answers from those in power. Guests were aware that they would be expected to account for any seeming inconsistencies in behavior and statements.

And there's a correlation between how much access a candidate grants the media and the tendency for gotcha journalism accusations to fly. In other words, the more time reporters can spend interviewing a candidate, the less likely uncomfortable moments are going to occur. As veteran political reporter Jules Witcover wrote in 2012 about the earlier decades of presidential coverage: "In dealing with the candidates and campaigns, reporters with personal access usually avoided the sort of 'gotcha journalism' that became vogue in the wake of Watergate (along with reporters' resultant quest for celebrity in the television era)."[15]

Having to explain: What politicians are frequently called on to do, much to their chagrin, after an especially serious gaffe or in the midst of a controversy.

★ No lawmaker wants to be caught in a position of having to explain something he or she already said. Politics is all about creating a positive first strong impression; you don't get a second chance. As the old political maxim has it, "If you're explaining, you're losing."

As a result, it was not good news for President Barack Obama in 2013 when news stories and broadcasts led with him "having to explain" the National Security Agency's eavesdropping on Americans and the numerous technical glitches in the Affordable Care Act (aka Obamacare) website. Nor was it seen as good news for House Republicans for having to explain why they hadn't taken up an immigration overhaul bill that passed the Senate on a bipartisan basis.

In the broader world, however, having to explain something political actually can be a positive. In a 2013 study published in *Psychological Science*, researchers at three universities found that explaining how a political policy works leads people to foster less extreme attitudes toward that policy—possibly because the act of explanation forces them to acknowledge that they didn't know as much as they thought they did about that policy. Significantly, the researchers found that happened with people across the political spectrum.[16]

Hot mic: See *Kinsley gaffe*.

Hypothetical: A common reporter's tactic for trying to get politicians to say something newsworthy by answering a "what-if" question.

★ Savvier officeholders and candidates usually avoid the temptation, though even the most seasoned politicians can fall into the hypothetical trap. One of the most memorable moments of Democrat Michael Dukakis' failed 1988 presidential bid was when CNN's Bernard Shaw asked at a debate: "If Kitty Dukakis were raped and murdered, would you favor an irrevocable death penalty for the killer?" Dukakis coolly cited his long-standing opposition to executions. That led his campaign manager, Susan Estrich, to acknowledge later: "It was a question about Dukakis' values and emotions. . . . When he answered by talking policy, I knew we had lost the election."[17]

As a result, politicians routinely duck legitimate questions by labeling the query as hypothetical. "They even seem to want credit for maintaining high standards by keeping this virus from corrupting the political discussion," political journalist Michael Kinsley wrote in 2003.[18]

The Iraq War proved an enduring topic on which politicians could reject hypothetical questions. At a Republican presidential primary debate in June 2007, former Massachusetts governor Mitt Romney was asked about whether, in hindsight, going to war in Iraq was a mistake. Romney criticized the question saying it was a "non-sequitur" as well as "unreasonable" and "hypothetical."[19]

More recently, Michigan journalists sought to pin down GOP governor Rick Snyder on his stance on gay-rights issues. When asked point-blank, "Is being gay a good reason to be fired?" Snyder told reporters in October 2013: "That's a broad statement, so it'd depend on the particular facts of the situation. That's a hypothetical, that's very general in that context." To which the reporter responded, according to MLive.com: "People are being fired because they're gay, though. That's not hypothetical."[20]

"I misspoke": An awkward all-purpose political excuse covering a multitude of sins, especially those that touch off an unintended furor. It is a close euphemistic relative of the time-honored chestnut "Mistakes were made."

★ As English journalist Steven Poole, author of the 2007 book *Unspeak: How Words Become Weapons, How Weapons Become a Message, and How That Message Becomes Reality*, wrote: "It is useful to say one 'misspoke.' You acknowledge that what you said was absolute balls [a Britishism for utter nonsense], but the fault is not your own, as it would be if you had lied or been wrong. No, the fault is somehow in the faculty of speech itself, something going wrong in the course of that complex magic between brain, lip and others' ears."[21]

Though the phrase has been around for centuries, it entered the political lexicon in 1973 when Ronald Ziegler, Richard Nixon's press secretary, sought to atone for his previous inaccuracies about Watergate by declaring, "I misspoke myself."

When Mitt Romney told CNN in 2012, "I'm not concerned about the very poor," it was a line that fed the ongoing *meme* that he was out of touch. Two days later, he corrected himself: "It was a misstatement; I misspoke."[22] That same year, Missouri GOP Senate candidate Todd Akin said after his remarks on "legitimate rape" caused a political firestorm: "In reviewing my off-the-cuff remarks, it's clear that I misspoke in this interview and it does not reflect the deep empathy I hold for the thousands of women who are raped and abused every year."[23]

But Republicans aren't the only mis-spokespeople. Four years earlier, Hillary Clinton was found to have embellished a tale of her running from her plane to a vehicle because of threats of sniper fire. She sought to clarify: "What I was told was that we had to land a certain way and move quickly because of the threat of sniper fire. So I misspoke—I didn't say that in my book or other times, but if I said something that made it seem as though there was actual fire, that's not what I was told. I was told we had to land a certain way, we had to have our bulletproof stuff on because of the threat of sniper fire."[24]

Kinsley gaffe: A category of verbal flub akin to *committing candor* coined by veteran political journalist Michael Kinsley, who wrote a column describing as a gaffe "when a politician tells the truth—some obvious truth he isn't supposed to say."[25] (The word gaffe, incidentally, is French for "clumsy remark," and didn't really come into use until the early twentieth century; its popularity skyrocketed in the late 1980s and early 1990s.)

★ Mitt Romney committed a Kinsley gaffe for the ages in his 2012 presidential bid by lamenting the "47 percent" of Americans he contended would never back him because they were too dependent on government programs, and just lazy. The GOP nominee didn't realize he was being videotaped, at a Florida fundraiser, and the recording didn't emerge until months after the comments. President Barack Obama's campaign exploited the gaffe to the hilt, painting Romney as an out-of-touch plutocrat.

One of the most prevalent forms of a Kinsley gaffe is the "hot mic," when a politician says something not intended for public consumption to a live microphone that he or she mistakenly believes is off. Examples of hot mic gaffes are legion; the most infamous is President Ronald Reagan's 1984 joke that he had signed legislation "that will outlaw Russia forever. We begin bombing in five minutes." That quip made Reagan a hero to defense *hawks*, but the consequences usually are far more negative. In September 2000, Republican presidential candidate George W. Bush made waves before a campaign rally while joshing with running mate Dick Cheney when he described *New York Times* reporter Adam Clymer as a "major league asshole." Cheney's response was equally memorable: "Oh yeah, he is, big time." To the Bush operation's chagrin, a hot mic picked up the moment, leading to days of unfavorable news coverage. But the swaggering Texan didn't seem too sorry about the vulgarity: "I regret that a private comment I made to the vice presidential candidate made it through the public airways. I regret everybody heard what I said."[26]

Once in the White House, Bush was disciplined about keeping private comments private. But Obama has had a tougher go of it. What was supposed to be a private exchange between Obama and Russian president Dmitry Medvedev in 2012 got picked up. "On all these issues, particularly on missile defense, this, this can be solved but it's important for him to give me space," Obama said during a summit in South Korea. "This is my last election. After my election, I have more flexibility."[27] And then there was Obama's November 2011 supposedly private exchange with then French president Nicolas Sarkozy the G-20 summit. The pair was discussing Israeli prime minister Benjamin Netanyahu. "I cannot bear Netanyahu; he's a liar," Sarkozy complained. Responded Obama, "You're fed up with him, but I have to deal with him even more often than you."[28]

Master of disaster: Once used to describe *operatives* who could adroitly handle crises, it has mutated in the media to become a laudatory term for elected officials who can capitalize on catastrophic occurrences.

★ The late Hunter S. Thompson observed that politics "is the art of controlling your environment." Political leaders relish few things more than demonstrating they're in control, that they can manage especially unmanageable situations. Floods, fires, hurricanes, snowstorms, shootings, and other epic conflagrations afford them that opportunity in spades. It's certainly become another of the key benchmarks the media uses to assess a politician.

Needless to say, reputations can be won or lost based on how they handle a disaster. Herbert Hoover's successful presidential bid was based in large part on how he dealt with flood relief in Mississippi in 1927 while serving as commerce secretary. Meanwhile, George W. Bush's second White House term was undone in no small measure by Hurricane Katrina. Political scientists

John T. Gasper and Andrew Reeves concluded in a study that voters are indeed prone to respond to badly managed situations "by punishing both presidents and governors for weather events, which are well beyond human control."[29]

Few understand this better than New Jersey governor Chris Christie, who was blasted after not coming home from a Disney World vacation in 2010 when a massive snowstorm blanketed the Garden State. When Hurricane Sandy struck two years later, he hastily canceled another Florida trip and enthusiastically squired President Obama around the damage (something that raised many eyebrows within his own party). *Time* magazine put him on its cover with the sobriquet "Master of Disaster." And when a massive fire hit the Seaside Heights boardwalk months later, the state's biggest newspaper, the *Star-Ledger*, pulled out the description again.[30]

Media terms: Unless you're a member of the Fourth Estate, you're probably as interested in the news media's inner workings as you are in Baltic grain production. And yet, these terms have become so ubiquitous—in said media as well as the various TV shows and movies attempting to depict the "real" Washington—that we wanted to mention some of them.

LOGISTICS AND EVENTS

- An **avail** or **presser** is the modern term for a news conference.
- A **stakeout** is a place where reporters wait to talk to politicians, as well as the event itself.
- A **gaggle** is the term for both a flock of geese and an informal event featuring a group of reporters, most often at the White House, in which TV cameras are barred. (When a gaggle gets overly crowded, it can become a **scrum** or, more colorfully, a **clusterfuck**.)
- A **pen and pad** is a news conference prohibiting video as well as photos.
- **Backgrounders** are briefings in which a person—often a

senior administration official—speaks *on background* and can't be quoted by name.

- The **pool** is the predesignated group of journalists traveling with a president or candidate; a **pool spray** is a brief photo opportunity held before a meeting. (When a campaign or office decides no more news will be made in a given day, it will announce a **lid**.)

ARTICLES

- A **process story** is a staple of Beltway-centric publications delving into how a policy is made, without examining the pros and cons of said policy. Process stories sometimes are dubbed **snowflakes**—they generate buzz but "kind of dissolve on contact" and have little substance or staying power, says *National Journal*'s Ron Brownstein, originator of the expression.

- A **tick-tock** is a behind-the-scenes reconstruction of how a major deal or other news event occurred.

- A **thumbsucker** is a detailed work of journalism that often appears in a Sunday newspaper or prominent section of a website. (A variation is the **goat choker**, an article so mercilessly long that it's intended more to bolster the writer's ego than it is to edify readers.)

- A **hit piece** is one that takes an extremely critical look at its subject.

- A **beat sweetener** or **source greaser**, in contrast, is a flattering profile intended to develop credibility with a prospective official or staffer. (*Slate* once parodied this genre by holding a contest of imaginary BS/SG stories; the winning entry saluted Kim Jong Il's appointment to President George W. Bush's election-reform commission by noting the North Korean dictator's "own electoral experience" in which he took 99.99957 percent of the vote.[31])

PHRASES

- **"It remains to be seen . . ."**: Essentially, the writer or speaker has no idea.

- **"The honeymoon is over":** Journalists inevitably will use the first thing that goes wrong during an officeholder's term to haul this out in the form of a question: "Is the honeymoon over?"
- **"What I'm hearing . . .":** As Ben Schott and Mark Leibovich noted in the *New York Times*, this can mean "What I think" among the pundit class.[32]
- **"Kabuki theater":** The all-purpose journalistic shorthand for the ritualistic preening and posturing of politicians. As *Slate*'s Jon Lackman observed, it's popular because it sounds funny, childish, foreign, and incomprehensible—but it's wrong. The actual Japanese event "does indeed use stylized gestures, expressions, and intonations, but it's far from empty and monotonous."[33]
- **"To be sure":** A preemptive anticipation of someone disagreeing with a pundit's central argument by making a minor concession.
- **"Quixotic":** Like the windmill-tilting hero of Cervantes' novel, this is the polite way of describing any effort that doesn't have a prayer.

Meme: A piece of political content with the potential to go *viral* online. Funny images and captions commenting on the day's events prove particularly infectious.

★ This distinctly twenty-first-century phenomenon provides new ways to view routine campaign events. Presidential debates, in particular, are meme-fodder. In 2012, even those who didn't watch the three in-person face-offs between President Barack Obama and Republican challenger Mitt Romney, would have been familiar with Big Bird, binders, and bayonets.

Those words were barely out of the candidates' mouths before Internet memes began appearing on Facebook, Twitter, and Tumblr feeds, where they quickly went viral. After threatening to defund PBS in the first debate, Big Bird became an albatross for Romney—though he was otherwise considered a winner in the faceoff against Obama.

Narrative: The all-important (at least to the media) way of framing a campaign, a presidency, or anything else in politics. The Austin, Texas-based Global Language Monitor declared "the narrative" the top political buzzword of 2010.

★ Narratives are the folklore of politics. Intellectual historian George Hoare sees narratives as "simplified but 'generally correct' aspects of popular knowledge which are used to identify, delineate and understand political phenomena. . . . The narrative of Left Versus Right is a signal example: it ranges over time and space as well as a multiplicity of different groups."[34]

When a scandal or something unpleasant hits someone, it's automatically suggested that he or she "lost control of the narrative" and consequently isn't able to effectively convey his or her competence and/or trustworthiness. Nowhere was this more true than in the many problems accompanying the rollout of the Affordable Care Act (aka Obamacare) website in fall 2013. "At some level, the White House lost control of the narrative on this," said Democratic strategist Chris Lehane. "They, for whatever reason, continue to be playing defense on the subject."[35]

But why has the narrative become so important? Observers see it as a result of the balkanization of the media in a highly polarized political climate. "Today's audiences are no longer satisfied with choosing their own news outlets," *Chicago Tribune* columnist Clarence Page wrote. "They also want to choose their own versions of the reality that news covers. Whether they realize it or not, they're shopping for their own 'narrative.'"[36]

Nerd prom: The White House Correspondents' Association televised annual dinner, featuring big-name guests ranging from Henry Kissinger to *Hustler* mogul Larry Flynt, music or comedy from a well-known entertainer (Jay Leno, Ray Charles), and, generally, some well-scripted jokes from the commander in chief that are often in the *comic self-deprecation* vein.

★ *Mediaite*'s Rachel Sklar credited Ana Marie Cox of Wonkette .com with popularizing the term "nerd prom" for the dinner; previously it had applied to the San Diego Comics Convention.[37] As has been written endlessly, the event has come to symbolize official Washington's unhealthy obsession with celebrities as well as its aloofness from the rest of the country (even though the vast majority of D.C. journalists have never suited up for a dinner). For those reasons, some media outlets, most prominently the *New York Times*, have chosen not to attend.

It wasn't always that way, though. Our friend Susan Milligan of *U.S. News and World Report* summed it up best: The dinner "used to be a fun and elegant evening during which journalists and their sources shared a meal and behaved like actual human beings instead of adversaries. But with each passing year, the dinner is starting to look more like an after-party at the Oscars. And what's worse, the reporters hosting the event end up in supporting roles as groupies, degrading both themselves and the profession."[38]

"The next . . .": Just as politics is about successfully defining your opponent, political journalism is about defining politicians. One of the easiest ways to do that is to compare an up-and-coming figure to an established one. The usual convention is via a question: "Is so-and-so the next so-and-so?"

★ And so, in recent years, the following Democrats have been yanked into discussions about who'll become "the next Barack Obama":

- New Jersey senator Cory Booker
- Massachusetts senator Elizabeth Warren
- San Antonio mayor Julian Castro
- Colorado governor John Hickenlooper
- California attorney general Kamala Harris
- Atlanta mayor Kasim Reed

There's also Republicans Ted Cruz of Texas, Rand Paul of Kentucky, and Marco Rubio of Florida, less for ideological reasons than other similarities (all are members of the Senate, where Obama came from, and Cruz and Rubio are minorities). Cruz's central role in the 2013 government shutdown debate and emergence as a tea party hero, naturally, led to stories about who would become the next Cruz—including, as *Slate* predicted in a subsequent headline, "Basically Every GOP Candidate."[39]

On background: A way for elected officials and their spinners to feed reporters information they want out publicly, without having their names attached.

★ Journalists and flacks have widely varying interpretations about the definition of *on background*. Some journalists feel it means they can't use the information unless they can get it elsewhere. Others contend they can report with the information, but without in any way attributing it, or even vaguely suggesting, that it came from a source.

Lawmakers routinely hold background briefings for journalists to get out their messages. Sometimes White House officials openly tout information they want in the public domain, without identifying the source. In June 2013, the Obama White House press secretary's office hosted a blatantly titled "Background Briefing by Senior Administration Officials on Afghanistan—Via Conference Call."[40]

On message: The ability of politicians to repeat for media consumption the same phrases over and over, no matter what question they're asked. In other words, answering the question they *want* to answer rather than the one they were actually asked.

★ In a political campaign, a candidates' message contains the ideas that the candidate wants to share with the voters. The message often consists of several talking points about policy issues. The points summarize the main ideas of the campaign and are repeated frequently in order to create a lasting impression with the voters. When Senator Maria Cantwell (D-WA) came across a nine-year-old reference she made to the importance of agriculture to her state in 2013 that she continues to use to this day, she was quick to point it out to her staff. "I said to them, 'See how on-message I was even back in 2004?' I was surprised," she told us.[41]

Most campaigns prefer to keep the message broad in order to attract the most potential voters. A message that is too narrow can alienate voters or slow the candidate down with explaining details. In 2008 Democratic presidential nominee Barack Obama ran on a consistent, simple message of "change" throughout his campaign.

The current House majority leader, Virginia Republican Eric Cantor, got where he is in large part because of his disciplined on-message articulation of conservative themes. He's become one of the biggest champions in his party of the idea that if the GOP successfully broadcasts its message, it can win over broad segments of a skeptical public. "We have to apply our principles in a way that translates to understanding that we actually are focusing and trying to help people and meet the needs that they have," he told the *New Yorker* in an on-message quote in 2013.[42]

Parse: A Talmudic-like dissection of a politician's statements, often done by the media and bloggers, to see if they're lying. The Online Etymology Dictionary dates it from the 1550s as a verb of the Middle English *pars*, "to state the parts of speech in a sentence."

★ Many elected officials are lawyers by training and skilled at using precise words to avoid making a statement that is technically lying, but far from what reasonable people would consider the whole truth. And at the highest levels of government, attorneys instruct those in power on exactly what to say and what *not* to say. President Bill Clinton was the undisputed champion of parsing. The very term "Clintonian" suggests a slippery approach to truth telling. The Monica Lewinsky scandal brought into common parlance debates about what the meaning of "*is*" is."

Fifteen years later reporters were parsing another lack-of-past-tense White House statement. President Barack Obama's press secretary, Jay Carney was being peppered with questions about U.S. surveillance activities on foreign leaders. Those included a report that intelligence agencies had hacked into the cell phone of German chancellor Angela Merkel and listened in. The United States "is not monitoring and will not monitor her communications," Carney said. Observers noted he fell short of disclosing any *past* practices.[43]

Sometimes political allies of a candidate try to parse a difficult-to-explain statement, looking for a more charitable explanation. In September 2012, Republican presidential nominee Mitt Romney left GOP supporters scratching their heads concerning his statement about a group of Americans he derided as moochers on government services.

Other Republicans, the Associated Press reported, "are having a hard time parsing what Romney meant by saying that 47 percent of Americans don't pay income taxes and think the government should take care of them."[44]

"The question we should be asking . . .": One of the biggest maxims for politicians in dealing with the media is that you don't always answer the question that you were asked; you answer the one you *want* asked. It's a rhetorical *pivot* away from potentially dangerous territory onto safer ground while staying *on message*.

★ Senate minority leader Mitch McConnell is especially practiced at this. In his 2009 biography of McConnell, *Republican Leader*, John David Dyche wrote that "the idea of an off-the-cuff comment is anathema to him."[45] When McConnell was asked on Fox News in July 2012 how thirty million uninsured Americans should be given health care, he responded: "That is not the issue. The question is how to go step by step to improve the American health care system. It is already the finest health care system in the world."[46]

Watch any presidential debate and you'll see numerous examples of this. In a 2008 debate, Democrat John Edwards was asked whether he considered Russia a friend or a foe. After a perfunctory nonanswer, he moved to what he wanted to talk about:

"I think the question we should be asking ourselves is, how does America change the underlying dynamic of what's happening in the world? . . . I think for that to occur, the world has to see America as a force for good again, which is why I talked about leading an effort to make primary school education available to 100 million children in the world who don't have it, in the Muslim world, in Africa, in Latin America."[47]

One way to avoid questions is to pose a series of rhetorical questions about the situation. Maryland attorney general Doug Gansler did just that in October 2013, when he had to fend off a series of awkward questions about his presence at his son's recent high school graduation party at a Delaware beach resort where excessive drinking took place. "Assume for purposes of discussion that there was widespread drinking at this party," Gansler said. "How is that relevant to me? . . . The question is, do I have any moral authority over other people's children at beach week in another state? I say no."[48] The problem for Gansler was that most everyone else said yes. Indeed, Gansler helped to arrange the party and promulgate special "rules" about what the kids could and could not drink.

Quote approval: Public officials' efforts to preapprove comments made to reporters before stories run.

★ Back in the 1930s, President Franklin Delano Roosevelt became the first president to hold regularly scheduled news conference, but only with the stipulation that the president's aides be able to preapprove his direct quotes. And while the idea of having a source preapprove quotes offends many journalistic sensibilities, it still happens. A July 2012 *New York Times* story revealed that the campaigns of President Barack Obama and Republican rival Mitt Romney insisted that they be granted veto power over any quotes that appeared in articles. According to the story, reporters were assenting to the demands. That led the *Times* itself to ban the practice. It "puts so much control over the content of journalism in the wrong place," Executive Editor Jill Abramson told the paper's public editor, Margaret Sullivan.[49]

As Reuters media columnist Jack Shafer noted, the practice of quote approval tends to flourish in places like the White House, Capitol Hill, Silicon Valley, Wall Street, and Hollywood where reporters are abundant and sources are far fewer, giving them more leverage. He cited his favorite example of when people in those places venture on to less familiar turf: Deputy Defense Secretary Paul Wolfowitz in 2004 tried to give an interview to reporters from several publications in Omaha, Nebraska, on the condition that he be referred to only as a "senior Defense Department official." The reporters refused, and Wolfowitz conducted his news conference by name.[50]

Senior administration official/United States official: Terms that Washington journalists have used in print, on air, and online for decades to protect their most coveted sources. Though there is no exact definition, a senior administration official generally is a cabinet member, high-level subcabinet member, or someone in the president's office (presidents can have as many as two dozen assistants).

★ The White House and other agencies often will conduct background briefings—in which the details of a specific proposal are discussed—and request that such an identity be conferred upon the briefer in the ensuing news articles.

Even people who don't mind using their names will sometimes deploy the title. "I was quoted as a 'senior administration official' even before I became a senior administration official," Joe Lockhart, who was press secretary under President Bill Clinton, once told *Politico*. "No one in the government wants to be a 'junior administration official,' and no one in the press wants to quote one."[51]

A "United States official" often is someone from a national security agency (the CIA, Pentagon, FBI) who requests, or requires, even greater anonymity in order to speak about sensitive matters. But those officials sometimes use the "administration" guise. In October 2013, former National Security Agency and CIA director Michael Hayden gave interviews to a variety of reporters aboard an Acela train. Another Acela passenger, Democratic political strategist Tom Matzzie, overheard Hayden giving the interviews on background on the condition that he be referred to as a "former senior administration official"—and promptly *tweeted* the development.

A variant is the anonymous source quoted as being "familiar with the thinking" of the unreachable subject of an article.

Strategery: Will Ferrell, in one of his earliest *Saturday Night Live* impersonations of George W. Bush, used this made-up word to describe Bush's most persuasive argument for his 2000 campaign. But it has retained its staying power among pundits as a winking code word for what they regard as highly off-kilter decision making.

★ Rush Limbaugh uses the term in a mocking way toward Democrats, but he's not alone. In February 2013, liberal MSNBC host Rachel Maddow used Republican objections to reauthorizing the Violence Against Women Act, which the Democratically controlled Senate had passed but which the Republican-controlled House had not taken up: "Now, to be clear, this is kind of strategery fail in legislating."[52] (The House did later pass the extension, and it was signed into law.) And a year earlier, when Newt Gingrich dropped out of the presidential race and Mitt Romney met with him, Fox News' Steve Doocy asked: "What do you think that means? Do you think it means Cabinet, or does it mean 'strategery?'"[53]

And NASCAR driver Michael Waltrip used the phrase "some of that Sarah Palin strategery" while doing commentary during a March 2013 race. That prompted an angry tweet from the ex-Alaska governor and political lightning rod: "Get some 'strategery' and check your facts before you shoot off your mouth." An embarrassed Waltrip—a conservative—took to Twitter to apologize: "You are one of my fav people on earth."[54]

Talking points: The script for staying *on message*.

★ Talking points were once a closely held secret. The most famous instance of their inadvertently being made public was when President George H. W. Bush, campaigning in 1992, blurted out "Message: I care," something that had been written on a cue card. When Bush spoke it, it was seen as transparent pandering and fed the *narrative* that he was out of touch. These days, though, campaigns and offices openly send them out as a way of conveying an undiluted message. The Democratic National Committee even e-mails its talking points to anyone who signs up online.[55]

Viral: Getting a news story or some other piece of information about politics to be seen by a large group of people. The goal is to spread the information online like a virus would spread among humans. Sometimes these are lengthy news articles or analyses, other times simplistic-yet-funny videos showing a politician in an embarrassing moment.

★ The 2008 presidential election was the first in which viral material played a key role. A fall 2008 *Politico* story detailing the Republican National Committee's spending habits on behalf of vice presidential nominee Sarah Palin's wardrobe went viral, helping the Democratic ticket. Another *Politico* story in which GOP nominee John McCain couldn't say how many houses he and his wife owned also didn't help the Republicans' chances.

That same election cycle included the first CNN-YouTube presidential debates, calling on users of the video site to pose questions. In this debate, the opinions of viral video creators and users were taken seriously.

There were also several memorable viral videos that appeared during the campaign. In June 2007, "I Got a Crush . . . on Obama," a music video featuring a girl claiming to have a crush on presidential candidate Barack Obama appeared. Unlike previously popular political videos, it did not feature any celebrities and was purely user generated. The video garnered many viewers and gained attention in the mainstream media.

Politicians themselves are becoming increasingly savvy about exploiting the relative ease of making their own content go viral. The *New Republic* reported in November 2013 that freshman senator Elizabeth Warren had taken a hands-on role in managing her public profile. The populist Massachusetts Democrat had, during the 2012 campaign, "traveled with at least three staffers: Her body man and press secretary, as is the case for most candidates, but also a digital director, whose job it was to capture Warren's choicest words on video, then upload the clips to YouTube and circulate them via social media. 'She's engaged in videos, e-mails, everything,' says an aide. 'She plays an integral role in the content we send out.'"[56]

Walk back: Attempts by politicians and press handlers to limit the damage done by dumb, embarrassing, and stupid statements.

It's a politely euphemistic way to address the subject of lying or deception without having to use those rather unseemly words.

★ Walk back is derived from "walking back the cat," which William Safire notes has been used in diplomatic circles to signify retreating from a previously held position in negotiations.[57] In the spy world, it also means reexamining old analyses based on new information.

While lawmakers and candidates sometimes try to deny outright embarrassing words, in the age of cell-phone cameras and video and other recording devices, it's become increasingly difficult to pull that off. Sometimes, even anonymous quotes can force walk-backs. During the October 2013 government shutdown, the *Wall Street Journal* quoted about political tactics that Team Obama figured would bring congressional Republicans to heel. "We are winning," a senior administration official said, bragging that the length of the shutdown "doesn't really matter to us." The point: the political pain would be on the other side, and the president, who wasn't running for reelection, thought "what matters is the end result." But the White House quickly backed off the senior administration official's blind quote, with Press Secretary Jay Carney tweeting that "potus wants the shutdown to end now," and Obama himself later said "no one is winning" while the government is shut down. Republicans seized on the original quote in the *Journal*. "This isn't some damn game,"

House Speaker John Boehner said indignantly at a press conference.[58]

Any discussion of political walk-backs must include Senate Democratic leader Harry Reid. The Nevada Democrat spent decades in politics, and by the time he ascended to the peak of his power during the Obama presidency he didn't particularly care who was offended by his tart tongue. Still, throughout the years Reid's staff made heroic, if mostly failed, efforts to walk back the senator's more controversial statements. During the same government shutdown, Reid drew flak after ineloquently responding to a question from CNN's Dana Bash about kids with cancer who, due to the government lockdown, were unable to undergo clinical trials run by the National Institutes of Health. (Bash: "But if you can help one child who has cancer, why wouldn't you do it?" Reid: "Why would we want to do that? I have 1,100 people at Nellis Air Force Base that are sitting home. They have a few problems of their own."[59]) Reid's press aides quickly issued a clarifying statement, but Republicans knew a good sound bite when they heard it.

Reid himself has at times admitted to verbal excesses and walked back his own statements. On the Senate floor in October 2013, the Senate majority leader delivered a striking mea culpa, saying he and his colleagues had simply gotten too personal and nasty in their debates. A day earlier, Senator John Cornyn had scolded Reid for attacking Senator Ted Cruz, a fellow Texas Republican, by name as they debated the government shutdown. Cornyn read directly from the Senate rules that prohibit members from impugning each other's motives or conduct.

Zinger: A supposedly spontaneous clever debate one-liner that shifts momentum toward the candidate who uttered it.

★ Former president George W. Bush, interviewed for a PBS special on presidential debates about his 2000 face-offs with Al Gore, discussed their importance. "I think Ronald Reagan in 1980 came up with some zingers and that became the measure of success to a certain extent. . . . Unless there is the zinger or the kind of the cute line or whatever, the quotable moment, there's no victor in a sense," Bush said.[60]

Debate zingers do go down in political history. There's 1988 Democratic vice presidential nominee Lloyd Bentsen telling Republican rival Dan Quayle, "You're no Jack Kennedy." Or Reagan in 1980 dismissing President Jimmy Carter with "There you go again." But in the Internet age, it's become increasingly difficult to get in a well-executed zinger. Journalists are on watch for scripted talking points. And finding the proper moment to deliver a zinger—always a difficult task—has become even harder.

Before the first 2012 president debate, the *New York Times* reported that Republican nominee Mitt Romney was preparing "a series of zingers" against President Barack Obama: "Mr. Romney's team has concluded that debates are about creating moments and has equipped him with a series of zingers that he has memorized and has been practicing on aides since August. His strategy includes luring the president into appearing smug or evasive about his responsibility for the economy."[61] Unfortunately for Republicans, Romney was unable to rattle off few genuine zingers that stuck. His best moments in that first debate—which he was widely acknowledged to have won—were due in part to Obama's lethargic performance.

Acknowledgments

This book distills years of interacting and watching politicians ply their trade. That includes interviewing officeholders, candidates, spinners, flacks, consultants, and assorted other hangers-on while watching hundreds of hours of c-span, among other activities.

We're particularly thankful for the dozens of people who helped with the research—especially former senators Robert Bennett and Byron Dorgan, former representatives Martin Frost and Michael Arcuri, former Republican National Committee chairman Michael Steele, and state senator Tim Mathern. Also Jeff Greenfield, Brian Donahue, David Rosen, John Feehery, Jim Manley, Alan Schroeder, Geoff Nunberg, Rick Wilson, Wayne Fields, Allan Louden, Paul Stob, Eric Woodard, Bob Benenson, Kathy Kiely, Jackie Koszczuk, Jill Lawrence, Ron Brownstein, Ron Fournier, Jim O'Sullivan, Bethany Albertson, Mike Fulton, Judy Hasson, and Steve Terrell. Plus the Hill staffers and lobbyists who asked to remain anonymous.

David would like to thank his family for their everlasting support—his father, Brian Mark, and sister, Rachael, and brother-in-law, Elliott Feigenbaum. Also, his Politix and Topix colleagues—particularly Managing Editor Mary Noble—for their indulgence as he and Chuck pulled together this book. Chuck would like to thank his extremely tolerant wife, Liisa Ecola.

We'd also like to salute our agent, John Willig, and our editor at UPNE, Steve Hull, for working through this project with us.

Notes

INTRODUCTION

1 Kevin Richert, "The Dark Art of Radiator-Capping," *Idaho Education News*, March 26, 2013, http://www.idahoednews.org/the-edge -blog/the-dark-art-of-radiator-capping/.

2 *A Way with Words*, "Hog House," http://www.waywordradio.org/hog _house_6/.

3 Jim O'Sullivan e-mail.

4 George Orwell, "Politics and the English Language," https://www .mtholyoke.edu/acad/intrel/orwell46.htm.

5 Julie Coleman, *The Life of Slang* (New York: Oxford University Press, 2012), 3.

6 Geoffrey Nunberg, *Talking Right: How Conservatives Turned Liberalism Into a Tax-Raising, Latte-Drinking, Sushi-Eating, Volvo-Driving, New York Times–Reading, Body-Piercing, Hollywood-Loving, Left-Wing Freak Show* (New York: PublicAffairs 2006), 3.

7 Global Language Monitor, "Top Political Buzzwords Paint a Different Picture Than the Campaigns," July 12, 2012, http://www.language monitor.com/obama/top-political-buzzwords-paint-a-different -picture-than-the-campaigns/.

CHAPTER 1. BED-WETTERS, SHERPAS, SQUISHES, AND OTHER PERSONALITY TYPES

1 Mark Leibovich, *This Town: Two Parties and a Funeral—Plus, Plenty of Valet Parking!—In America's Gilded Capital* (New York: Blue Rider Press, 2013), 232.

2 McConnell floor speech, June 25, 2013, http://beta.congress.gov /congressional-record/2013/06/25/senate-section/article/S5104-2.

3 Jake Tapper, "VP Biden Says Republicans Are 'Going to Put Y'all Back in Chains," ABCNews.com, August 14, 2012, http://abcnews .go.com/blogs/politics/2012/08/vp-biden-says-republicans-are -going-to-put-yall-back-in-chains/.

4 Jillian Rayfield, "GOP Rep: Libya Is Worse Than Watergate," Salon
.com, October 1, 2012, http://www.salon.com/2012/10/01/gop_rep
_libya_is_worse_than_watergate_for_obama/.

5 Brian Montopoli, "Alan Grayson 'Die Quickly' Comment Prompts
Uproar," CBSNews.com, September 30, 2009, http://www.cbsnews
.com/news/alan-grayson-die-quickly-comment-prompts-uproar/.

6 Susan F. Rafsky, "Representative Newt Gingrich: From Political Gue-
rilla to Republican Folk Hero," *New York Times*, June 15, 1988, http://
www.nytimes.com/1988/06/15/us/washington-talk-working-profile
-representative-newt-gingrich-political-guerrilla.html?src=pm.

7 Ashley Parker and Jonathan Weisman, "Conservatives Take Turns
Standing Up to the Speaker," *New York Times*, September 19, 2013,
http://www.nytimes.com/2013/09/20/us/politics/conservatives-take
-turns-standing-up-to-boehner.html.

8 *Wall Street Journal*, "The Bedwetter Caucus," August 16, 2012, http://
online.wsj.com/news/articles/SB100008723963904441847045775892
62998551978.

9 David Plouffe, "November Doesn't Need to be a Nightmare," *Washington Post*, January 24, 2010, http://articles.washingtonpost.com
/2010-01-24/opinions/36818470_1_meaningful-health-insurance
-reform-jobs-health-care.

10 Joe Nocera, "The Last Moderate," *New York Times*, September 5,
2011, http://www.nytimes.com/2011/09/06/opinion/the-last-moder
ate.html?src=tp.

11 WordCraft, November 11, 2004, http://wordcraft.infopop.cc
/Archives/2004-11-Nov.htm.

12 R. J. Duke Short, *Centennial Senator: True Stories of Strom Thurmond from the People Who Knew Him Best* (Columbia, SC: University
of South Carolina Press, 2009), 395.

13 Daniel Halper, "Love: Obama Played Cards during Osama Raid:
'I Can't Watch This Entire Thing,' Obama Said," *Weekly Standard*,
August 14, 2013, http://www.weeklystandard.com/blogs/love-obama
-played-cards-during-osama-raid-i-can-t-watch-entire-thing-obama
-said_748413.html.

14 Ashley Parker, "Starting the Day, and Ending It, at Romney's Side,"

New York Times, April 6, 2012, http://www.nytimes.com/2012/04
/07/us/politics/mitt-romneys-assistant-seldom-leaves-his-side
.html.

15 Alex Roarty, "Meet the New Republican Flamethrowers," *National Journal*, November 18, 2013: http://www.nationaljournal.com/maga
zine/meet-the-new-republican-flamethrowers-20131118.

16 Transcript of *The Diane Rehm Show*, October 1, 2013, http://the
dianerehmshow.org/shows/2013-10-01/federal-government-shuts
-down/transcript.

17 See "Jon Stewart on Crossfire," *Crossfire*, October 15, 2004, 7:24,
posted by "Alex Felker," January 16, 2006, http://www.youtube.com
/watch?v=aFQFB5YpDZE.

18 See "Bullshit Mountain," *Crossfire*, October 15, 2004, 10:12, posted
by "Alex Felker," January 16, 2006, http://www.youtube.com/watch
?v=UfCBurnHCh8.

19 Jennifer Steinhauer, "On the Sunday Morning Talk Shows, a Rather
Familiar Cast of Characters," *New York Times*, June 8, 2013, http://
www.nytimes.com/2013/06/09/us/politics/on-sunday-talk-shows
-a-familiar-cast-of-characters.html.

20 Paul Waldman, "If It's Sunday, It's John McCain," *American Prospect*,
March 19, 2012, http://prospect.org/article/if-its-sunday-its-john
-mccain.

21 James Dao, "Using a Lobbyist's Pull from the Governor's Seat," *New
York Times*, February 21, 2006, http://www.nytimes.com/2006/02
/21/national/nationalspecial/21barbour.html.

22 Kinsley quoted in Geoffrey Nunberg, *Talking Right: How Conservatives Turned Liberalism into a Tax-Raising, Latte-Drinking, Sushi-
Eating, Volvo-Driving*, New York Times–*Reading, Body-Piercing,
Hollywood-Loving, Left-Wing Freak Show* (New York: PublicAffairs,
2006), 87.

23 Speech of Joseph McCarthy, February 9, 1950: http://historymatters
.gmu.edu/d/6456.

24 National Public Radio *Talk of the Nation* transcript, October 26,
2010, http://www.npr.org/templates/story/story.php?storyId
=130837426.

25 Quoted in http://raggedthots.blogspot.com/2009_04_26_archive
.html.

26 Geoffrey Nunberg interview with authors, November 2013.

27 Nunberg, *Talking Right*, 108.

28 "Paul Corbin, 75, Dies; Robert Kennedy Aide," *New York Times*,
January 4, 1990, http://www.nytimes.com/1990/01/04/obituaries
/paul-corbin-75-dies-robert-kennedy-aide.html.

29 Ed O'Keefe, "Tom DeLay Conviction Overturned by Texas Court,"
Washington Post, September 19, 2013, http://www.washingtonpost
.com/blogs/post-politics/wp/2013/09/19/tom-delay-conviction
-overturned-by-texas-court/.

30 *Times-Picayune*, "Lobbyist Livingston Not Welcome at House Opening Day," January 8, 2011, http://www.nola.com/politics/index.ssf
/2011/01/lobbyist_bob_livingston_not_we.html.

31 "In Search of Republican Grown-Ups," *New York Times*, October 24,
2013, http://www.nytimes.com/2013/10/25/opinion/in-search-of
-republican-grown-ups.html.

32 Alex Altman, "Handicapping the Veepstakes: Is Rob Portman the
Answer to Republicans' Palin Problem?" *Time*, April 19, 2012, http://
swampland.time.com/2012/04/19/handicapping-the-veepstakes-is
-rob-portman-the-answer-to-republicans-palin-problem/.

33 Rob Portman interview with authors, October 2013.

34 "President Obama Delivers Victory Speech After Winning 2012 Election," YouTube video, from a speech delivered November 7, 2012,
posted by "tomthunkit," http://www.youtube.com/watch?v=Of4MF
HUXUxw.

35 William Safire, "On Language: 'Happy Warrior,'" *New York Times*,
June 13, 2004, http://www.nytimes.com/2004/06/13/magazine/the
-way-we-live-now-6-13-04-on-language-happy-warrior.html.

36 Robert Costa, "Boehner's Brief Rally," *National Review Online*, September 28, 2013, http://www.nationalreview.com/corner/359814
/boehners-brief-rally-robert-costa.

37 See "Chickenhawks" Floor Speech By Sen. Frank Lautenberg, C-SPAN,
9:09, February 24, 2004, posted by "Andrew Pang," June 3, 2013,
http://www.youtube.com/watch?v=QJcFDVi2nrQ.

38 Ezra Klein, "Now Is the Time to Be an Infrastructure Hawk, Not a Deficit Hawk," *Washington Post*, June 5, 2013, http://www.washing tonpost.com/blogs/wonkblog/wp/2013/06/05/now-is-the-time-to -be-an-infrastructure-hawk-not-a-deficit-hawk/.

39 Jack Shafer, "Infrastructure Madness," *Slate*, April 21, 2009, http:// www.slate.com/articles/news_and_politics/press_box/2009/04 /infrastructure_madness.html.

40 Fred Barnes, "The Democrats and the Loony Left," *Weekly Standard*, August 2, 2004.

41 John Feehery, "How About a Little Respect, Barry?" *Daily Caller*, March 1, 2010, http://dailycaller.com/2010/03/01/how-about-a -little-respect-barry/.

42 Bryant Jordan, "Lawmaker Calls VA Official a Political Operative," Military.com, September 20, 2013, http://www.military.com/daily -news/2013/09/20/lawmaker-calls-va-official-a-political-operative .html.

43 Flanagan Consulting LLC website, http://www.flanaganconsulting .com/.

44 David Mark, *Going Dirty: The Art of Negative Campaigning* (New York: Rowman & Littlefield, 2006), 58.

45 John F. Kennedy speech transcript, September 14, 1960, http://www .pbs.org/wgbh/americanexperience/features/primary-resources/jfk -nyliberal/.

46 Congressional Progressive Caucus website, "What Is CPC?" http:// 1.usa.gov/IRYFXu.

47 Media Matters website, "About Us," http://mediamatters.org/about.

48 David Sirota, "What's the Difference between a Liberal and a Pro- gressive?" *Huffington Post*, October 19, 2005, http://www.huffington post.com/david-sirota/whats-the-difference-betw_b_9140.html.

49 See "Harry Reid Pits 'Reasonable' Republicans Against Tea Party Extremists in Senate Debate," YouTube video, 1:24, from Senate floor speech October 4, 2013, posted by "NewsM," October 4, 2013, https://www.youtube.com/watch?v=Y5jvRRHZzVs.

50 Harry Reid floor speech, July 8, 2013, http://thomas.loc.gov/cgi-bin /query/z?r113:S08JY3-0004:/.

51 Jim Haddadin, "Republican Gubernatorial Hopeful Smith 'Not Driven by Ideology,'" Fosters.com, April 12, 2012, http://www.fosters .com/apps/pbcs.dll/article?AID=/20120412/GJNEWS_01/70412 9851.

52 John Feehery, "Nine Insults I've Been Getting on Twitter Lately and What I Think of Them," TheFeeheryTheory.com, October 3, 2013, http://www.thefeeherytheory.com/twitter-wars/.

53 Wayne Fields interview with authors, November 2013.

54 Reg Henry, "The Sorry Republicans, Me Included," *Newsday*, January 18, 2012, http://www.newsday.com/opinion/oped/henry-the -sorry-republicans-me-included-1.3461495.

55 Dan Coats, "Anatomy of a Nomination: A Year Later, What Went Wrong, What Went Right and What We Can Learn from the Battles over Alito and Miers," *Hamline Journal of Public Law and Policy* 28 (2006–7): http://heinonline.org/HOL/LandingPage?handle=hein .journals/hplp28&div=18&id=&page=.

56 Mike Memoli, "Sherpa Plays Crucial Role in Nomination Process," *Real Clear Politics*, May 29, 2009, http://www.realclearpolitics.com /articles/2009/05/29/sherpas_play_crucial_role_in_confirmation _process_96733.html.

57 Tom Korologos, "How to Scale The High Court," *Washington Post*, May 24, 2009, http://www.washingtonpost.com/wp-dyn/content /article/2009/05/22/AR2009052202034.html.

58 Carnegie Endowment for International Peace transcript, July 15, 2013, http://carnegieendowment.org/files/071513_brainard_tran script.pdf.

59 Nick Wing, "Sarah Palin: 'Barack Obama is a Socialist,' Communism Could Be Coming," *Huffington Post*, December 4, 2012, http://www .huffingtonpost.com/2012/12/04/sarah-palin-obama-socialist_n _2237163.html.

60 Igor Volsky, "How Romney Spent All Day Calling Obama a Foreigner," ThinkProgress.org, July 17, 2012, http://thinkprogress.org /politics/2012/07/17/537131/how-romney-spent-all-day-calling -obama-a-foreigner/.

61 See "Newsweek Covers Says We Are All Socialists Now," American Glob.com, February 9, 2009, http://americanglob.com/2009/02/09/newsweek-cover-says-we-are-all-socialists-now/.

62 David Remnick, "On and Off the Road with Barack Obama," *New Yorker*, January 27, 2014, http://www.newyorker.com/reporting/2014/01/27/140127fa_fact_remnick.

63 Billy Wharton, "Obama's No Socialist. I Should Know," *Washington Post*, March 15, 2009, http://articles.washingtonpost.com/2009-03-15/opinions/36769306_1_socialist-party-usa-barack-obama-new-york-times.

64 "Senator Ted Cruz Surprises the FreedomWorks Texas Summit with a Special Speech," YouTube video from a speech delivered April 26, 2013, posted by FreedomWorks, http://www.youtube.com/watch?feature=player_embedded&v=geHPipl6mt8#!.

65 Hamilton, Nigel. *Bill Clinton: Mastering the Presidency* (New York: PublicAffairs, 2007), 139.

66 Daniel Libit, "Meet the Make-Believe Strategists of TV," *Politico*, June 24, 2008, http://www.politico.com/news/stories/0608/11319.html.

67 William Safire, "Strategist, Rising," *New York Times*, August 5, 2007, http://www.nytimes.com/2007/08/05/magazine/05wwln-safire-t.html.

68 Chuck McCutcheon and Christina Lyons, eds., *CQ's Politics in America 2010* (Washington, DC: CQ Press, 2009), 934.

69 Alana Goodman, "Romney Pounces on Santorum's 'Team Player' Blunder," *Commentary*, February 23, 2012, http://www.commentarymagazine.com/2012/02/23/romney-pounces-on-santorum-blunder/.

70 Martin Kaste, "When Politicians Slip, Video Trackers Are There," NPR.org, April 23, 2012, http://www.npr.org/2012/04/23/151060718/behind-the-scene-to-the-next-debacles-video-trackers.

71 *New York Times* slideshow, "Texas Right Offers Fast Embrace to G.O.P. Newcomer," November 15, 2011, http://www.nytimes.com/slideshow/2011/11/15/us/TEDCRUZ.html.

72 Justin Sink, "Republican Tweets That Dems 'Lost a True Believer' in

Chavez," *The Hill*, March 6, 2013, http://thehill.com/blogs/twitter -room/other-news/286497-stockman-deleted-tweet-democrats-lost -a-true-believer-in-chavez.

73 Jason Zengerle, "Wanna Be Veep? Okay, But This Is Going to Hurt," *GQ*, July 2012, http://www.gq.com/news-politics/politics/201208 /mitt-romney-vice-president-gq-july-2012.

74 Rick Wilson interview with authors, November 2013.

75 Cass R. Sunstein, "How to Humble a Wing Nut," *Bloomberg View*, May 20, 2013, http://www.bloomberg.com/news/2013-05-20/how -to-humble-a-wing-nut.html.

76 See http://www.zazzle.com/american_wacko_bird_and_proud_of _it_shirt-235819591338427307.

77 "Clinton: 'I Believe I Am a Workhorse,'" NBC's *Meet The Press*, January 14, 2007, http://www.nbcnews.com/video/meet-the-press /22635148.

78 Transcript of Rep. Brad Sherman on NBC's *Meet the Press*, June 25, 2012.

79 For the 2012 edition, see http://www.washingtonian.com/articles /people/best-and-worst-of-congress-2012/.

80 Tim Fleck, "The Insider," *Houston Press*, May 14, 1998, http://www .houstonpress.com/1998-05-14/news/the-insider/.

CHAPTER 2. "WITH ALL DUE RESPECT, I DEEPLY REGRET HOLDING YOU IN MINIMUM HIGH REGARD": ONLY-IN-POLITICS EXPRESSIONS

1 Wayne Fields interview with authors, November 2013.

2 David Lawder, "U.S. House Republicans Commit to Delay of Obamacare Tax Provision," *Reuters*, October 23, 2013, http://mobile .reuters.com/article/politicsNews/idUSBRE99M0N920131023.

3 Becky Pallack, "McCain Touches on Variety of Topics at Town Hall," *Arizona Daily Star*, November 26, 2013, http://azstarnet.com/news /local/govt-and-politics/mccain-touches-on-variety-of-political -topics-at-town-hall/article_ff927e0f-8270-5266-9af3-40cb43c 6336e.html.

4 White House.gov, "Press Briefing by Press Secretary Jay Carney,"

October 17, 2013, http://www.whitehouse.gov/the-press-office/2013
/10/17/press-briefing-press-secretary-jay-carney-101713.

5 David Harsanyi, "Pelosi on Bipartisanship: Then and Now," *Denver Post*, February 6, 2009, http://blogs.denverpost.com/thespot/2009
/02/06/pelosi-on-bipartisanship-then-and-now/.

6 Judy Woodruff, "Is It Compromise . . . or Selling Out?" PBS.org, May 10, 2012, http://www.pbs.org/newshour/rundown/2012/05/is-it
-compromise-or-selling-out.html.

7 Sam Brownback interview with authors, March 2004.

8 Stephen F. Hayes, "Walker to Romney: Go Big and Go Bold," *Weekly Standard*, June 6, 2012, http://www.weeklystandard.com/blogs
/walker-romney-go-big-and-go-bold_646734.html#.

9 See "Bold Ideas Are Politically Shrewd, But Mostly, 'Bold' Is Just a Clothes Detergent," *UppityWisconsin.org*, May 31, 2011, http://www
.uppitywis.org/blogarticle/bold-ideas-are-politically-shrewd-mostly
-just-clothes-detergent.

10 See "Mitt Romney's Bold Running Mate Pick," *The Colbert Report*, August 13, 2013, http://www.colbertnation.com/the-colbert-report
-videos/417826/august-13-2012/mitt-romney-s-bold-running-mate
-pick.

11 Ed O'Keefe and David A. Farenthold, "Gabrielle Giffords Speaks at Senate Hearing on Gun Violence: 'You Must Act. Be Bold'" *Washington Post*, January 30, 2013, http://articles.washingtonpost.com/2013
-01-30/politics/36623733_1_gun-violence-checks-for-gun-buyers
-gun-laws.

12 Bruce Stokes, "No Truce in Class Warfare," *National Journal*, July 20, 2011, http://www.nationaljournal.com/daily/no-truce-in-class
-warfare-20110720.

13 Gordon T. Anderson, "Buffett Speaks: Berkshire Chairman's Annual Letter Attacks CEOs, Funds, Bush Tax Policies and the Trade Deficit," *CNNMoney*, March 8, 2004, http://money.cnn.com/2004/03/06/pf
/buffett_letter/.

14 Dain Fitzgerald, "Santorum: Talk of 'Middle Class' Is Marxism," *Politix*, August 14, 2013, http://politix.topix.com/homepage/7482
-santorum-talk-of-middle-class-is-marxism.

15 Jonathan Martin, "George W. Bush on Dick Cheney: 'It's Been Cordial,'" *Politico*, April 24, 2013, http://www.politico.com/story/2013/04/george-bush-on-dick-cheney-its-been-cordial-90545.html.

16 Carl M. Cannon, "Clinton Draws Line on Budget," *Baltimore Sun*, September 26, 1995, http://articles.baltimoresun.com/1995-09-26/news/1995269066_1_clinton-train-wreck-blackmailed.

17 Richard G. Zimmerman, *Call Me Mike: A Political Biography of Michael V. DiSalle* (Kent, OH: Kent State University Press, 2002), 177.

18 Jake Miller, "House Republicans 'Deeply Troubled' by Rice," CBS News.com, November 19, 2012, http://www.cbsnews.com/news/house-republicans-deeply-troubled-by-rice/.

19 Rachel Weiner, "Inhofe Blasts Hagel: 'Deeply Troubling,'" *Washington Post*, January 31, 2013, http://www.washingtonpost.com/blogs/post-politics/wp/2013/01/31/inhofe-blasts-hagel-deeply-troubling/.

20 Office of Speaker John Boehner, "Speaker Boehner Statement on U.S.-Iran Nuclear Talks," November 8, 2013, http://www.speaker.gov/press-release/speaker-boehner-statement-us-iran-nuclear-talks.

21 "George Bush & Will Ferrell on Global Warming," YouTube video from a WTBS special "Earth to America," July 10, 2007, posted by Adrian Choong, http://www.youtube.com/watch?v=I_kODETmro8.

22 Mark Preston, "Reid Apologizes for Racial Remarks about Obama During Campaign," CNN.com, January 9, 2010, http://www.cnn.com/2010/POLITICS/01/09/obama.reid/.

23 Lynn Sweet, "RNC, DNC Chiefs Battle on Bloomberg TV," *Chicago Sun-Times*, April 5, 2012, http://voices.suntimes.com/early-and-often/sweet/rnc-dnc-chiefs-battle-on-bloom/.

24 Max Pizarro, "Rothman Camp Attempts to Turn Pascrell's Championing of Public Option into Anti-Obama Line," *Politicker NJ*, March 23, 2012, http://www.politickernj.com/55799/rothman-camp-attempts-turn-pascrells-championing-public-option-anti-obama-line.

25 Office of Senator James Inhofe, "Inhofe: Obama's Oklahoma Visit Disingenuous," March 22, 2012, http://www.inhofe.senate.gov/newsroom/press-releases/inhofe-obamas-oklahoma-visit-disingenuous.

26 Jim Manley interview with authors, October 2013.

27 See "Top Republican Accuses Dems of 'Scare Tactics' to Influence
Women Voters," *The Hill*, March 21, 2012, http://thehill.com/video
/house/217425-top-republican-accuses-dems-of-scare-tactics-to
-influence-women-voters-.

28 Raymond Hernandez, "Cory Booker, Obama Surrogate, Criticizes
Bain Ad," *New York Times*, May 20, 2012, http://www.nytimes.com
/2012/05/21/us/politics/cory-a-booker-criticizes-obamas-bain-ad
.html.

29 David Jackson, "Clinton Added 2,300 Words to His Speech," *USA
Today*, September 6, 2013, http://content.usatoday.com/commu
nities/theoval/post/2012/09/clinton-added-2300-words-to-his
-speech/1#.UqOgYeIQQkE.

30 Ruth Walker, "Why Did President Obama Double Up on 'Double
Down'?" *Christian Science Monitor*, February 10, 2012, http://www
.csmonitor.com/The-Culture/Verbal-Energy/2012/0210/Why-did
-President-Obama-double-up-on-double-down.

31 Representative Eliot Engel floor speech, September 8, 2011, http://
www.gpo.gov/fdsys/pkg/CREC-2011-09-08/html/CREC-2011-09
-08-pt1-PgH5974-3.htm.

32 Jon Campbell, "Cuomo on Corruption: 'People Do Stupid Things,
Frankly,'" *LoHud.com*, April 3, 2013, http://polhudson.lohudblogs
.com/2013/04/03/cuomo-on-corruption-people-do-stupid-things
-frankly/.

33 See remarks of Rep. Glenn Thompson, "How Business Gets Done in
Washington," *Congressional Record*, February 9, 2011, http://beta
.congress.gov/congressional-record/2011/02/09/house-section
/article/H593-1.

34 Paula Poundstone, "The Poundstone Report," *Mother Jones*, March/
April 1995, http://www.motherjones.com/politics/1995/03/mother
jones-ma95-poundstone-report.

35 See "Newt Gingrich: Frankly, Not Mitt Romney's Biggest Supporter,"
http://www.youtube.com/watch?v=Z1jMaeoBrCs.

36 Ari Shapiro, "In GOP Primary Race, Can Steadiness Trump Passion?"
NPR.org, January 30, 2012, http://www.npr.org/2012/01/30/14608
3520/in-the-gop-primary-race-can-steadiness-trump-passion.

37 Katy Steinmetz, "The 2012 Candidates' Telling Verbal Tics," *Time*, December 16, 2011, http://swampland.time.com/2011/12/16/the-2012-candidates-telling-verbal-tics/.

38 CNN transcript of January 20, 2012 debate, http://transcripts.cnn.com/TRANSCRIPTS/1201/20/ddhln.01.html.

39 Dan Amira, "Fundamentally: Newt Gingrich's Favorite Word," *New York*, December 2, 2011, http://nymag.com/daily/intelligencer/2011/11/fundamentally-newt-gingrichs-favorite-word.html.

40 U.S. House Education & the Workforce Committee, "Kline Statement: HR 5, The Student Success Act," July 18, 2013, http://edworkforce.house.gov/news/documentsingle.aspx?DocumentID=342927.

41 Chris Matthews, "What Ronald Reagan and Tip O'Neill Could Teach Washington Today," *Washington Post*, January 11, 2011, http://www.washingtonpost.com/wp-dyn/content/article/2011/01/17/AR2011011703299.html.

42 Rush Limbaugh radio show transcript, January 18, 2011, http://www.rushlimbaugh.com/daily/2011/01/18/don_t_be_fooled_liberals_despised_reagan_and_were_not_civil_about_it.

43 Jessica Hagy, "Poor Things," November 5, 2010, http://thisisindexed.com/2010/11/poor-things-2/.

44 Clinton speech transcript, June 30, 1999, http://www.presidency.ucsb.edu/ws/?pid=57806.

45 Kelly Hardy, "ICANN San Francisco: A High-Class Problem," *DomainPulse.com*, April 4, 2011, http://www.domainpulse.com/2011/04/04/icann-san-francisco-a-high-class-problem-by-kelly-hardy/.

46 CNN transcript, October 16, 2013, http://transcripts.cnn.com/TRANSCRIPTS/1310/16/cg.02.html.

47 Transcript of President Obama in Everett, Washington, February 17, 2012, http://blogs.suntimes.com/sweet/2012/02/obama_at_boeing_dreamliner_pla.html.

48 Brendan Nyhan, "Will Hillary Escape a Pledge Not to Run for President?" *BrendanNyhan.com*, May 6, 2005, http://www.brendan-nyhan.com/blog/2005/05/will_hillary_es.html.

49 Arlette Saenz, "Veep Beat: Christie and Rubio Go on the Attack," ABCNews.com, May 21, 2012, http://abcnews.go.com/blogs/politics/2012/05/veep-beat-christie-and-rubio-as-attack-dogs/.

50 Ashley Killough, "Cuomo on 2016: 'I'm Focused on' Being Governor," CNN.com, June 22, 2013, http://politicalticker.blogs.cnn.com/2013/07/22/cuomo-on-2016-im-focused-on-being-governor/.

51 David Muto, "The Evening Brief: Texas Headlines for April 24, 2013," *Texas Tribune*, April 24, 2013, http://www.texastribune.org/2013/04/24/evening-brief-texas-headlines-april-24-2013/.

52 NBCNews.com, "Cruz: '100 percent of my focus is on the U.S. Senate,'" October 26, 2013, http://www.nbcnews.com/video/nbc-news/53385105#53385105.

53 Dan Collins, "Martha Stewart Focuses on Her Salad," CBSNews.com, June 26, 2002, http://www.cbsnews.com/news/martha-stewart-focuses-on-her-salad/.

54 John Kador, *Effective Apology: Mending Fences, Building Bridges and Restoring Trust* (San Francisco: Berrett-Koehler Publishers, 2009), 204.

55 Ibid., 204–5.

56 Josh Voorhees, "Pa. Governor Exchanges One Inappropriate Gay-Marriage Analogy for Another," *Slate.com*, October 4, 2013, http://www.slate.com/blogs/the_slatest/2013/10/04/tom_corbett_gay_marriage_pa_governor_compares_gay_marriage_to_brother_sister.html.

57 Lynn Bartels, "Colorado Lawmaker Joe Salazar Issues Apology over Rape Remark," *Denver Post*, February 18, 2013, http://www.denverpost.com/ci_22617884/lawmaker-issues-apology-over-rape-remark.

58 Dana Perino tweet, May 13, 2013, https://twitter.com/DanaPerino/status/334128451852316672.

59 "First Time In Recorded History The "Spend More Time With My Family" Excuse Was Believable," *Gawker.com*, http://gawker.com/348711/first-time-in-recorded-history-the-spend-more-time-with-my-family-excuse-was-believable.

60 Steven T. Dennis, "CIA Deputy Retires to Spend More 'Time with My Family,'" *Roll Call*, June 12, 2013, http://www.rollcall.com/news/cia _deputy_retires_to_spend_more_time_with_my_family-225573-1 .html.

61 Allen Louden interview.

62 Laura Vanderkam, "What Resigning to 'Spend More Time With Family' Really Means," AOL.com, September 17, 2013, http://jobs .aol.com/articles/2013/09/17/spend-more-time-with-family -euphemism/.

63 Ben Feller, "Obama's Favorite Phrases," *Huffington Post*, October 13, 2009, http://www.huffingtonpost.com/2009/10/13/obamas-favorite -phrases_n_318314.html.

64 David Espo, "Boehner: 'Let Me Be Clear: Tax Hikes Are Off the Table,'" Associated Press, June 24, 2011, http://www.gopusa.com /news/2011/06/24/boehner-let-me-be-clear-tax-hikes-are-off-the -table/.

65 Steinmetz, "The 2012 Candidates' Telling Verbal Tics."

66 E-mail interview with author, November 1, 2013.

67 Kansas State University, "Former Rep. Lee Hamilton Landon Lecture," March 29, 2005, https://www.k-state.edu/media/newsreleases /landonlect/hamiltontext305.html.

68 George Washington University, "Interview with Senator Eugene McCarthy—1968 Democratic Party Contender," July 11, 1996, http:// www2.gwu.edu/~nsarchiv/coldwar/interviews/episode-13/mccarthy 1.html.

69 Transcript of House floor debate, June 27, 2007, http://thomas.loc .gov/cgi-bin/query/F?r110:1: ./temp/~r110M0nzqW:e220001:.

70 Robert D. Novak, *Completing the Revolution: A Vision for Victory in 2000* (New York: Simon & Schuster, 2000).

71 Office of Representative Rosa DeLauro, "DeLauro Statement on Labor-HHS-Education Funding Legislation," http://delauro.house .gov/index.php?option=com_content&view=article&id=1016:delauro -statement-on-labor-hhs-education-funding-legislation&catid=2& Itemid=21.

72 Office of Governor Rick Perry, "Statement by Gov. Rick Perry on Pas-

sage of Pro-Life Legislation," July 13, 2013, http://governor.state.tx
.us/news/press-release/18746/.

73 Gene Green interview with authors, November 2013.

74 Aaron Blake, "McConnell: Reid Could Be Worst Senate Leader Ever,"
Washington Post, July 11, 2013, http://www.washingtonpost.com
/blogs/post-politics/wp/2013/07/11/mcconnell-nuclear-option-will
-be-reids-legacy/.

75 Anthony Bourdain, *Kitchen Confidential: Adventures in the Culinary
Underbelly* (New York: Ecco Press, 2000), 221.

76 See "The Godfather: Quotes," http://m.imdb.com/title/tt0068646
/quotes?qt=qt0361843.

77 CNN transcript, August 23, 2008, http://transcripts.cnn.com/TRAN
SCRIPTS/0808/23/smn.03.html.

78 Charlie Mitchell and Mark Wegner, "In A House Divided, Hastert
Savors Wins," *National Journal*, March 30, 2001, http://www.nation
aljournal.com/member/daily/congressdailyam-house-leadership-in
-a-house-divided-hastert-savors-wins-20010330.

79 William Safire, *Safire's Political Dictionary* (New York: Oxford University Press, 2008), 489.

80 George E. Condon Jr., "The Populist Pivot," *National Journal*, January 29, 2010, http://www.nationaljournal.com/member/daily/the
-populist-pivot-20100129.

81 Michael Falcone and Amy Walter, "The Note: Testing the Fragile
Front-Runner Theory," ABCNews.com, August 3, 2011, http://abc
news.go.com/blogs/politics/2011/08/the-note-testing-the-fragile
-front-runner-theory-mitt-romneys-opponents-take-aim/.

82 Alan Schroeder interview with authors, November 2013.

83 Heidi Stevens, "What's 'Radical' Really Mean?" *Chicago Tribune*,
January 19, 2011, http://articles.chicagotribune.com/2011-01-19/fea
tures/ct-tribu-words-work-radical-20110119_1_religious-radicals
-spectrum-term.

84 Office of Senator Harry Reid, "Reid Remarks on Republican Efforts
to Shut Down the Government," September 23, 2013, http://www
.reid.senate.gov/newsroom/reid_remarks_on_republican_efforts
_to_shut_down_the_government.cfm.

85 See "NBC Grills Cheney on Tea Party; Cheney Calls Obama 'Most Radical Operator' in DC," MRCTV.com, October 21, 2012, http://www.mrctv.org/videos/nbcs-grills-cheney-tea-party-cheney-calls-obama-most-radical-operator-dc.

86 National Public Radio *Talk of the Nation* transcript, October 26, 2010, http://www.npr.org/templates/story/story.php?storyId=130 837426.

87 C-SPAN, "Newsmakers with Senator Patrick Leahy," November 15, 2013, http://www.c-spanvideo.org/program/Sensen.

88 Edward Moyer, "Intelligence Chief Clapper Cites 'Casablanca' in Dismissing Merkel Mess," CNET, October 29, 2013, http://news.cnet.com/8301-13578_3-57609933-38/intelligence-chief-clapper-cites-casablanca-in-dismissing-merkel-mess/.

89 Jim Rutenberg, "Data You Can Believe In," *New York Times Magazine*, June 22, 2013, http://walmartcommunityvotes.com/news/view/82039.

90 Transcript of U.S. State Department press briefing, January 16, 2013, http://www.state.gov/r/pa/prs/dpb/2013/01/202928.htm.

91 Chris Cillizza, "Who Had the Worst Week in Washington? Attorney General Eric Holder," *Washington Post*, June 14, 2012, http://articles.washingtonpost.com/2012-06-14/opinions/35461089_1_contempt-vote-worst-week-eric-holder.

92 Ed Rogers, "Romney Attacks, More in Sorrow Than in Anger," *Washington Post*, September 28, 2012, http://www.washingtonpost.com/blogs/the-insiders/post/romney-attacks-more-in-sorrow-than-in-anger/2012/09/28/f9468402-097e-11e2-9eea-333857f6a7bd_blog.html.

93 Larry Eichel, "For a Lame Duck, Clinton Looms Large—Too Large—for Gore," *Philadelphia Inquirer*, August 13, 2000. http://articles.philly.com/2000-08-13/news/25592903_1_clinton-plan-bill-clinton-al-gore.

94 Jennifer Loven, "Bush Using Straw-Man Arguments in Speeches," Associated Press, March 26, 2006, http://www.twinpeaksgazette.com/community/topic-topicid=704.cfm.html.

95 David Espo, "Obama, Boehner Seek Cliff Talks Leverage," *Boston

Globe, December 1, 2012, http://www.boston.com/news/politics
/2012/12/01/analysis-obama-boehner-seek-cliff-talks-leverage
/QbskQhpihWAnE06ReVqnPK/story.html.

96 George E. Condon Jr., "Running Against Congress," *National Journal*, March 25, 2012, http://www.nationaljournal.com/member
/daily/running-against-congress-20120325.

97 Michael Luo, "The Thompson Sound Effects," *New York Times*, October 24, 2007, http://thecaucus.blogs.nytimes.com/2007/10/24/the
-thompson-sound-effects/.

98 David Segal, "Time to Hit the Brakes on That Cliché," *Washington Post*, April 30, 2008, http://www.washingtonpost.com/wp-dyn
/content/article/2008/04/30/AR2008043003607.html.

99 Erika Eichelberger, "GOP Staffer on Vitter Amendment: 'Congress Literally Threw Staff under the Bus,'" *Mother Jones*, September 30, 2013, http://www.motherjones.com/politics/2013/09/obamacare
-employer-contribution-exemption-vitter-amendment.

100 Transcript of Boehner floor speech, October 9, 2013, http://beta
.congress.gov/congressional-record/2013/10/09/house-section
/article/H6427-1.

101 Dave Barry, "The Epitome of Wordliness," *Miami Herald*, June 10, 2013, http://www.miamiherald.com/2013/06/10/946457/the
-epitome-of-wordliness.html.

102 Lois Frankel floor speech, September 28, 2013, http://thomas.loc
.gov/cgi-bin/query/z?r113:H28SE3-0042:.

103 Mike Quigley floor speech, March 20, 2013, http://www.gpo.gov
/fdsys/pkg/CREC-2013-03-20/html/CREC-2013-03-20-pt1-PgH
1635-4.htm.

104 Greg Richter, "GOP Congressmen: Republican Senators Need 'Backbone,'" *Newsmax.com*, October 14, 2013, http://www.newsmax.com
/NewsmaxTv/aaron-schock-paul-labrador-senate-republicans/2013
/10/14/id/531012.

105 "Transcript: Tribune Interview with Mayor Rahm Emanuel," *Chicago Tribune*, February 12, 2012, http://www.chicagotribune.com/news
/local/ct-met-transcript-emanuel-speed-camera-records-2-2012
0212,0,5143651,full.story.

106 "Bachmann: White House Team Living on Another Planet 'With All Due Respect,'" *National Journal*, July 8, 2011, http://www.national journal.com/politics/bachmann-white-house-team-living-on -another-planet-with-all-due-respect-20110708.

CHAPTER 3. GOING DOWNTOWN THROUGH THE OVERTON WINDOW TO PLAY IN THE ENDGAME: PEOPLE, PLACES, AND THINGS, BOTH REAL AND IMAGINED

1 Jeffrey Frank, *The Columnist* (New York: Simon & Schuster, 2001), 10–11.

2 Biden interview with authors, August 1996.

3 Ross Douthat, "The Great Disconnect," *New York Times*, June 22, 2013, http://www.nytimes.com/2013/06/23/opinion/sunday/douthat -the-great-disconnect.html.

4 Erick Erickson, "Why America Hates Washington," *RedState*, June 26, 2013, http://www.redstate.com/2013/06/26/why-america-hates -washington/.

5 Paul Stob interview with authors, October 2013.

6 Steve Holland and Mark Felsenthal, "Crisis Averted, Obama Says Americans 'Completely Fed Up' with Washington," Reuters, October 17, 2013: http://www.reuters.com/article/2013/10/17/us-usa-fiscal -obama-idUSBRE99G0R720131017.

7 Representative Ann Wagner floor speech, May 22, 2013, http:// thomas.loc.gov/cgi-bin/query/z?r113:H22MY3-0010:/.

8 Matthew Daly, "Obama Links Keystone Approval to Carbon Emissions," Associated Press, June 25, 2013, http://bigstory.ap.org/article /official-obama-link-pipeline-ok-emissions.

9 Mark Bloomfield, "The Art of 'The Ask,'" *The Hill*, May 5, 2009, http://thehill.com/business-a-lobbying/k-street-insiders/20183 -the-art-of-the-ask--be-kind-and-courteous.

10 Jacob Weisberg, "Chicago Style," *Slate*, July 13, 2013, http://www .slate.com/articles/news_and_politics/the_big_idea/2012/07/mitt _romney_s_campaign_is_attempting_to_link_barack_obama_to _the_corruption_of_chicago_style_politics_of_a_different_era_.html.

11 Mark Silva, "Obama's 'Chicago-Style Politics': Boehner," *Chicago*

Tribune, October 23, 2009, http://www.johnboehner.com/news
/tribune-obamas-chicago-style-politics-boehner.

12 Jennifer Rubin, "What the GOP Can Learn from Chris Christie,"
Washington Post, November 3, 2013, http://www.washingtonpost
.com/blogs/right-turn/wp/2013/11/03/what-the-gop-can-learn
-from-chris-christie/.

13 Clifton French, "Congressman Upton Reacts to Niece's *SI* Swimsuit
Cover," WSBT.com, February 13, 2012, http://articles.wsbt.com/2012
-02-13/si-swimsuit_31076104.

14 Jeff Nussbaum, "A Guy Walks into an Oval Office," *Slate*, April 30,
2010, http://www.slate.com/articles/news_and_politics/politics
/2010/04/a_guy_walks_into_an_oval_office.html.

15 Michelle Malkin, "Why Can't Obama Tell a Good Joke?" *Michelle
Malkin.com*, March 20, 2009, http://michellemalkin.com/2009
/03/20/why-cant-obama-tell-a-good-joke/.

16 FrontPage Magazine, "Senator Ted Cruz: Confronting the Threat of
Radical Islam," May 20, 2013, http://www.frontpagemag.com/2013
/frontpagemag-com/senator-ted-cruz-confronting-the-threat-of
-radical-islam/.

17 "Ted Cruz's Humble Portrait," *The Colbert Report*, July 30, 2013,
http://www.colbertnation.com/the-colbert-report-videos/428209
/july-30-2013/ted-cruz-s-humble-portrait.

18 Ruth Marcus, "One Syllable of Civility," *Washington Post*, November
22, 2006, http://www.washingtonpost.com/wp-dyn/content/article
/2006/11/21/AR2006112101223.html.

19 Libby Copeland, "President's Sin of Omission? (Dropped Syllable in
Speech Riles Democrats," *Washington Post*, January 25, 2007, http://
www.washingtonpost.com/wp-dyn/content/article/2007/01/24/AR
2007012402469.html.

20 National Public Radio, "Transcript: Mr. Bush on the Democratic
Majority," January 29, 2007, http://www.npr.org/templates/story
/story.php?storyId=7061016.

21 Ali Frick, "Rep. Kaptur Scolds GOP: 'Democrat Party' Doesn't Exist,"
ThinkProgress.org, March 3, 2009, http://thinkprogress.org/politics
/2009/03/03/36534/kaptur-democrat-party/.

22 The full list is at http://www.opensecrets.org/revolving/top.php ?display=Z.

23 Jonathan Strong, "Congressman on Obamacare Exemption: 'Go Home and Talk to Your Wife,'" *National Review Online*, September 18, 2013, http://www.nationalreview.com/corner/358876/congress man-obamacare-exemption-go-home-and-talk-your-wife-jonathan -strong.

24 John Dickerson, "'As I Was Saying to the President . . . ,'" *Slate*, January 23, 2006, http://www.slate.com/articles/news_and_politics/poli tics/2006/01/as_i_was_saying_to_the_president_.html.

25 Maureen Fan, "Walls of 'Power' Show off Political Clout," *Washington Post*, November 25, 2004, http://www.washingtonpost.com/wp-dyn /articles/A13396-2004Nov25.html.

26 Manley interview with authors, November 2013.

27 Albert R. Hunt, "Republican Insurgents Forget Their Political ABCs," Bloomberg View, October 6, 2013, http://www.bloomberg.com/news /2013-10-06/republican-insurgents-forget-their-political-abcs.html.

28 *Safire's Political Dictionary*, 61.

29 Jill W. Klausen, "5 Words and Phrases Democrats Should Never Say Again," *Daily Kos*, March 18, 2012, http://www.dailykos.com/story /2012/03/18/1075582/-5-Words-And-Phrases-Democrats-Should -Never-Say-Again.

30 Senator Mitch McConnell transcript, February 13, 2013, http://www .republican.senate.gov/public/index.cfm/floor-updates?ID=08667 46d-5def-49c3-a4b6-fbb42d83a20c.

31 See "Thaddeus McCotter Teaches Us How to 'Speak Democrat,'" http://www.youtube.com/watch?v=LPc9xG1sajI.

32 Representative Tom Rice transcript, March 21, 2013, http://rice .house.gov/media-center/press-releases/rice-the-republican-plan -offers-protections-across-the-spectrum-of.

33 Representative George Miller transcript, March 15, 2013, http://beta .congress.gov/congressional-record/2013/3/15/house-section/article /H1435-4.

34 See "Alito Mouths 'Not True' as Obama Criticizes Sup Ct for Opening

Floodgates to Special Interests," http://www.youtube.com/watch?v
=4pB5uR3zgsA.

35 Amy Chozick, "Planet Hillary," *New York Times Magazine*, January
24, 2014, http://www.nytimes.com/2014/01/26/magazine/hillary
-clinton.html?&module=ArrowsNav&contentCollection=Magazine
&action=keypress&region=FixedLeft&pgtype=article.

36 Joshua Green, "Inside the Clinton Shake-Up," *The Atlantic*, February
12, 2008, http://www.theatlantic.com/magazine/archive/2008/02
/inside-the-clinton-shake-up/306684/.

37 Eric Woodard interview with authors, November 2013.

38 George Packer, "Washington Man," *New Yorker*, October 29, 2012,
http://www.newyorker.com/reporting/2012/10/29/121029fa_fact
_packer.

39 William Douglas, "Newt Gingrich's Mouth Is Famous as a Verbal
Blowtorch," McClatchy Newspapers, December 15, 2011, http://www
.mcclatchydc.com/2011/12/15/133216/newt-gingrichs-mouth-is
-famous.html#storylink=cpy.

40 PBS *Frontline*, Frank Luntz interview, conducted November 13,
2006, http://www.pbs.org/wgbh/pages/frontline/hotpolitics/inter
views/luntz.html.

41 Joan Walsh, "Stay Classy, Frank Luntz," *Salon*, October 24, 2012,
http://www.salon.com/2012/10/24/stay_classy_frank_luntz/.

42 Hank Stephenson, "State Representative Stands by Her Comparison
of Obama to Hitler," *Arizona Capitol Times*, October 7, 2013, http://
azcapitoltimes.com/news/2013/10/07/state-representative-stands
-by-her-comparison-of-obama-to-hitler/.

43 Doug Heye, "The Left's Limited Outrage at Hitler Comparisons," *U.S.
News.com*, October 6, 2011, http://www.usnews.com/opinion/blogs
/doug-heye/2011/10/06/celebs-should-avoid-the-hitler-president
-comparison-be-it-bush-or-obama.

44 David Mark, *Going Dirty: The Art of Negative Campaigning* (New
York: Rowman & Littlefield, 2006), 221.

45 Marti Lotman, "Dershowitz: Iran Nukes Would Mark 'Neville Chamberlain Moment' for Obama," *Newsmax.com*, November 15, 2013,

http://www.newsmax.com/Newsfront/Dershowitz-Chamberlain
-Iran-nukes/2013/11/15/id/536955.

46 Robert Self, "Was Neville Chamberlain Really a Weak and Terrible
Leader?" BBC.co.uk, September 30, 2013, http://www.bbc.co.uk
/news/magazine-24300094.

47 Alan Greenblatt, "Morale Plummets for Federal Workers Facing
Unending Furlough," NPR.org, October 5, 2013, http://www.npr
.org/2013/10/05/229301173/morale-plummets-for-federal-workers
-facing-unending-furlough.

48 WAMU.org, "Analysis: Stop Calling Federal Employees 'Nonessential,'" October 4, 2013, http://wamu.org/news/13/10/04
/analysis_stop_calling_federal_employees_non_essential.

49 Mackinac Center for Public Policy, "The Overton Window," https://
www.mackinac.org/OvertonWindow.

50 Balloon Juice, "Lexicon (A–H)," http://www.balloon-juice.com
/balloon-juice-lexicon-a-h/#H.

51 "Driving Mr. Obama," TheAtlantic.org, http://assets.theatlantic.com
/static/mt/assets/podcasts/motorcade-smaller.jpg.

52 See "The Daily Show with Jon Stewart, Grover Norquist," http://
www.thedailyshow.com/watch/mon-march-12-2012/grover-norquist.

53 See "The Pledge: Grover Norquist's Hold on the GOP," http://www
.cbsnews.com/videos/the-pledge-grover-norquists-hold-on-the
-gop/.

54 Representative Scott Rigell website, November 13, 2012, http://rigell
.house.gov/news/documentsingle.aspx?DocumentID=312261.

55 Coral Davenport, "Out on the Town with Grover Norquist," National
Journal, September 1, 2012, http://www.nationaljournal.com/2012
-conventions/out-on-the-town-with-grover-norquist-20120901.

56 Safire's Political Dictionary, 612.

57 See "McCain: Obama Is a Decent Person," http://www.youtube.com
/watch?v=m_O7AjyWJWU.

58 Dan Murphy, "Commentary: An Orgy of Red Meat," Drovers Cattle
Network.com, September 4, 2012, http://www.cattlenetwork.com
/cattle-news/Commentary-An-orgy-of-red-meat-168507266.html.

59 Eric Lipton, "A Journey from Lawmaker to Lobbyist and Back

Again," *New York Times*, November 13, 2010, http://www.nytimes
.com/2010/11/14/us/politics/14coats.html.

60 Mary Beth Schneider, "Bio: Senate Race Is Coats' Greatest Challenge," *Indianapolis Star*, September 10, 2010, http://www.indystar
.com/article/20100907/NEWS05/9070327/.

61 Sarah McKinnon Bryner, "From Hired Guns to Hired Hands:
'Reverse Revolvers in the 111th and 112th Congresses," Center for
Responsive Politics report, July 2011, www.opensecrets.org/news
/Hired%20Guns%20to%20Hired%20Hands.pdf.

62 See "'Blame America First'—Jeane Kirkpatrick's 1984 GOP Convention Speech," YouTube video, 7:39, from the 1984 Republican
National Convention, posted by "Levan Ramishvili," February 14,
2012, http://www.youtube.com/watch?v=Dv8L-cuq17s.

63 Joe Garofoli, "Three Dirty Words: San Francisco Values," *San Francisco Chronicle*, November 3, 2006, http://www.sfgate.com/politics
/joegarofoli/article/THREE-DIRTY-WORDS-SAN-FRANCISCO
-VALUES-2467246.php.

64 *TheTurnerReport.com*, "Akin Advisor: Claire McCaskill Has San
Francisco Values," October 11, 2012, http://rturner229.blogspot
.com/2012/10/akin-advisor-claire-mccaskill-has-san.html.

65 Garofoli, "Three Dirty Words."

66 David Mark, "Ex-Congressman Blasts John Boehner," *Politix*, March
24, 2013, http://politix.topix.com/homepage/5239-ex-congressman
-blasts-john-boehner.

67 CBSNews.com, "Slam Dunk," April 26, 2007, http://www.cbsnews
.com/news/slam-dunk/.

68 Alan Freeman, "Nevada Voters Come Out for Bush and Brothels,"
Toronto Globe and Mail, November 9, 2004.

69 Michael Steele interview with authors, November 2013.

70 Jackie Koszczuk, "Ann Romney Insult Sparks Twitter War between
Top Politicos," *National Journal*, April 14, 2012, http://news.yahoo
.com/ann-romney-insult-sparks-twitter-war-between-top-183803
849.html.

71 Eni Mustafaraj and Panagiotis Metaxas, "From Obscurity to Prominence in Minutes: Political Speech and Real-Time Search," in Pro-

ceedings of the WebSci10: Extending the Frontiers of Society On-Line, April 26–27, 2010, http://journal.webscience.org/317/.

72 Jennifer Epstein, "Poll: Americans Confused by Budget," *Politico*, March 2, 2011, http://www.politico.com/news/stories/0311/50486 .html.

73 Website of House Speaker John Boehner, "Speaker Boehner: A Growing Economy Is Our Best Weapon against Poverty and Hunger," September 19, 2013, http://www.speaker.gov/press-release/speaker -boehner-growing-economy-our-best-weapon-against-poverty -hunger.

74 Jonathan Cohn, "The Recovery Act Was Virtually Free of Waste, Fraud and Abuse. That's Too Bad," *New Republic*, October 4, 2010, http://www.newrepublic.com/blog/jonathan-cohn/78149/stimulus -recovery-spending-waste-fraud.

75 Emi Kolawole, "Angle Attacks Reid Over 'Coked-up Stimulus Monkeys,'" *Washington Post*, August 3, 2010, http://voices.wash ingtonpost.com/44/2010/08/angle-attacks-reid-over-coked-.html.

76 White House website, "Policies to Crack Down on Waste, Fraud and Abuse": http://www.whitehouse.gov/health-care-meeting/proposal /whatsnew/waste-fraud-abuse.

77 See *MotherJones.com*, "Full Transcript and Audio of Mitch McConnell's Campaign Meeting on Ashley Judd," http://www.motherjones .com/politics/2013/04/mcconnell-transcript.

CHAPTER 4. ON A GLIDE PATH WITH AN ODD COUPLE TO NUT-CUTTING TIME: THE LEGISLATIVE PROCESS

1 Peter Coy, "Did Larry Summers Get Borked? Not Really," Bloomberg Businessweek, September 16, 2013, http://www.businessweek.com /articles/2013-09-16/did-larry-summers-get-borked-not-really.

2 "Sounds: Bork," *Economist*, December 12, 2012, http://www.econo mist.com/blogs/johnson/2012/12/sounds.

3 See "Video: President Barack Obama Lauds Congress Fiscal Cliff Deal," Telegraph.co.uk, http://www.telegraph.co.uk/news/worldnews /barackobama/9775148/President-Barack-Obama-lauds-Congress -fiscal-cliff-deal.html.

4 U.S. Government Accountability Office, "Glossary of Terms Used in the Federal Budget Process," http://www.gao.gov/new.items /do5734sp.pdf.

5 "Parody," *The Weekly Standard*, December 1995.

6 Robert Reich, "Why Giving Republican Bullies a Bloody Nose Isn't Enough," *RobertReich.org*, October 12, 2013, http://robertreich.org /post/63873198693.

7 Steve Inskeep and Shankar Vedantam, "Why Compromise Is a Bad Word in Politics," NPR.org, March 13, 2012, http://www.npr.org /2012/03/13/148499310/why-compromise-is-terrible-politics.

8 Andrew Kacynski, "Congresswoman Uses Steak, Vodka and Caviar to Hammer Republicans on Food Stamp Cuts," *BuzzFeed*, September 19, 2013, http://www.buzzfeed.com/andrewkaczynski/democratic -congresswoman-uses-steak-vodka-and-caviar-to-hamm.

9 Darren Goode, "Dems Ask EPA to Move on Greenhouse Gas Regulations," *National Journal*, April 24, 2007.

10 Associated Press, "Senate OKs 700-Mile Border Fence," FoxNews .com, September 29, 2006, http://www.foxnews.com/story/2006 /09/29/senate-oks-700-mile-border-fence/.

11 Paul Kane, "House Republicans Broken into Fighting Factions," *Washington Post*, June 3, 2013, http://articles.washingtonpost.com /2013-06-03/politics/39711961_1_house-republicans-house-speaker -john-a-boehner.

12 Chuck Schumer transcript from Senate floor debate, June 26, 2013, http://beta.congress.gov/congressional-record/2013/06/26/senate -section/article/S5205-2.

13 White House transcript, "Remarks by the President and Vice President on Gun Violence," January 16, 2013, http://www.whitehouse .gov/the-press-office/2013/01/16/remarks-president-and-vice -president-gun-violence.

14 Manley interview, November 2013.

15 *National Journal*, "Outlook Still Murky for Broadband Vote," November 27, 2001, http://www.nationaljournal.com/member /daily/congressdailyam-telecommunications-outlook-still-murky -for-broadband-vote-20011127.

16 Dan Friedman, "Bernanke's Renomination Hits a Bump in the Road," *National Journal*, January 22, 2010, http://www.national journal.com/member/daily/bernanke-s-renomination-hits-a-bump -in-the-road-20100122.

17 Scott Wong, "Harry Reid: Gang of Six Plan 'Happy Talk,'" *Politico*, November 29, 2011, http://www.politico.com/news/stories/1111 /69339.html.

18 Ben Zimmer, "Happy Landings on the 'Glide Path,'" *VisualThesaurus .com*, December 9, 2008, http://www.visualthesaurus.com/cm/word routes/happy-landings-on-the-glide-path/.

19 Orrin Hatch speech transcript, July 29, 2011, http://www.gpo.gov /fdsys/pkg/CREC-2011-07-29/html/CREC-2011-07-29-pt1-PgS5057 .htm.

20 Charles Babington, "Hastert Launches a Partisan Policy," *Washington Post*, November 27, 2004, http://www.washingtonpost.com/wp-dyn /articles/A15423-2004Nov26.html.

21 Susan Ferrechio, "The Hastert Rule (According to Dennis Hastert)," *Washington Examiner*, September 20, 2013, http://washington examiner.com/the-hastert-rule-according-to-dennis-hastert /article/2536140.

22 Eleanor Clift, "Denny Hastert Disses the 'Hastert Rule': It 'Never Really Existed," *Daily Beast*, October 3, 2013, http://www.thedaily beast.com/articles/2013/10/03/denny-hastert-disses-the-hastert -rule-it-never-really-existed.html.

23 See MSNBC.com news release, "Exclusive: Nancy Pelosi: 'The Hastert Rule Isn't a Rule, It's an Excuse,'" November 3, 2013, http:// www.nbcumv.com/mediavillage/networks/msnbc/pressreleases?pr =contents/press-releases/2013/11/03/exclusivenancyp1467546.xml.

24 Emily Heil, "Hideaways—The Senate's Hottest Real Estate," *Roll Call*, January 20, 2011, http://www.rollcall.com/features/Welcome -Congress_2011/welcome_congress/-202612-1.html.

25 Derek Wallbank, "Senatorial Seclusion: An Inside View of Capitol Hideaways," *MinnPost*, September 8, 2010, http://www.minnpost .com/dc-dispatches/2010/09/senatorial-seclusion-inside-view -capitol-hideaways.

26 CBSNews.com, "Boehner Echoes Obama on Sequester Talks: 'Hope Springs Eternal,'" February 25, 2013, http://www.cbsnews.com /videos/boehner-echoes-obama-on-sequester-talks-hope-springs -eternal/.

27 Associated Press, "Lawmaker Wants Voting Age Dropped to 17," June 23, 2008, http://news.google.com/newspapers?nid=2245& dat=20080623&id=eQRSAAAAIBAJ&sjid=uzQNAAAAIBAJ& pg=7163,4798602.

28 Anthony York, "Torricelli to Senator: 'I'm Going to Cut Your Balls Off!'" Salon.com, April 30, 2011, http://www.salon.com/2001/04/30 /blue_56/.

29 *National Journal's Hotline*, "White House 2000: Kerrey—Can He Carry It Off?" Septemebr 16, 1997, http://www.nationaljournal.com /member/hotline/white-house-2000-kerrey-can-he-carry-it-off --19970916.

30 *National Journal*, "Top News," October 1, 2010, http://www.national journal.com/njonline/no_20101001_9899.php.

31 Mathern interview, November 2013.

32 Dennis Byrne, "It's Nut-Cutting Time for Rep. Bill Foster," *Chicago-Now*, April 15, 2013, http://www.chicagonow.com/dennis-byrnes -barbershop/2013/04/its-nut-cutting-time-for-rep-bill-foster/.

33 Arlette Saenz, "Nuclear Flashback: When Harry Reid and Mitch McConnell Sang Different Tunes," ABCNews.com, July 14, 2013, http://abcnews.go.com/blogs/politics/2013/07/nuclear-flashback -when-harry-reid-and-mitch-mcconnell-sang-different-tunes/.

34 U.S. Senate Democrats website, "Fact Check: Minority Leader McConnell and Republican Obstruction," September 4, 2007, http:// democrats.senate.gov/2007/09/04/fact-check-minority-leader -mcconnell-and-republican-obstruction/.

35 Bennett interview with authors, November 2013.

36 Catherine Hollander, "Know What It Means to Be 'On the Flagpole'?" *National Journal*, July 30, 2013, http://www.nationaljournal.com /daily/know-what-it-means-to-be-on-the-flagpole-20130730.

37 Dennis Hastert, *Speaker: Lessons from Forty Years in Coaching and Politics* (Washington, DC: Regnery Publishing, 2004), 112.

38 Kathryn Pearson, "'One Minute Attack Speeches Becoming Routine in U.S. House," *MinnPost*, September 22, 2009, http://www.minn post.com/politics-policy/2009/09/one-minute-attack-speeches -becoming-routine-us-house.

39 Richard Connelly, "Talky? You Bet!" *Houston Press*, February 12, 2004, http://www.houstonpress.com/2004-02-12/news/talky-you -bet/.

40 Sherrod Brown, *Congress from the Inside: Observations from the Majority and Minority* (Kent, OH: Kent State University Press, 2004), 93.

41 Robert M. Andrews, "Now It Can Be Said: The Other Body Is the Senate," Associated Press, January 31, 1987, http://www.apnews archive.com/1987/Now-It-Can-Be-Said-The-Other-Body-is-the -Senate/id-6079b37808d2af6ffe22d80da8dcc5a1.

42 Arcuri interview with authors, October 2013.

43 John Feehery, "Return to Regular Order," *The Hill*, January 13, 2013, http://thehill.com/opinion/columnists/john-feehery/276071-return -to-regular-order.

44 Visclosky interview.

45 Darren Goode, "Senate Republicans Slow-Walk Global Warming Measure," *National Journal*, June 4, 2008, http://www.national journal.com/daily/senate-republicans-slow-walk-global-warming -measure-20080604.

46 See "Boehner: Obama 'Slow-Walking' to Fiscal Cliff," *ABC News*, 2:08, posted by "bulcevap," December 11, 2012, http://www.youtube.com /watch?v=emfD4XVZRak.

47 *Safire's Political Dictionary*, 668.

48 Naureen Khan, "Obama Goes 'Small-Bore' on Gun Control," AlJazeera.com, August 29, 2013, http://america.aljazeera.com/ articles/2013/8/29/obama-admin-quietlyrollsoutsmallboregun controlmeasures.html.

49 Kelly Ayotte transcript, ABC's *This Week with George Stephanopolous*, July 15, 2012, http://abcnews.go.com/Politics/week-transcript -mayor-rahm-emanuel-sen-kelly-ayotte/story?id=16763931&page=5.

50 NPR.org, "After Leaving Senate, Snowe Is Still 'Fighting for Common

Ground,'" May 13, 2013, http://www.npr.org/2013/05/13/182640887
/after-leaving-senate-snowe-is-still-fighting-for-common-ground.

51 Jay Rockefeller floor speech transcript, February 17, 2011, http://
thomas.loc.gov/cgi-bin/query/z?r112:S17FE1-0014.

52 Ron Wyden floor speech transcript, September 11, 2013, http://beta
.congress.gov/congressional-record/2013/9/11/senate-section/article
/S6350-4.

53 John Boehner tweet, https://twitter.com/SpeakerBoehner/status
/403637535479320576.

54 FoxNews.com, "Guy Benson: GOP Needs to Tackle 'Train Wreck'
That's ObamaCare," October 16, 2013, http://www.foxnews.com
/politics/2013/10/16/guy-benson-gop-needs-to-tackle-entitlements
-soaring-debt/.

CHAPTER 5. DEAD MONEY, DOG WHISTLES, AND DROPPIN'
THE G'S: THE LINGO OF CAMPAIGNS AND ELECTIONS

1 U.S. Department of Defense Joint Publication 1-02, "Department of
Defense Dictionary of Military and Associated Terms," http://www
.dtic.mil/doctrine/new_pubs/jp1_02.pdf.

2 Steve Martin, *Born Standing Up* (New York: Scribner, 2007), 142–43.

3 Brian Donahue interview with authors, November 2013.

4 Alex Wade, "Good and Bad Reviews: The Ethical Debate Over 'Astroturfing,'" *The Guardian*, January 11, 2011, http://www.theguardian
.com/media-tech-law/astroturfing-posting-fake-reviews.

5 *WordSpy.com*, "Grasstops," http://wordspy.com/words/grasstops
.asp.

6 Political Transcript Wire, "Former Rep. Newt Gingrich is Interviewed on MSNBC," December 29, 2011.

7 University of California–Santa Barbara American Presidency Project,
"The Post-Convention Bounce in Voters' Preference, 1964–2012,"
http://www.presidency.ucsb.edu/data/convention_bounces.php.

8 Steven Shepard, "Researcher Examines Variation of the 'Bradley
Effect,'" *National Journal*, May 18, 2012, http://www.nationaljournal
.com/2012-presidential-campaign/researcher-examines-variation
-of-the-bradley-effect-20120518.

9 Al Kamen, "A Tip Sheet for The Would-Be Nominee," *Washington Post*, January 23, 2013, http://articles.washingtonpost.com/2013 -01-23/politics/36504019_1_senate-seat-president-obama -appointments.

10 Drew Katchen, "Barney Frank: I'm Interested in Being Temporary Mass. Senator," NBCNews.com, January 4, 2013, http://www.nbc news.com/id/50362758/#.UqyhdY1OBV4.

11 Jim VandeHei and Dan Balz, "Kerry Picks Edwards as Running Mate," *Washington Post*, July 7, 2004, http://www.washingtonpost .com/wp-dyn/articles/A30354-2004Jul6.html.

12 Jim Galloway, "David Johnson and His Troubled Strategic Vision Promise Crosstabs with Every Poll," *Atlanta Journal-Constitution*, September 27, 2009, http://blogs.ajc.com/political-insider-jim -galloway/2009/09/27/strategic-vision-promises-crosstabs-with -every-poll/.

13 Brian M. Rosenthal, "Washington Ballot Issues Draw Money from Near, Afar," *Seattle Times*, November 2, 2003, http://seattletimes .com/html/localnews/2022180905_electionspendingxml.html.

14 Dan Brekke, "State Levies Fines in Epic Campaign Money-Laundering Case," *KQED News Fix*, October 24, 2013, http://blogs. kqed.org/newsfix/2013/10/24/fppc-fine-campaign-money-launder ing-case.

15 David Latt, "Sarah Palin's Dead Cat Bounce," *Huffington Post*, October 12, 2008, http://www.huffingtonpost.com/david-latt/sarah -palins-dead-cat-bou_b_133929.html.

16 Amy Sullivan, "Do the Democrats Have a Prayer?" *Washington Monthly*, June 2003, http://www.washingtonmonthly.com/features /2003/0306.sullivan.html.

17 Bethany Albertson, "Dog-Whistle Politics, Coded Communication and Religious Appeals," paper for the University of Chicago and Princeton University, May 31, 2006, www.princeton.edu/csdp/events /Albertson053106/Albertson053106.pdf.

18 Rick Perlstein, "Exclusive: Lee Atwater's Infamous 1981 Interview on the Southern Strategy," *The Nation*, November 13, 2012, http://www

.thenation.com/article/170841/exclusive-lee-atwaters-infamous-1981
-interview-southern-strategy.

19 Fox News network transcript, September 19, 2012.

20 Rick Wilson interview with authors, November 2013.

21 Michael D. Shear, "White House Rebuts Allegation That Big Donors Get Special Perks," *Washington Post*, October 27, 2009, http://articles .washingtonpost.com/2009-10-27/politics/36911738_1_white-house -obama-administration-donors.

22 Meredith Jessup, "Obama Discriminates Against the Letter G," *The Blaze*, September 25, 2011, http://www.theblaze.com/blog/2011/09 /25/why-does-obama-discriminate-against-the-letter-g/.

23 Grace Wyler, "CREEPY: Mitt Romney Is Asking for Hugs from Southern Girls," *Business Insider*, March 13, 2002, http://www .businessinsider.com/mitt-romney-asks-for-hugs-from-southern -girls-2012-3.

24 Patrick Gavin, "Lipton: Obama Shouldn't Drop His G's," *Politico*, June 8, 2012, http://www.politico.com/news/stories/0612/77203 .html.

25 Erin McClam, "The Making of Hillary Clinton: 15 Moments That Define Her Public Life," NBCNews.com, February 1, 2013, http:// usnews.nbcnews.com/_news/2013/02/01/16791796-the-making-of -hillary-clinton-15-moments-that-define-her-public-life.

26 Huma Khan, "'I Won: President Obama Works to Be Bipartisan but Shows There Are Clear Limits," ABCNews.com, January 23, 2009, http://abcnews.go.com/blogs/politics/2009/01/i-won-president/.

27 PBS *NewsHour* transcript, "Gore Urges Congress to Take Action on Climate Change," PBS.org, March 21, 2007, http://www.pbs.org /newshour/bb/environment/jan-june07/gore_03-21.html.

28 "Sen. Harkin on Filibuster: 'We've Got to Change The Rules,'" NPR transcript, November 20, 2013, http://m.npr.org/news/Politics /246409440?start=10.

29 Steven T. Dennis, "Pelosi Defends Democrats' Vetting of Stimulus Plan," *Roll Call*, January 22, 2009, http://www.rollcall.com/news /-31650-1.html.

30 Daniel Halper, "Nancy Pelosi: 'Elections Shouldn't Matter as Much as They Do,'" *Weekly Standard*, April 12, 2011, http://www.weekly standard.com/blogs/nancy-pelosi-elections-shouldnt-matter-much -they-do_557307.html.

31 Glen Johnson, "Romney Announces Exploratory Committee," *Boston Globe*, April 11, 2011, http://www.boston.com/news/politics/political intelligence/2011/04/romney_announce_2.html.

32 Mark Kellam and Jason Wells, "As Campaigns Wind Down, Rhetoric and Accusations Heat Up," *Glendale News-Press*, November 5, 2012, http://articles.glendalenewspress.com/2012-11-05/news/tn-gnp -1105-as-campaigns-wind-down-rhetoric-and-accusations-heat-up _1_d-silver-lake-assemblyman-mike-gatto-campaigns-wind/2.

33 See "Harry Reid Rips Conspiracy Theorists: I WILL Vote for Dianne Feinstein Assault Weapon Ban," YouTube video, 1:52, posted by "Les Grossman" April 17, 2013, http://www.youtube.com/watch?v =kRwwwXqghyY.

34 *This American Life* transcript, "Take the Money and Run for Office," March 30, 2012, http://www.thisamericanlife.org/radio-archives /episode/461/transcript.

35 Shushannah Walshe, "Paul Ryan Meeting with Sheldon Adelson in Vegas," ABCNews.com, August 14, 2012, http://abcnews.go.com /blogs/politics/2012/08/paul-ryan-meets-with-sheldon-adelson -at-vegas-event/.

36 Kitty Felde, "It's Jeff Denham's Party (for His Party) and He'll Invite LeAnn Rimes If He Wants To," *Southern California Public Radio*, January 4, 2011, http://www.scpr.org/blogs/kitty-felde/2011/01/04 /2509/its-jeff-denhams-party-his-party-and-hell-invite-l/.

37 Eric Lipton and Ben Protess, "Banks' Lobbyists Help in Drafting Financial Bills," *New York Times*, May 23, 2013, http://dealbook .nytimes.com/2013/05/23/banks-lobbyists-help-in-drafting -financial-bills/?_r=0.

38 Linda Dorcena Forry for State Senate, "Help Me Kick This Off!," http://myemail.constantcontact.com/Help-me-kick-this-off-.html ?soid=1112524074139&aid=AMFkSKFaZpk.

39 Melissa Silverberg, "Drake: Campaign for Arlington Heights Leader Is about 'The Future,'" *Daily Herald.com*, April 7, 2013, http://www .dailyherald.com/article/20130403/news/704039995/.

40 Laura Figueroa, "Thomas Suozzi, Adam Haber Attend Democrats' Spring Fundraiser," *Newsday*, April 15, 2013, http://www.newsday .com/long-island/nassau/thomas-suozzi-adam-haber-attend -democrats-spring-fundraiser-1.5078828.

41 Robert Draper, "Can the Democrats Catch Up in the Super-PAC Game?" *New York Times Magazine*, July 5, 2012, http://www.nytimes .com/2012/07/08/magazine/can-the-democrats-catch-up-in-the -super-pac-game.html.

42 Stuart Rothenberg, "Obama's New Political Reality Is Bad News for Dems in 2014," *Roll Call*, May 14, 2013, http://blogs.rollcall.com /rothenblog/obamas-new-political-reality-is-bad-news-for-dems -in-14/.

43 Bethany Albertson interview with authors, November 2013.

44 John Sides and Lynn Vavreck, *The Gamble: Choice and Chance in the 2012 Presidential Election* (Princeton, NJ: Princeton University Press, 2013), 1.

45 Mark Silva, "Getting Primaried: The Dreaded Verb," *Bloomberg.com*, December 14, 2012, http://go.bloomberg.com/political-capital/2012 -12-14/getting-primaried-the-dreaded-verb/.

46 FoxNews.com, "Palin Says Fiscal Conservatives Are 'More Energized Than Ever,'" October 17, 2013, http://www.foxnews.com/politics /2013/10/17/palin-says-fiscal-conservatives-more-energized-than -ever-after-end-budget/.

47 Lisa Murkowski interview with authors, November 2013.

48 Rick Wilson interview with authors, November 2013.

49 Ben Feller, "Obama Tells Students: 'Don't Boo. Vote,'" Associated Press, September 2, 2012, http://news.yahoo.com/obama-tells -students-dont-boo-vote-202042464--election.html.

50 Frank Bruni, "Show Us Your Woe," *New York Times*, May 18, 2013, http://www.nytimes.com/2013/05/19/opinion/sunday/bruni-show -us-your-woe.html.

51 Larry J. Sabato, "Do Endorsements Matter?" *Wall Street Journal*, January 24, 2013, http://online.wsj.com/news/articles/SB100014240 5297020380650457717888241663792 6.

52 University of California–Santa Barbara American Presidency Project, "2012 General Election Endorsements By Major Newspapers," http://www.presidency.ucsb.edu/data/2012_newspaper_endorsements.php.

53 Chris Cillizza, "The Fix Archive: Fix Endorsement Hierarchy," *Washington Post*, http://voices.washingtonpost.com/thefix/fix-endorse ment-hierarchy/.

54 Rich Galen, "Happy New Year!" CNSNews.com, September 30, 2013, http://cnsnews.com/commentary/rich-galen/happy-new-year.

55 Bernie Becker and Erik Wasson, "Top Tax-Writer Baucus Shows His Hand with Senate Budget Vote," *The Hill*, March 26, 2013, http://thehill.com/homenews/senate/290491-top-tax-writer-baucus-shows -his-hand-with-budget-vote.

56 Byron Dorgan interview with authors, October 2013.

57 Noam Schreiber, "The Internal Polls That Made Mitt Romney Think He'd Win," *New Republic*, November 30, 2012, http://www.new republic.com/blog/plank/110597/exclusive-the-polls-made-mitt -romney-think-hed-win.

58 American Principles In Action, "Building a Winning GOP Coalition: The Lessons of 2012," October 2013, http://www.americanprinciples inaction.org/gop-autopsy-report-2013/.

59 Tom Serres, "No Debate: Offline Is the Rocket Fuel of Online Political Giving," *Huffington Post*, October 22, 2012, http://www.huffing tonpost.com/tom-serres/online-political-fundraising_b_2001868 .html.

60 Chuck McCutcheon, "Black Knights and Dead Parrots: Monty Python and the Presidential Race," *National Journal*, June 26, 2012, http://www.nationaljournal.com/politics/black-knights-and-dead -parrots-monty-python-and-the-presidential-race-20120626.

61 Zeke Miller, "Mitt Romney Inc.: The White House That Never Was," *Time*, June 2, 2013, http://swampland.time.com/2013/06/02/mitt -romney-inc-the-white-house-that-never-was/.

62 Ben Smith, "A Haircut Tip," *Politico*, November 10, 2009, http://www.politico.com/blogs/bensmith/1109/A_haircut_tip.html.

63 Brett Logiurato, "Fox News' Chris Wallace: 'As Soon as We Announced Ted Cruz as a Guest, Republicans Wanted Us to Hammer Him,'" *Business Insider*, September 23, 2013, http://www.businessinsider.com/chris-wallace-ted-cruz-fox-news-shutdown-government-obamacare-defund-2013-9.

64 Stacy Kaper, "Obama's Housing Plan May Be about Optics, Not Substance," *National Journal*, March 6, 2012, http://www.nationaljournal.com/member/economy/obama-s-housing-plan-may-be-about-optics-not-substance-20120306.

65 Ben Zimmer, "Optics," *New York Times Magazine*, March 4, 2010, http://www.nytimes.com/2010/03/07/magazine/07FOB-onlanguage-t.html.

66 Martin Frost interview with authors, November 2013.

67 Charlie Spiering, "Ted Cruz, Mike Lee Vow to Keep On Keeping On against Obamacare," *Washington Examiner.com*, October 17, 2013, http://washingtonexaminer.com/ted-cruz-mike-lee-vow-to-keep-on-keeping-on-against-obamacare/article/2537346.

68 Dan Amira, "Romney Can't Quote 'Bean Bag' Aphorism Correctly," *New York*, January 30, 2012, http://nymag.com/daily/intelligencer/2012/01/romney-cant-quote-bean-bag-aphorism-correctly.html.

69 Amanda Marcotte, "Sanford Supporters Go Weirder with Accusatory Push Poll about Colbert Busch," *Slate*, May 2, 2013, http://www.slate.com/blogs/xx_factor/2013/05/02/elizabeth_colbert_busch_linked_to_abortion_crime_and_debt_in_bizarre_south.html.

70 Jamie Hanlon, "Hypothetically Tweaking," UniversityOfAlberta.com, October 5, 2011, http://news.ualberta.ca/newsarticles/2011/10/hypotheticallytweaking.

71 Amanda Terkel, "Virginia Robocalls Accuse Terry McAuliffe of Backing 'Abortion on Demand," *Huffington Post*, November 5, 2013, http://www.huffingtonpost.com/2013/11/05/virginia-robocalls_n_4219898.html.

72 Sarah Lai Stirland, "Anti-Robocall Crusader Pushes for a Crackdown

on Political Phone Droids," *Wired*, July 23, 2008, http://www.wired
.com/threatlevel/2008/07/anti-robocall-c/.

73 Steve Brusk, "Democrat Kathy Hochul Wins House Seat in New York
Special Election," CNN.com, May 25, 2011, http://www.cnn.com/2011
/POLITICS/05/25/new.york.special.election/.

74 David Smith and Thomas L. Brunell, "Special Elections to the U.S.
House of Representatives: A General Election Barometer?" *Legislative Studies Quarterly* 35, no. 2 (May 2010), www.utdallas.edu
/~tbrunell/papers/Special_Elections_LSQ_FINAL.pdf.

75 Gregory Cowles, "Inside the List," *New York Times*, February 17, 2013,
http://www.nytimes.com/2013/02/17/books/review/inside-the-list
.html.

76 John Harwood tweet, October 13, 2013, https://twitter.com/JohnJ
Harwood/status/389537537347178496.

77 Dennis Prager, "November Is a Plebiscite on the American Revolution," *Townhall*, May 1, 2012, http://www.dennisprager.com/novem
ber-is-a-plebiscite-on-the-american-revolution/.

78 Jonathan Cohn, "The Most Important Election of Our Lives," *New
Republic*, November 4, 2012, http://www.newrepublic.com/article
/109648/case-re-electing-obama-and-feeling-good-about-it.

79 Nathan L. Gonzales, "Six Things Losing Candidates Say," *Roll Call*,
August 22, 2013, http://blogs.rollcall.com/rothenblog/six-things
-losing-candidates-say/.

CHAPTER 6. HAVING TO EXPLAIN BLOWBACK
ON THE TICK-TOCK: THE MEDIA AND SCANDALS

1 Douglas Brinkley, "Joe Biden: The *Rolling Stone* Interview," *Rolling
Stone*, May 9, 2013, http://www.rollingstone.com/politics/news/joe
-biden-the-rolling-stone-interview-20130509.

2 Caitlin McDevitt, "Kid Rock on Why He Stumped for Mitt," *Politico*,
June 19, 2013, http://www.politico.com/blogs/click/2013/06/kid
-rock-on-why-he-stumped-for-mitt-166620.html.

3 CNN.com, "Clinton Weighs In on Bin Laden, War in Iraq," July 9,
2004, http://www.cnn.com/2004/ALLPOLITICS/07/09/clinton/.

4 Henry C. Jackson, "Some Candidates Mum on Tough Policy Ques-

tions," Associated Press, October 15, 2012, http://bigstory.ap.org
/article/some-candidates-mum-tough-policy-questions.

5 David A. Farenthold, "House Conservatives Face Up to Their Defeat,"
Washington Post, October 16, 2013, http://www.washingtonpost.com
/politics/house-conservatives-face-up-to-their-defeat/2013/10/16
/00c745b8-3697-11e3-80c6-7e6dd8d22d8f_story.html.

6 Maureen Dowd, "When Myths Collide in the Capital," *New York
Times*, May 11, 2013, http://www.nytimes.com/2013/05/12/opinion
/sunday/dowd-when-myths-collide-in-the-capital.html.

7 Brett Logiurato, "Cory Booker Campaign Slams *National Review*
after Allegations That He Made Up a Drug-Dealing Friend," *Business Insider*, August 30, 2013, http://www.businessinsider.com/cory
-booker-t-bone-national-review-drug-dealer-2013-8.

8 Mike Nizza, "D.C. Madam's List Yields a Senator," *New York Times*,
July 10, 2007, http://thelede.blogs.nytimes.com/2007/07/10/dc
-madams-list-yields-a-senator/.

9 Chuck McCutcheon, "Abramoff Still Biggest Thorn in Lobbying
Industry's Side," *CQ Press' First Street Research Group*, March 15,
2012.

10 Chung Joo Chung et al., "Exploring Online News Credibility: The
Relative Influence of Traditional and Technological Factors," *Journal
of Computer-Mediated Communication* 17 no. 2 (January 13, 2012),
onlinelibrary.wiley.com/doi/10.1111/j.1083-6101.2011.01565.x/pdf.

11 See "Gov Getting News He Won Puerto Rico," http://www.youtube
.com/watch?v=dsSe3pjCWUA&list=PLE5A1ADBF716CF98F.

12 Peter Hamby, "Did Twitter Kill the Boys on the Bus?" Joan Shorenstein Center on the Press and Public Policy, September 2013, http://
shorensteincenter.org/wp-content/uploads/2013/08/d80_hamby
.pdf.

13 *Larry King Live* transcript, CNN.com, September 30, 2008, http://
transcripts.cnn.com/TRANSCRIPTS/0809/30/lkl.01.html.

14 Dylan Byers, "Santorum Accuses Media of Double Standard,"
Politico, February 17, 2012, http://www.politico.com/blogs/media
/2012/02/santorum-accuses-media-of-double-standard-114843
.html.

15 Jules Witcover, "Twitter Is Killing Political Journalism," *Baltimore Sun*, September 8, 2013, http://articles.baltimoresun.com/2013-09-08/news/bs-ed-witcover-twitter-20130908_1_campaign-coverage-mitt-romney-campaign-reporters.

16 Association for Psychological Science news release, "Extreme Political Attitudes May Stem from an Illusion of Understanding," April 29, 2013, http://www.psychologicalscience.org/index.php/news/releases/extreme-political-attitudes-may-stem-from-an-illusion-of-understanding.html.

17 Roger Simon, "Questions That Kill Candidates' Careers," *Politico*, April 20, 2007, http://www.politico.com/news/stories/0407/3617.html.

18 Michael Kinsley, "In Defense of Hypothetical Questions," *Slate*, October 2, 2003, http://www.slate.com/articles/news_and_politics/readme/2003/10/just_supposin.html.

19 Republican presidential debate transcript, CNN.com, June 5, 2007, http://transcripts.cnn.com/TRANSCRIPTS/0706/05/se.01.html.

20 Melissa Anders, "Michigan Gov. Rick Snyder Pushed for Opinions on Gay Rights Issues," *MLive.com*, October 24, 2013, http://www.mlive.com/politics/index.ssf/2013/10/michigan_gay_civil_rights_disc.html.

21 Steven Poole, "Misspeak," *Unspeak.net*, March 25, 2008, http://unspeak.net/misspeak/.

22 Maggie Haberman, "Romney: I Misspoke on 'Very Poor,'" *Politico*, February 2, 2013, http://www.politico.com/blogs/burns-haberman/2012/02/romney-i-misspoke-on-very-poor-113342.html.

23 Anthony Bartkewicz, "Mitt Romney and Paul Ryan Rebuke Todd Akin's Comments on 'Legitimate Rape' and Pregnancy Despite Ryan's Anti-Abortion History," *New York Daily News*, August 20, 2012, http://www.nydailynews.com/news/politics/mitt-romney-paul-ryan-rebuke-todd-akin-comments-legitimate-rape-pregnancy-ryan-anti-abortion-history-article-1.1140200.

24 Ron Allen, "Word of the Day: 'Misspoke,'" NBCNews.com, March 25, 2008, http://firstread.nbcnews.com/_news/2008/03/25/4438889-word-of-the-day-misspoke.

25 "Word of the Week: Kinsley Gaffe," *Fritinancy*, August 22, 2011, http://nancyfriedman.typepad.com/away_with_words/2011/08/word-of-the-week-kinsley-gaffe.html.

26 M. J. Stephey, "Top 10 Hot Mic Moments: Bush's Major League Mistake," *Time*, March 27, 2012, http://content.time.com/time/specials/packages/article/0,28804,1821563_1821568_1821597,00.html.

27 Larry Downing, "Obama Tells Russia's Medvedev He'll Have More Flexibility after Election," *Reuters*, May 26, 2012, http://www.reuters.com/article/2012/03/26/us-nuclear-summit-obama-medvedev-idUSBRE82P0JI20120326.

28 Karl Vick, "Sarkozy to Obama: 'I Cannot Bear Netanyahu. He's A Liar," *Time*, November 9, 2011, http://world.time.com/2011/11/09/sarkozy-to-obama-i-cannot-bear-netanyahu-hes-a-liar/.

29 John T. Gasper and Andrew Reeves, "Make It Rain? Retrospection and the Attentive Electorate in the Context of Natural Disasters," *American Journal of Political Science* 55, no. 2 (April 2011), andrewreeves.org/sites/default/files/rain.pdf.

30 Jenna Portnoy, "Once Again, Christie Thrives amid Crisis as Seaside Fire Reminiscent of Sandy," *The Star-Ledger*, September 17, 2013, http://www.nj.com/politics/index.ssf/2013/09/christie_sandy_response.html.

31 Timothy Noah, "A Beat-Sweetener Sampler," *Slate*, April 8, 2009, http://www.slate.com/articles/news_and_politics/chatterbox/2009/04/a_beatsweetener_sampler.html.

32 Ben Schott and Mark Leibovich, "Washington Words," *New York Times*, September 6, 2013, http://www.nytimes.com/interactive/2013/09/08/opinion/sunday/ben-schott-washington-words.html.

33 Jon Lackman, "It's Time to Retire 'Kabuki,'" *Slate*, April 14, 2010, http://www.slate.com/articles/life/the_good_word/2010/04/its_time_to_retire_kabuki.html.

34 George Hoare, "Telling Stories about Politics: The Concept of Political Narrative and 'Left Versus Right,'" paper presented at University of Oxford graduate workshop, September 18, 2010, http://www.academia.edu/340888/Telling_stories_about_politics_the_concept_of_political_narrative_and_Left_Versus_Right.

35 Niall Stanage and Amie Parnes, "Gloomy Anniversary for Obama," *The Hill*, November 6, 2013, http://thehill.com/homenews/adminis tration/189375-gloomy-anniversary-for-obama.

36 Clarence Page, "How Stories, True or Not, Drive Politics," *Chicago Tribune*, September 15, 2010, http://articles.chicagotribune.com /2010-09-15/news/ct-oped-0915-page-20100915_1_narrative -obama-muslim-drive-politics.

37 Rachel Sklar, "The Origin of the Term 'NerdProm': Ana Maria Cox and Twitter," Mediaite.com, May 5, 2010, http://www.mediaite.com /online/the-origin-of-the-term-nerdprom-ana-marie-cox-and -twitter/.

38 Susan Milligan, "The Real Problem with the White House Corre-spondents' Dinner," U.S.News.com, May 2, 2012, http://www.usnews .com/opinion/blogs/susan-milligan/2012/05/02/the-real-problem -with-the-white-house-correspondents-dinner.

39 David Weigel, "Meet the Next Ted Cruz: Basically Every GOP Candi-date," *Slate*, October 21, 2013, http://www.slate.com/blogs/weigel /2013/10/21/meet_the_next_ted_cruz_basically_every_gop_candi date.html.

40 White House website, "Background Briefing by Senior Administra-tion Officials on Afghanistan—Via Conference Call," http://www .whitehouse.gov/the-press-office/2013/06/18/background-briefing -senior-administration-officials-afghanistan-conferen.

41 Maria Cantwell interview with authors, November 2013.

42 Ryan Lizza, "Can Eric Cantor Redeem the Republican Party and Himself?" *New Yorker*, March 4, 2013, http://www.newyorker.com /reporting/2013/03/04/130304fa_fact_lizza.

43 Rebecca Kaplan, "W.H.: U.S. Not Monitoring German Chancellor Angela Merkel's Phone," CBSNews.com, October 23, 2013, http:// www.cbsnews.com/news/wh-us-not-monitoring-german-chancellor -angela-merkels-phone/.

44 Kasie Hunt, "Mitt Romney: '47 Percent' Comments 'Were Just Com-pletely Wrong,'" Associated Press, October 5, 2012, http://www.huff ingtonpost.com/2012/10/04/mitt-romney-47-percent_n_1941423 .html.

45 John David Dyche, *Republican Leader: A Political Biography of Senator Mitch McConnell* (Wilmington, DE: ISI Books, 2009), 7.

46 See "McConnell: We Can Defeat ObamaCare in November," FoxNews .com, July 1, 2012, http://video.foxnews.com/v/1715039029001 /mcconnell-we-can-defeat-obamacare-in-november/.

47 "The Democrats' First 2008 Presidential Debate," *New York Times*, April 27, 2007, http://www.nytimes.com/2007/04/27/us/politics /27debate_transcript.html?pagewanted=15&_r=1st=cse%22 Surgical%20Strike%22&scp=34.

48 Chris Gentilviso, "Maryland Attorney General: I Had No 'Moral Authority' to Stop Underage Drinking at My Son's Party," *Huffington Post*, October 24, 2013, http://www.huffingtonpost.com/2013/10/24 /doug-gansler-underage-drinking_n_4156285.html.

49 Margaret Sullivan, "In New Policy, the Times Forbids After-the-Fact 'Quote Approval,'" *New York Times*, September 20, 2012, http:// publiceditor.blogs.nytimes.com/2012/09/20/in-new-policy-the -times-forbids-after-the-fact-quote-approval/.

50 Jack Shafer, "Banning Quote Approval Sounds Good, but Can It Work?" Reuters, September 21, 2012, http://blogs.reuters.com/jack shafer/2012/09/21/banning-quote-approval-sounds-good-but-can -it-work/.

51 Mike Allen, "Who's That Senior Administration Official?" *Politico*, January 30, 2007, http://www.politico.com/news/stories/0107/2548 .html.

52 *Rachel Maddow Show* transcript, February 28, 2013, http://www .today.com/id/51009273/ns/msnbc-rachel_maddow_show/#.Uq4uz I1OBV4.

53 *Kilmeade and Friends* transcript, April 26, 2012.

54 Jeff Gluck, "Sarah Palin Angered by Michael Waltrip Comment," *USA Today*, March 13, 2013, http://www.usatoday.com/story/sports /nascar/2013/03/13/sarah-palin-michael-waltrip-nascar-strategery /1983835/.

55 Democratic Party.org, "Sign Up for Talking Points," http://my.demo crats.org/page/s/talkingpoints.

56 Noam Scheiber, "Hillary's Nightmare? A Democratic Party That

Realizes Its Soul Lies with Elizabeth Warren," *New Republic*, November 10, 2013, http://www.newrepublic.com/article/115509/elizabeth-warren-hillary-clintons-nightmare.

57 *Safire's Political Dictionary*, 785.

58 Gregory Korte, Catalina Camia, and Aamer Madhani, "Shutdown Day 4: Progress on Back Pay, but No End in Sight," *USA Today*, October 5, 2013, http://www.usatoday.com/story/news/politics/2013/10/04/government-shutdown-congress/2922297/.

59 Ashley Killough, "Reid to CNN: 'Boehner's Job Is Not as Important as Our Country," *CNN Political Ticker*, October 3, 2013, http://politicalticker.blogs.cnn.com/2013/10/03/reid-boehners-job-is-not-as-important-as-our-country/.

60 "Debating Our Destiny," PBS website, September 8, 2008, http://www.pbs.org/newshour/bb/politics/july-dec08/destiny_09-08.html.

61 Peter Baker and Ashley Parker, "Before Debate, Tough Crowds at the Practice," *New York Times*, September 28, 2012, http://www.nytimes.com/2012/09/29/us/politics/cramming-and-pruning-for-first-presidential-debate.html.

List of Terms